DATE DUE

DEC 05 '97			

HIGHSMITH 45-220

Contemporary Issues in
Corporate Governance

Allen & Overy is one of the UK's leading international law firms. It has over 100 partners and 1,100 staff working in eleven major centres on three continents: London, Brussels, Dubai, Hong Kong, Madrid, New York, Paris, Prague, Singapore, Tokyo, and Warsaw. It has associated offices in Beijing and Budapest. Internationally, Allen & Overy works closely with Gide Loyrette Nouel, a leading French firm, and with Loeff Claeys Verbeke, a multinational law firm specializing in Dutch and Belgian Law.

Allen & Overy sponsors the Chair of Corporate Law at Oxford University, whose current holder is Professor D. D. Prentice.

Contemporary Issues in Corporate Governance

Edited by

D. D. PRENTICE
Allen & Overy Professor of Corporate Law,
University of Oxford
Fellow of Pembroke College, Oxford

and

P. R. J. HOLLAND
Partner, Allen & Overy

CLARENDON PRESS · OXFORD
ALLEN & OVERY
1993

Oxford University Press, Walton Street, Oxford OX2 6DP
Oxford New York Toronto
Delhi Bombay Calcutta Madras Karachi
Kuala Lumpur Singapore Hong Kong Tokyo
Nairobi Dar es Salaam Cape Town
Melbourne Auckland Madrid
and associated companies in
Berlin Ibadan

Oxford is a trade mark of Oxford University Press

Published in the United States
by Oxford University Press Inc., New York

British Library Cataloguing in Publication Data
Data available

Library of Congress Cataloging in Publication Data
Contemporary issues in corporate governance/edited by D. D. Prentice
and P. R. J. Holland.
p.   cm.
"The origins of this book lie in the Second Oxford Law Colloquium,
held in St. John's College, Oxford, on 10–11 September 1992,
organized by the Faculty of Law of the University of Oxford and
Allen & Overy"—Pref.
1. Corporate governance—Law and legislation—Great Britain—
Congresses. 2. Corporate governance—Law and legislation—
Congresses. I. Prentice, David D. (Daniel David) II. Holland,
P. R. J. (Peter R. J.) III. Oxford Law Colloquium (2nd: 1992)
IV. University of Oxford. Faculty of Law. V. Allen & Overy (Firm)
KD2089.A75C66 1993
346.41'0668—dc20
344.106668   93-443
ISBN 0-19-825859-3

Typeset by Cotswold Typesetting Ltd, Gloucester

Printed in Great Britain
on acid-free paper by
Biddles Ltd, Guildford and King's Lynn

PREFACE

The origins of this book lie in the Second Oxford Law Colloquium held in St John's College, Oxford, on 10–11 September 1992, organized by the Faculty of Law of the University of Oxford and Allen & Overy.

The Oxford Law Colloquium arose out of the mutual desire of academics and practitioners to promote a conference in the nature of a high-level workshop in which distinguished speakers would present the structure and conceptual framework of a chosen subject in the context of its practical application, and identify policy issues and trends in legal thinking. The subject chosen is intended to permit the exploration of fundamental concepts, principles, policies, and trends in particular fields of law of mutual interest and importance. Academic and practical issues are brought together in the exposition and detailed discussion of the chosen subject and in case studies discussed in specialist groups. The Colloquium is intended, *inter alia*, to (i) stimulate a high level of debate by an exchange of views and information among experts; (ii) concentrate on fundamental concepts, policies, and trends rather than on the minutiae of English law; (iii) adopt an international and comparative approach to the subject, with particular emphasis on European developments; (iv) blend academic and practitioner knowledge and skills; and (v) provide an opportunity to influence legal policy.

The topic of this Colloquium, corporate governance, is one that is currently highly topical but which has a long intellectual pedigree. Since the formation of the joint-stock company there has been a continuing debate as to the structure of corporate governance and the controls, both legal and institutional, that are, or should be, exercised over corporate management. This debate, if it is to provide any illumination, must be informed by an appreciation of the regulatory, financial, and commercial environment in which companies carry on business. A bare analysis of the relevant legal structures and rules without a clear understanding of the wider commercial and financial context within which these rules operate will provide an impoverished picture of the *status quo* and an inadequate basis for assessing the need for reform. A major purpose of this Colloquium was to try to analyse, and provide information about, this wider picture both at a national and a comparative level. This is an area in which knowledge of the attitudes and practices of managers and investors is vital in assessing the validity of the differing theories on corporate governance, and the Colloquium provided an opportunity for this information to be obtained.

The contributors to this volume are drawn from both the practising and the academic world, and bring their own specialist knowledge to bear on their chosen subjects. We have also benefited from contributions relating to the United States and Europe, and this has added a valuable international and comparative perspective to this volume.

We would like to express our gratitude to the contributors for complying with the very tight deadlines which were laid down for them, and to the Governor of the Bank of England, Mr Robin Leigh-Pemberton, for providing the foreword following this preface.

Pembroke College   D. D. Prentice
Oxford

Allen & Overy   P. R. J. Holland
9 Cheapside
London

December 1992

FOREWORD

The collapse of the command economies of the Communist world has left market-based systems as victors in the field. At the same time it has sharpened our perception that there are many elements which contribute to their efficiency and many different ways of producing a satisfactory result. Stable macro-economic conditions are the foundation of long-term prosperity; a sound educational system and adequate investment in training are essential if people are to have a chance of realizing their full potential.

Even when these conditions are satisfied, much depends on the system by which companies are governed. In the short term almost anything goes; we can see that in any country under any circumstances some companies will prosper whilst others fail. We cannot expect all companies to live for ever.

Having a sound system of corporate governance is no substitute for individual skill and ability. What it does provide is a framework within which the able can drive a company forward and in which problems can be addressed in a timely way. Its role is to foster this entrepreneurial drive within a framwork of accountability. It does not suppress individuality but secures for the medium and longer term the lasting benefits that individual skills produce.

We stand so close to our own system and take for granted so many of its features that it is especially valuable to consider the practice in other countries as a means of putting a spotlight on the differences. I therefore particularly welcome, alongside the wide and diverse range of expert views from many leading British authorities, the contributions from abroad.

Much depends on the good and better governance of our companies. It is a subject which will continue to deserve careful study—as a prelude to action. I welcome the initiative that resulted in the Colloquium and commend these essays, which are lasting evidence of its value.

Robin Leigh-Pemberton
Bank of England

CONTENTS

Part V. The Role of Litigation

LIST OF CONTRIBUTORS

LORD ALEXANDER OF WEEDON, QC, Chairman, National Westminster Bank PLC.

PROFESSOR DR THEODOR BAUMS, Professor of Law, University of Osnabrück, Germany.

SIR ADRIAN CADBURY, Chairman, Committee on Financial Aspects of Corporate Governance.

PAUL L. DAVIES, Reader in the Law of the Enterprise, University of Oxford; Fellow of Balliol College, Oxford.

PADDY LINAKER, Deputy Chairman, M&G Group PLC.

MARTIN LIPTON, Senior Partner, Wachtell, Lipton, Rosen & Katz, New York.

MORRIS PANNER, Associate at Watchell, Lipton, Rosen & Katz

ALAN PAUL, Partner, Allen & Overy; Secretary of the Takeover Panel 1985–8.

PROFESSOR D. D. PRENTICE, Allen & Overy Professor of Corporate Law, University of Oxford; Fellow of Pembroke College, Oxford.

PAUL RUTTEMAN, Senior Partner, Ernst & Young.

G. P. STAPLEDON, Keith Murray Senior Postgraduate Scholar, Lincoln College, Oxford; Solicitor, South Australia.

PROFESSOR EDDY WYMEERSCH, Professor of Law, University of Ghent, Belgium.

LIST OF TABLES

LIST OF FIGURES

TABLE OF CASES

United States

TABLE OF INTERNATIONAL LEGISLATION

France

Germany

Netherlands

Part I
An Overview of the Corporate Governance Debate

The purpose of this part is relatively self-evident: it is intended to highlight some of the themes that have informed the debate on corporate governance both in the United Kingdom and in other jurisdictions. As Professor Eddy Wymeersch points out, the debate has not been as active in other EC jurisdictions as it has been in Anglo-Saxon jurisdictions. This may be attributable to the structures of the financial markets, and this is one of the themes that his essay develops. In fact it was a general theme of the Colloquium that corporate governance issues can only be satisfactorily examined in the context of the commercial and financial environments in which companies operate.

1

THE CORPORATE GOVERNANCE DISCUSSION IN SOME EUROPEAN STATES

Eddy Wymeersch

Introduction

The purpose of the present report is to give an overview of the discussion on corporate governance as it seems to be developing in some of the Continental European states.

Under the heading of 'corporate governance' the issue is still relatively new. Most jurisdictions do not have an equivalent term to 'corporate governance', and therefore use the English expression, it not being certain whether the content thereby is meant to be the same. Therefore, this overview should be read with a few reservations in mind.

A first reservation relates to the sources of information. Corporate governance has been, sometimes explicitly, but most of the time implicitly, discussed for a very long time. These discussions have often related to specific aspects of the subject, especially where interests of particular parties were involved. Less widespread and structured is the discussion of the corporate governance issue as encompassing the entire functioning and distribution of power within the large corporation.

Apart from these factual discussions, and the negotiations going on at the moment of legislative reforms that have occurred in several states, the corporate governance discussion could be measured in terms of legal publications and statements relating to the subject. The following overview will essentially be based on that method.

The overview will deal with aspects of the corporate governance discussion in Belgium, France, Germany, and the Netherlands. It is already very difficult to give a view of the discussion in one's own country. It would be hazardous to attempt to give an overview for other countries. Anyone familiar with comparative law knows how difficult it is to interpret laws and regulations dealing with another country's legal system. The following overview has to be read under that express proviso.

Corporate Governance is Not an Explicit Issue

Corporate governance, as such, is not an explicit issue in Belgium France and the Netherlands. However, there are differences, especially with respect to the co-determination issue, this is very much a topic in Germany and in the Netherlands,[1] but totally absent from the political and legal debate in Belgium. Labour participation is more widely discussed, and schemes are being developed.[2]

Specific issues that can be linked to the governance theme have been brought to light as a consequence of the aggressive takeovers that have shaken most of these countries. Hence, one finds a renewed interest for the role of the shareholder, especially the investor, but also for rules better to protect his interests. The technicalities of takeover regulation are intertwined with the rules on defensive techniques,[3] and these raise fundamental issues about the corporate structure. Even green-mailing practices have received attention.[4]

More constant themes of interest continue to be the rules on groups of companies,[5] and directly related, the rules on conflicts of interests. Now that the implementation of the Fourth, Seventh, and Eighth EC directives is largely effected, interest in the accounting and auditing rules will subside for a while, although one sees new accounting themes calling for attention.[6]

One could conclude that in several states scattered efforts to better frame governance of corporations have been undertaken but this without an explicit general pattern or framework. Also, little research has been going on to better identify the factual functioning of the large European corporation, and the interplay between the different classes of shareholders and the management.[7]

[1] See *inter alia* the constructions by, P. G. Van Den Hoek, 'Variaties op de structuurregeling big contract', and by P. F. Van Der Heijden, 'Het medezeggingschapscovenant', in *Ondernemingsrechtelijke contracten* (Kluwer, 1991), 81 ff.

[2] See the changes in Belgian Company Law, esp. of art. 52septies and of art. 52ter; for an analysis: B. Dubois and M. Delcour, 'De financiële participatie der werknemers', in Braeckmans and Wymeersch (eds.), *Het gewijzigde vennootschapsrecht* (Maklu, Antwerp, 1992), 273–323. For an overview of the French situation, Y. Guyon, *Droit des affaires*, t. 1, 7ème edn., nos. 397 *et seq.*

[3] Focusing on this aspect: J. M. M. Maeijer and K. Geens (eds.), *Defensive Measures Against Hostile Takeover in the Common Market* (Martinus Nijhoff, 1990); K. Geens *Openbaar bod en beschermingscontructies* (Biblo, Kalmthout, 1988); for Germany: K. J. Hopt, 'Präventivmass-nahmen zur Abwehr von Übernahme- und Beteiligungsversuchen', *WM* (1991), Sonderheft 'Festgabe für Th. Heinsius', 22; R. Vatinet, 'Les Défenses anti-OPA', *Rev.Sociétés* (1987), 539; C. T. Ebenroth and R. Schrupkowski, 'Die Abwehr von Unternehmensübernahmen in der Schweiz in Lichte europäischer Herausforderungen', *ZVgl.RWiss.* 90 (1991), 319–89.

[4] See in Germany: W. Schlaus, 'Auskauf opponierender Aktionäre', *AG* (1988), 113; K -P. Martens, 'Die Vergleichs- und Abfindungsbefugnis des Vorstands gegenüber opponierden Aktionären', *AG* (1988), 118.

[5] See the reports commissioned by the EC Commission, in E Wymeersch (ed.), *Groups of Companies in the EEC* (de Gruyter, 1993); also the recent comparative-law overviews published in Germany in *ZGR*, 20 (1991), vols. 2 and 3; more generally: Commission Droit Vie Des Affaires (CDVA), *Modes de rapprochement structurel des entreprises* (Story-Scientia, Brussels, 1988).

[6] See e.g. the discussion about the accounting for goodwill.

[7] However, one should mention the studies by e.g. P. De Woot and X. Desclée De Maredsous, *Le Management stratégique des groupes industriels* (Economica, Paris, 1984) M. Bauer, *Qui gouverne les groupes industriels? Essai sur l'exercice du pouvoir du et dans le groupe*

Therefore it may be useful to attempt to give an overview of the differences between the corporate structures in the states compared.

Differences in the Corporate Structure and Present Status of Share Distribution

If one talks about the corporations in the jurisdictions compared, one should bear in mind that one is talking about quite different factual situations. The national laws do to a certain extent take into consideration these differences. At the level of European harmonization, however, the harmonized rules are considered applicable to all entities within the different countries, leading to tensions and inadequate answers to each country's specific needs. The proposal for a Thirteenth Directive is an example: why introduce regulations on takeovers in countries that have never seen such a transaction? Subsidiarity may be the answer.

Germany

A first difference relates to the number of companies limited by shares and the importance of these in the financing mechanism.

It is well known that the German *Aktiengesellschaft* is not easily comparable to the French or Belgian *société anonyme*, nor to the Dutch *naamloze vennootschap*.

The mere figures underline this difference: in Germany, according to one source,[8] there were 2,682 *Aktiengesellschaften*, of which 501 were stock-exchange listed. It seems that 90 per cent of these listed companies are majority owned by one or more active or controlling shareholders.[9] Only sixty to seventy companies are really publicly traded companies, representing the largest German corporations.[10] It would be useful to relate these figures to the market capitalization, in order to obtain a better idea of the relative importance of these really public companies.

Institutional investors in Germany still prefer to invest in bonds, especially government bonds. So, for example, investment funds hold only 16.5 per cent of their portfolio in shares. For the insurance companies the figure was 10 per cent and for the pension funds 3 per cent. The role of

---

industriel (Seuil, Paris, 1981) also Anne Vincent and Jean-Pierre Martens, 'L'Europe des Groupes: Présence et stratégies en Belgique', *CRISP*, Bruxelles (Dec. 1991); Anne Vincent, 'Les groupes d'entreprises en Belgique; Le domaine des principaux groupes privés', *CRISP*, Bruxelles (Nov. 1990).

[8] For further details and refinement about the German situation, one should refer to T. Baums, Ch. 10 below.

[9] See *A.* Gottschalk, 'Der Stimmrechtseinfluss der Banken in Aktionärsversammlungen der Grossunternehmen', *WSI Mitteilungen*, 6 (1988), 294 ff.

[10] Another source indicated that only thirty-nine companies have 75 per cent of their shares in the hands of the public. There are fears that the majority may be foreign owned: see U. Schneider, 'Auf dem Weg des Pensionkassenkorporatismus', 35, *AG* (1990), 317.

enterprise-linked pension liabilities offers alternative long-term financing and constitutes a strong competitor with capital financing.[11]

Over the longer term, however, the role of these institutional investors has been increasing. So, for the period 1960–90, the private investor's share dwindled from 27 per cent to 17 per cent, the share of the public sector being reduced from 14 per cent to 5 per cent. On the other hand, the institutional investors, especially the insurance and pension funds (from 3 per cent to 12 per cent) along with the credit institutions (6 per cent to 10 per cent) have increased their holdings, while foreign ownership increased significantly (from 6 per cent to 14 per cent), leading to worries about foreign dominance.[12]

The role of institutional investors in Germany is relatively limited compared to the still-dominant influence exercised by the banking system. The banks are reported to own about 10 per cent of the German listed companies. However, their influence is much more important due to their right to vote with the shares deposited with the bank. The influence of the individual bank—as opposed to the banking system, that is, from the three major banks—seems to have decreased during these last years, due to enhanced competition in the lending markets.[13]

FRANCE

The French market authorities have paid ample attention to the distribution of shares in stock-exchange listed companies. These enquiries are part of the larger programme to revamp corporate life and promote share ownership, whether direct or indirect, by individuals. It seems, however, that while the number of securities holders is increasing, the number of individual shareholders is decreasing.

Table 1.1 gives an overview of share ownership, in terms of market capitalization, in French companies.

The number of French listed companies—only a tiny fraction of the total of about125,000 *sociétés anonymes* existing in France—has been decreasing these last years, while more and more foreign companies are listed in Paris.[14]

On the other hand the COB reported that the number of securities investors had increased from 2.4 million in 1979 to 14 million in 1991, 5.5 million to 6 million francs having directly invested in shares, and 11 million in investment funds.

Also the traditional portfolio composition has been investigated by the Banque de France.

[11] See on these issues Baums, Chap. 10.

[12] See Schneider n. 10; F. Kübler, 'Institutional Investors and Corporate Governance: A German Perspective', to be published in T. Baums (ed.), *Conference on Institutional Investors* (Osnabrück, July 1992 de Gruyter, Berlin, 1993).

[13] Details in T. Baums, 'Should banks own industrial firms? Remarks from the German perspective', *Rev. banque* (1992), 249.

[14] See Table 1.2.

TABLE 1.1. *Share ownership in French companies* (% of market capitalization)

	1987	1988	1989	1990
Individuals	37.6	37.0	34.7	36.0
Institutional investors	26.3	26.8	20.3	21.5
Industrial/Commercial enterprises	24.4	20.1	21.4	24.1
Associations	1.1	0.8	0.4	0.7
Foreign	10.6	15.3	23.2	17.7

Note: State, agencies, State enterprises ±20 to 24%.

TABLE 1.2. *Listed companies in France*

	1988	1989	1990	1991	1992
French issuers	608	606	577	551	534
Foreign issuers	205	223	225	231	226
Turnover (bill.ff)	412	667	626	614	na
Market capitalization (billion ff)	1,350	1,952	1,570	1,779	na

Source: COB. *Bulletin* (1992), Supplément 51 and 62.

TABLE 1.3. *French portfolio composition* (%)

	French shares	French bonds	Foreign securities	Investment funds
Physical persons	14.0	64.4	6.7	14.9
Institutional investors	32.6	26.3	7.1	34.0
Non-residents	67.4	22.0	7.7	2.9
Business enterprises	15.6	28.9	3.7	51.8

BELGIUM

In Belgium, there are 102,231 *sociétés anonymes*, of which only 169 enjoyed a stock-exchange listing.[15] Of these, fifty-five or 32.54 per cent have only a minority of their shares listed, the remaining shares being held in firm

[15] The first figure relates to 15 Dec. 1991; the second to 1 Nov. 1992.

hands. As of the end of 1990, of the then 141 companies that had to report,[16] 59 (or 42 per cent) had one or a group of majority-controlling shareholders, while in 108 cases the majority of the shares were held by identified shareholders, most of whom either took part in the control of the company, or belonged to the opposition to the controlling shareholders.[17] Only a small minority of listed companies would not be owned by clearly identified or controlling shareholders: ten out of the twenty most important companies obviously have the majority of their shares effectively put on the market.[18]

Very little research has been done on the role of institutional investors, mainly due to the fact that the information is not available, but also to the widespread perception that most institutional investors are linked to financial groups and hence would not be able to act independently. However, one can assess the presence of institutional investors in listed companies as follows.

In terms of market capitalization, institutional investors held about 22 per cent of all Belgian shares, insurance companies accounting for 9 per cent, UCITS 8.5 per cent, pension funds 3 per cent, and credit institutions 1.3 per cent. These figures are unfortunately not very reliable, as little detailed public information is available. Also, one should take into account the Belgian banks managed Luxembourg Funds, about which no figures appear to be available.

On the other hand, most institutional investors belong to, or are managed by, management teams belonging to banks, or to financial groups that dominate the Belgian economic scene. Full independence of action or judgement, therefore, will only occur on extreme occasions.[19] Monitoring action thereby can be presumed to be limited although not non-existent. Recently, for example, UCITS sued the purchaser of a controlling block of shares for not extending a mandatory bid to all shareholders.[20]

In some listed companies the employees own significant stakes (for example, Petrofina, BBL), but this is not a prevalent phenomenon.

The state or its agencies[21] seldom own shares in listed companies, except

---

[16] Up to 1 Jan. 1991, only companies with a capital of 250 million or more BEF had to report (art. 12, s. 3, L. 2 Mar. 1989). The rule has been extended to all listed companies.

[17] One does not have information about the agreements that have been entered into between shareholders. But it is safe to assume that reporting shareholders are either part of a voting agreement, or are acting in concert.

[18] See *Bulletin Bank Brussels Lambert*, no. 2,259 (Mar. 1992).

[19] For an analysis of the questions raised by the UCITs' links to the financial groups, see e.g. E. Wymeersch and M. Kruithof, 'Belangentegenstellingen bij het beheer van gemeenschappelijke beleggingsfondsen', *Bank- en Financiewezen* (1989), no. 5, 303–21.

[20] See Bruxelles, 6 Aug. 1992, DAOR, no. 25 (1992), 63 and Trib. Comm. Brussels, 3, Sept. 1992, DAOR, no. 25 (1992), 93 in the so-called *Wagon-lits* case. See also the previous decisions in the same case: Trib. Comm. Brussels, 22 Nov. 1991, DAOR, no. 21 (1991), 95; Pres. Trib. Comm. Brussels, DAOR, no. 21 (1991), 195 and Trib. Comm. Brussels, 4 Dec. 1991, DAOR (1991), no. 21, 119.

[21] These are the so-called Public Investment Companies, L. 2 Apr. 1962, of which there are four, one national and three regional ones.

their controlling interests in companies which they had to rescue (FN, Barco) or which have been transformed from the former state-run business (airline, railways, telecommunication, post office). In other closely held corporations these agencies would normally take a minority interest.[22]

The conclusion of the foregoing overview[23] could be a relatively simple warning: in discussing rules of company law in a comparative perspective, one should fully take into account the quite substantial factual differences existing between the different national settings. This could be considered as being of relatively little importance in dealing with the issues that have been harmonized in the First and Second Directives, but it has led to tensions in the field of accounting,[24] and will create renewed difficulties in putting into effect the draft Fifth Directive if adopted.

The Corporate Governance Debate

In attempting to give an overview of the present debate on issues of corporate governance, one must distinguish the national from the European level.

AT THE NATIONAL LEVEL

Corporate governance reasoning in each of EC member states focuses on different issues since it is directly related to the ownership structure and embedded in the enterprise culture of these states. One could summarize the present position as follows.

DISTRIBUTION OF SHAREHOLDINGS

The 'Berle and Means' type of corporation, with widely scattered ownership and a predominantly self-perpetuating board, is mainly an Anglo-Saxon phenomenon, prevalent both in North America, in the UK, and in Australia, but it is not the dominant European continental pattern of enterprise. Of course, any generalization calls for further qualifications and each company constitutes a different case. The following analysis, therefore, is an imperfect generalization. There are continental companies that possess some or many of the characteristics of the 'Berle and Means' corporation, but statistically these remain a dwindling minority while significant variances from the said pattern would dominate.

Correspondingly, in Belgium, the Netherlands, and France one predominantly finds companies that, although listed on the stock exchange, are closely held and often minority controlled, whether by the founding family,

---

[22] See the prevailing financing technique used in implementating *inter alia* of the Textile reorganization plan: RD no. 20 of 23 Mar. 1982 and RD of 7 May 1985.

[23] No information has been obtained in time about the Netherlands; see for some indication: W. J. Slagter, 'Institutional Investors and Corporate Governance in the Netherlands', to be published in Baums (ed.), *Conference on Institutional Investors* (Osnabrück, July 1992).

[24] e.g. the EC Directive, 8 Nov. 1990, 90/640/EEC, OJ L 317, 16 Nov. 1990, 57–9.

by financial holdings, or by other interests acting together. Ownership and control can often be traced back to an identifiable person or group of persons.

In Belgium the evidence indicates that, but for a handful of companies, control is held by a single party. These figures do not take into account the undisclosed existence of voting agreements, or syndicates of shareholders, often entered into between the members of the controlling families or groups. In addition, as a consequence of the law of 18 July 1991, protective mechanisms against takeovers have been authorized, further increasing the number of the companies the controlling shares of which are in firm hands.[25] Markets had largely anticipated this reinforcement of existing *de facto* control, and no price movements were noticeable upon the introduction of the said protective mechanisms.[26]

In the Netherlands a comparable situation exists, mainly as a consequence of the widespread use of protective clauses and mechanisms, especially the use of 'preference shares': even if the majority of the shares is listed and traded on the markets, the purchaser of these shares would normally not afford power, as the preference shares would be the only ones entitled to nominate members to the board. The stock exchange has attempted to reduce their impact, but does not seem to have been very effective.[27] Therefore takeovers would be unsuccessful most of the time except with the consent of the former controlling shareholder.

In the other states compared the situation would not be very dissimilar, although the techniques followed would differ. In France the state plays a leading role, often indirectly through one of the state organisms such as the Caisse de Dépôts (CDC).[28] Leading business groups, including banks and insurance companies, are also linked to the state sector and cannot freely act against the will of the public authorities.

In Germany the prevalence of bank-led monitoring in most large enterprises seems to be the striking characteristic.[29]

STRUCTURE OF THE GOVERNING BODIES

Of the four legal systems compared, three have introduced the two-tier

---

[25] Some companies have, for instance, massively issued warrants, placed in the hand of secure partners, or convertible bonds with a very low issue price but convertible in relatively large amounts of shares.

[26] According to an unpublished event study undertaken by A. M. Henderick, at the University of Ghent.

[27] See on this topic, the position taken by the Association of Securities Issuing Enterprises (VEUO) with respect to defensive measures, published in *N.V.* (1991), 81; and the reaction of the Ministry of Finance: 'Notitie van de Minister van Financiën en de Staatssecretaris van Justitie inzake beschermingsconstructies bij beursgenoteerde vennootschappen', *N.V.* (1991), 82. J. B. A. Hoyinck, 'Partieel bod aan de Fusiecode toegevoegd', *Tijdschrift voor Verenigingen, Vennootschappen en Stichtingen* (1991), 67; M. W. den Boogert, 'Partieel bod en tenderbod in SER fusiegedragsregels', *N.V.* (1991), 231; P. J. Dortmond, 'De Nieuwe bijlage X bij het fondsenreglement', *N.V.* (1991), 215, with the text of the new regulation appended.

[28] Controlling about 20 per cent of the market capitalization.

[29] See T. Baums, Ch. 10 below.

board, Belgium having planned a reform to that effect which appears to have been abandoned.[30]

Germany

Most noticeably, German law imposes the two-tier board, composed of the *Aufsichtsrat* and the *Vorstand*. Essential to the understanding of the system are the rules relating to co-determination.[31] For large enterprises and enterprises belonging to the coal and steel sector, half of the Aufsichtsrat members have to be elected by the shareholders, the other half by the employees. However, the shareholders maintain the last say, whether as a consequence of the chairman's casting vote, or due to the rule subjecting major company related decisions to their agreement.

The Netherlands

A different situation exists in the Netherlands, where the members of the *Raad van Commissarissen* are appointed by co-optation, but are subject to a right of refusal of both the shareholders or the employees.[32]

In both cases it is often stressed that a takeover bid on the company would be effectively impracticable as a consequence of the presence of the employee representatives. Therefore, co-determination has become popular even with the spokesmen of the large companies and their shareholders.

France

In France the two-tier structure has been introduced in the Companies Act, but remains optional.[33] The Conseil de Surveillance consists of shareholder-elected members and appoints the members of the Directoire. The Directoire takes care of the actual management of the company, while the Conseil de Surveillance supervises the Directoire, and authorizes certain important transactions, for example those involving a conflict of interest.[34]

Co-determination has been introduced but remains optional, except for the state-owned enterprises. (One third of directors in State-owned enterprises are employees.)[35]

Belgium

Belgium has kept the unitary structure, the board being elected by the majority of the shareholders. Labour representation is very rare to non-existent. Effective management lies with those board members who have

---

[30] See the bill introduced in Parliament on 3 Dec. 1979, Kamer van Volksvertegenwoor-digers, 1979–80, no. 387/1.
[31] There are three systems of co-determination: Montan-Mitbestimmungsgesetz 1951; Betriebsverfassungsgesetz 1952 (2/3–1/3); Mitbestimmungsgesetz 1976 (1/2–1/2), for enterprises with more than 2,000 employees.
[32] This is the so-called *structuurwet*, presently art. 153 *et seq.*, Book 2, Civil Code.
[33] Art. 188 *et seq.*, L. 24 July 1966.
[34] Art. 143, L. 24 July 1966.
[35] See for details, Y. Guyon, *Droit des affaires*, no. 403 *et seq.*, op. 41 *et seq.*

been appointed to the executive committee. The board chairman would in many cases be a dominant personality, different from the president of the executive committee, who is a full-time director. Although legally not provided for, the role of the full board is rather that of a supervisory board, meeting a limited number of times a year.

Independent directors are rather rare on the Belgian scene, board members being elected *de facto* by the controlling shareholder, most of the time the controlling holding company.

At the EC Harmonization Level

Corporate governance issues have received ample attention in the European Community's harmonization Directives. A few of these provisions should be mentioned here.

The second Directive has set a definite pattern of creditor protection.[36] Some specialists fear that this over-protective attitude to creditors is causing adverse effects on shareholders and may in the longer term hamper capital formation and hence weaken European industry. These choices have been made without thorough previous studies of the possible effects of the measures on the financing of enterprises.

Recently the Community enacted a prohibition on the subscription of shares of a parent company by a subsidiary.[37] Here again, for purposes of creditor protection, the subject is taken out of its broader context of group law and was directly inspired by the issue of whether a company might defend its independence against a takeover bidder by diluting its share capital as a consequence of a subscription by a subsidiary. The catalyst was the Belgian Société Générale affair.[38] But once more, harmonization was attempted piecemeal, as the Community did not have a consistent doctrine dealing with defensive mechanisms.[39]

The Fourth, Seventh, and Eighth Directives could also be viewed in a governance perspective, since the drawing-up of reliable and comparable accounts, along with comprehensive and professional auditing, are essential instruments in the internal relationship between directors and shareholders, but also indispensable devices for any monitoring action, whether by banks, institutional investors, markets, or the public authorities.[40] Furthermore, in several of the Continental countries these accounting documents are

[36] For an extensive comparative analysis see J. N. Schutte. *Harmonisatie van het kapitaalbeschermingsrecht in de EEG* (Kluwer, 1990).

[37] Amended proposal to the 2nd Directive Com (90) 631 Final, OJ C 8, 12 Jan. 1991, 5–6.

[38] For the facts see the description made by A. Benoit-Moury, and the decisions reprinted in *Journal des Tribunaux* (1988), 217–40.

[39] See about the Bangemann Statement: K. Van Hulle, 'De voorstellen van Europese richtlijnen inzake openbaar bod en beschermingsconstructies', in K. Geens, *et al.*, *Openbaar bod en beschermingsconstructies* (Biblo, 1990), 179 ff.

[40] See H. Niessen, 'Zur Angleichung des Bilanzrechts in der Europäischen Gemeinschaft', *RabelsZ* (1984), 82.

required to serve the overriding general interest in the monitoring of large corporations and enterprises. In Belgium and France this aspect is often expressly referred to. One should further mention the German 1971 *Publizitätsgesetz*, extending accounting and reporting obligations to all larger enterprises whatever their form, a law driven by public-interest monitoring considerations. Also similarly inspired are the Belgian accounting rules applicable to all enterprises, whatever their form, including non-profit enterprises.[41]

The proposed Fifth Directive on the structure of the corporation is undoubtedly the central piece of harmonization in the field of governance.[42] Apart from the traditional stumbling-block of co-determination, which has delayed adoption of this Directive for a very long time, one could mention the many other governance rules that would have to be harmonized once the Directive were adopted.

Without fully analysing the proposed Directive, one should mention the rules dealing with the structure of the board, especially as to the member states' choice between the one-tier and two-tier boards. The Directive also proposes to determine some basic principles for the 'administrative organ': procedures for dealing with conflicts of interest; the appointment of executive and non-executive directors, the latter being entitled to dismiss the former; the possibility of appointing committees; and so on.

On the other hand, the proposal contains basic rules for the general meeting of shareholders, some of which are fundamental for the future development of corporate governance ideas. Voting rights would have to be proportional: the rule of "one share, one vote" would be adopted. In the United States this rule has stirred a lasting debate; in Europe it is part of the harmonization discussion. Voting agreements would be validated. The directors are to be elected by the majority of the shareholders. Minority shareholders will be granted a right to bring a derivative action if they own at least 5 per cent of the shares.

An amendment to the original proposal for a Fifth Directive would restrict certain protective techniques such as limiting voting rights, nomination privileges for certain preferred shares relating to the majority of the board, or increased majorities relating to the appointment or dismissal of directors.[43]

Two further proposals would have a considerable impact on the life of companies. The adoption of both of them seems at present improbable.

The proposed thirteenth Directive,[44] dealing with takeover bids,

---

[41] See art. 1, L. 17 July 1975.

[42] For an overview: P. H. Westermann, 'Tendenzen der gegenwartigen Mitbestimmungsdiskussion in der Europäischen Gemeinschaft', *RabelsZ* (1984), 123.

[43] See Second Amended Proposal of 20 Dec. 1990 for a 5th Directive Com(90) 629, OJ C 7, 11 Jan. 1991, 4–6. See also Directive 92/101/EEC, 23 November 1992, OJEC, L3790/ 28 November 1992, 64.

[44] Amended proposal for a 13th Directive, Com(90) 416 Final, OJ C 240, 26 Sept. 1990, 7–30. Numerous comments have been written about this proposal.

contains at least two rules that cause uneasiness and controversy in many of the states. The mandatory bid (Art. 4), according to which, after the acquisition of a third of the shares the acquiror would be obliged to bring a bid for all the remaining shares, reflects the present legal tradition in four of the states. It seems debatable whether this rule relates to market organization, or to company law, more specifically to the rules on groups of companies, as has convincingly been argued in some of the states.[45] In the latter case the rule, in a modified form, would have to be included in the future proposal for a Ninth Directive. The rule prohibiting defensive techniques by the board of directors in case of a takeover (Art. 8) is also part of the proposed harmonization as the rule exists in several states. However, the rule is far from evident, especially if one takes into account the US practice obliging the board of directors to take the necessary measures to enhance the shareholder's value, and eventually to oppose the bid if the board has solid reasons to believe that its own policy proposals offer a better prospect. The rule may have a different meaning in the more market-oriented company structure, as one sees in the UK. On the Continent, the real meaning is to prevent the board from entering into negotiations that would run contrary to the will of the controlling shareholder, thereby guiding the entire control negotiation for the benefit of the latter.[46]

Strikingly enough, while regulating (rare) takeovers is absorbing all the reform effort, little is being done about the protective techniques used in may of the Continental states to avoid the company being taken over. The above-mentioned amendment to the Second Directive, and the changes to the proposed Fifth Directive, would aim at reducing the existing high barriers against takeovers. In several of the states these issues attracted interest from both legal doctrine and actual practice, resulting in many companies becoming practically unassailable. Complaints about the uneven playing field are heard. However, even if aggressive takeovers are hampered, the market for corporate control continues to function, not on the public market-place, but along the lines of private negotiations, acquisitions of controlling blocks, mergers, and other comparable techniques.

The once-planned Ninth Directive on groups of companies deserves special mention here.[47] Although it becomes more and more apparent that the rules on groups of companies belong to the essential devices in regulating

---

[45] See in Germany: P. Hommelhoff and D. Kleindiek, 'Takeover Richtlinie und europäisches Konzernrecht', AG (1990), 106; in Belgium E. Wymeersch, The Mandatory Takeover Bid: A Critical View in Hopt and Wymeersch (eds.), *Takeovers in Europe* (Butterworths, London, 1992), 351 at 365.

[46] See for this analysis: Wymeersch *op. cit.* 351 at 363–5.

[47] The text of the proposal was never officially published. However, the most recent draft version can be found in CDVA (n. 5 above), 223, with comments by U. Immenga and the present author.

companies' conduct, the Community's attempts failed. The German-inspired preliminary proposal was too far away from the actual practice in the other states. In the meantime, rules relating to group relationships were developed both by the national legislators and by national case law.[48] A coherent and more predictable set of rules on group relationships remains, however, very necessary

The conclusion of this sketchy overview can be short.[49] Although started in the mid-sixties, the Community's harmonization programme has in fact paid ample attention to the issue of governance of the companies in Europe. It has, however, reasoned essentially in terms of harmonizing the existing national rules, without questioning the existing regulations nor allowing for a rethinking of the existing structures. This approach has incited states to pre-emptively modify their regulations,[50] while the petrifying effect, once the directive is adopted, risks the prevention for a long period of time of any change in the framework in which the harmonization had been produced.

Since the 1960s corporate Europe has changed considerably. The impact of securities regulation has lead to a two-pronged regulatory system, the factual significance of which is very divergent in the different European states. Whether company law harmonization can be continued without allowing for a more clear differentiation between rules for listed and rules for unlisted companies is open to doubt.

Also striking is the absence, at least in the Continental European systems, of facts-based analysis including so-called 'event studies' relating to company life and decisions.[51] This difference seems due to the limited significance of stock exchange prices in Continental Europe, where control and eventually most of the shares are in firm hands, rather than to the unawareness or inefficiency of Continental European research.

Overview of the Most Active Issues

In this part I will attempt to give an overview of some of the issues that appear to be most active in the jurisdictions reviewed. The overview is

---

[48] For an overview of these developments, see *Groups of Companies in the EC* (de Gruyter, Berlin, 1993), with reports by Immenga, Prentice, Guyon, Timmermans and Timmerman, Spada, Embid Irujo, and the present author.

[49] For a sharper view on many of these issues, see R. M. Buxbaum and K. J. Hopt, *Legal Harmonization and the Business Enterprise*. (Berlin, 1988), and R. M. Buxbaum, G. Hertig, K. J. Hopt, and A. Hirsch, *European Business Law* (Berlin, 1991).

[50] This case, although impossible to prove, could be illustrated by pointing at the dates at which new legislation was enacted on topics dealt with at the Community level. The 1966 French Companies Act, also the 1965 German reregulation, may be viewed in that perspective; but one could also mention the many states remodeling their insider regulation while negotiating at the Community on a harmonization directive.

[51] One of the few publications in this field is K. Byttebier, *Het vijandige overnamebod, Een rechtsvergelijkend onderzoek naar de economische wenselijkheid en juridische haalbaarheid van een disciplinaire overnamemarkt*, reviewing the American and UK research (due to be published early 1993 Maklu, Antwerp).

mainly based on legal literature and therefore cannot possibly give the full picture of the governance discussion.

IN FRANCE

In 1966 France enacted its new Company Law. Although many of its articles were similar to the previously existing rules, the 1966 law constituted a major search for a better equilibrium within the company structure. Notwithstanding the many later changes, the former objective obviously has been achieved, and no calls for a fundamental overhaul of the law have been heard.

Therefore issues that are controversial in other states have been settled in France, obviously in a satisfactory way. One could mention items such as the one-tier or two-tier board, French law allowing for either of these; labour representation, imposed on the state enterprises but not on the private ones; rules on conflicts of interest,[52] on minority rights, and on class action.[53] The business judgement rule is being more and more expressly formulated in French case law.[54]

Since 1966 this law has been repeatedly changed, mostly on minor points and in these last years to take better account of the increasing pressure from the financial markets. French company law needs more and more to be read in conjunction with financial regulations, laid down in different laws and decrees and in a broad range of regulations enacted by government agencies such as the Commission des Opérations de Bourse and the Conseil des Bourses de Valeurs. One of the present points of discussion is the incoherence of both sets of rules: definition, concepts, and objectives are different if one looks at the rule from the company law angle as opposed to the financial markets angle. The situation has become increasingly complex as new government agencies have been put into place. In the fields of market regulation, and especially of take-over bids, the Conseil des Bourses de Valeurs has received extensive powers, especially to exempt from certain regulatory requirements, thus making it a quasi-judicial body. On some issues the Commission des Opérations de Bourse is also involved, resulting in divergent decisions between both agencies.

Among the fields in which this friction between financial regulation and company law is the most visible, one should mention the corporate control market, standing here for takeover bids and changes of control, whether by private transfer of a controlling block of shares, by management buy-out, or as a consequence of a withdrawal right.[55] The mandatory takeover bid has

---

[52] Art. 101, Companies Law of 24 July 1966.
[53] Art. 226, Companies Law of 24 July 1966.
[54] See the formulation by Y. Guyon, *Droit des affaires*, o.c., no. 456, p. 468.
[55] These different forms have been regulated in the CBV regulation approved by decree of 28 Sept. 1989; for comments see: A. Viandier, *OPA-OPE, Garantie de cours—retrait* (Litec, 1991); T. Forschbach, 'L'offre publique obligatoire', *Rev. dr. bancaire et de la bourse* (1990),

been the most controversial and discussed topic. Up to May 1992 French regulation had a requirement calling for a two-thirds bid upon acquisition of a third of the shares.[56] This led to protests by minority shareholders, especially in the Pinault takeover of *Le Printemps*.[57] The contested bid of Perrier also caused strain on the system: the tribunal had to intervene—and, did so quite satisfactorily—to investigate whether 'auto-control' systems were compatible with the law, whether concerted action had been undertaken, or even the law on insider dealing violated.[58]

In the direct wake of the takeover discussions one should mention the controversies about the notion of 'concerted action',[59] and about the exemptive powers of the CBV, especially rejecting the offer price as inadequate even if above the market price.[60] Previously defensive techniques were discussed,[61] and the law was adapted on certain points.[62]

Among the most conspicuous items in which no comprehensive reform has been realized, one should cite the subject of the law of groups of enterprises. The legislature has obviously abandoned the idea of introducing the grand reform, as planned in the early 1970s,[63] but has enacted some piecemeal rules dealing with parent and subsidiary relationships, including rules on cross shareholdings[64] and outlawing the formerly popular auto-control.[65] Case law has in the meantime extensively dealt with the issue, and the results constitute a rather well balanced system. In one of the leading cases, dealing with the question of whether mere ownership-related companies could financially assist each other, it was held that

financial assistance to which one of the group companies had agreed in favour of another group enterprise should be based on a common economic, social, or financial

179; A. Pézard, 'La nouvelle réglementation française des offres publiques d'achat', *Rev. Banque* (1990), 675; C. Gavalda, 'Commentaire de la loi du 2 aouf6t 1989 concernant l'amélioration de la transparence et de la sécurité du marché financier', *Rev. Sociétés* (1990), 1.

[56] See art. 5–3–1 of the regulation, approved by Decree 28 Sept. 1989, as modified by Decree 15 May 1992; see: D. Carreau and J-Y. Martin, 'La réforme du régime des offres publiques', *Rev. Sociétés* (1992), 451.

[57] See Paris 10 Mar. 1992, *Rev. Sociétés* (1992), 345; M. Vasseur, 'Les leçons de l'arrêt de la cour d'appel de Paris en date du 10 mars 1992 rendu dans l'affaire Pinault-Printemps', *Rev. Sociétés* (1992), 229.

[58] See the Cob Report, mentioned in Wymeersch (n. 45 above), 116 ff.; See Cob, 'Délit d'initié; transmission d'une enquête de la COB au parquet', *Bulletin*, no. 238 (July–Aug. 1990). There is autocontrol when a company directly or indirectly holds its own shares (Corian, M. and Viandier, A., Droit des sociétés, Lites, Paris, no. 1963.

[59] Schmidt and Baj, 'Réflexions sur la notion d'action de concert', *Rev. dr. bancaire et de la bourse* (1991), 86; P. Le Cannu, 'L'action de concert', *Rev. Sociétés* (1991), 675.

[60] See about this issue in general, Cass., 23 Oct. 1990, *Rev. Sociétés* (1991), 356, nte Le Cannu.

[61] See n. 3 above; G. Parléani, 'Les pactes d'actionnaires', *Rev. Sociétés* (1991), 1.

[62] See art. 180, al. 3, Company Law of 1966, as modified by L. 2 Aug. 1989 dealing with certain poison pills.

[63] The so-called proposition Cousté, analysed by its author in 'Vers un nouveau statut des groupes des sociétés', *Gaz. Palais* (1985), 1, 333–4.

[64] See art. 358, *et seq.* L. 24 July 1966.

[65] See on the subject: A. Viandier, 'Securité et Transparence du Marché Financier', J.C.P., Ed. G, 1989, I, 3420, 132.

interest, to be assessed in the light of a group-wide policy; while not devoid of any return nor disruptive of the equilibrium between the liabilities of all companies concerned nor exceeding the financial capacities of the burdened group entity.[66]

At present much attention is directed towards the de-regulation issue: it has been proposed to parliament to introduce a *société anonyme simplifiée*, which, as a subsidiary, would have the exterior appearance of the company limited by shares, the internal organization being largely left to the contractual arrangements that have been put into place.[67]

The issue of governance as far as it relates to monitoring corporate conduct has not yet received very much attention in France. The role of institutional investors has not been systematically studied,[68] mainly due to the fact that the most important ones are state-owned bodies (especially the Caisse de Dépôts et Consignations and its affiliates). However, changes may be forthcoming, and some people expect that for example, under US influence, attention will be focused on the remuneration of corporate leaders.

In Germany

Although still mainly bank monitored, it would seem that the main German enterprises are paying more attention to the impact of the securities markets and their regulations. This change is sometimes linked to the decreasing role of the banks in enterprise financing, taking place against a background of increased competition between the banks. Also, flotations of securities have become more frequent, not against the wishes of the banks, but rather under their guidance, as solvency ratios are putting heavier burdens on their profitability.

The renewed importance of the securities market and the increased competition has lead the German banking industry to agree on a new pattern of regulation of the market, based on an integrated stock exchange and on integration of the clearing system. At the same time, the supervision of the markets would be re-regulated and reorganized. However, newcomers to the markets are still very rare, and, notwithstanding the considerable efforts, remain difficult to attract.

As a consequence of the increasing importance of institutional invest-

[66] Cass., 4 Feb. 1985, *Rev. Sociétés* (1985), 648; Dalloz (1985), 478, nte D. ohl (Rozenblum case); in the same sense: Cass., 13 Feb. 1989, *Rev. Sociétés* (1989), 693; Cass., 23 Apr. 1991, *Rev. Sociétés* (1991), 785, nte B. Bouloc (Broche). The literature has remained abundant in this field: F. Ichon, Fusion d'échelles d'intérêts et convention d'unité de compte, JCP, Ed. E., 1990, 15839; Ch. Dolfuss, La fiscalité des sociétés holding en Europe, Dalloz, 1991, 191; D. Plantamp, L'originalité du groupe de sociétés au sens de l'art. L 439-1 du code du travail, Dalloz, 1991, Chr. 69.

[67] See C. Duculoux-Favard, 'La société anonyme simplifiée, une idée nouvelle des juristes français', *Rivista delle società* (1991), 319.

[68] One of the first studies being by Y. Guyon, 'Les investisseurs institutionnels en droit français', to be published in T. Baums (ed.), *Conference on Institutional Investors* (Osnabrück, July 1992).

ment, including foreign investment, some writers have expressed their worries about the disappearance of the traditional monitoring by the banks, especially in cases in which crisis interventions is necessary, as these previously took place under direct bank guidance. The company may become difficult to manage since other corporate potential monitors would not offer sufficient guidance. Also, the risk has been voiced that no stable majorities in the general meeting will exist, resulting in a further destabilization of companies. A call for a powerful shareholdership has been made while a more intense use of existing mechanisms, for example, aimed at revitalizing the general meeting, has been considered. The potential role of institutional investors at present is not considered a viable alternative to the previously existing bank monitoring. More impetus is coming from the enterprise-linked pension funds, where interest of labour and capital are parallel.

The issue of takeovers is not one that is currently debated in Germany.[69] Companies are being taken over not on the public market, but as a consequence of private negotiation between present and future controlling shareholders. Some transactions however, come very close to a takeover, such as the Continental—Pirelli fight and the attempt by Krupp to take over Hoesch. These transactions did not, however, result in an aggressive bid. Defensive issues are therefore more frequently discussed, *inter alia*, the maximum voting rights which shareholders are allowed to possess (*Höhststimmrechte*).[70]

The law of groups of companies is still one of the major issues in German company law debates.[71] Although it is sometimes conceded that present regulation of the group law is not satisfactory as far as the *de facto* groups are concerned, more attention has been paid to the qualified *de facto* GmbH group, to which the rules of the *Aktiengesetz* are not applicable as such but to whom the supreme court has applied rules that are very akin to the ones applicable to the companies limited by shares.

Recently, in connection with the merger and division directives being planned for implementation, much attention has been drawn on to these issues, especially as these could be destructive of German enterprise culture.[72]

---

[69] However, excellent studies have been published: see Assmann, Basaldua, Bozenhardt, and Peltzer, 'Übernahmeangebote', *ZGR*, Sonderheft 9 (1990).

[70] See T. Baums, 'Höhststimmrechte', *AG* (1990), 221.

[71] See, for, the recent literature: M. R. Theisen 'Rücklagenbildung im Konzern', 156 *ZHR* (1992), 185; R. Hütteman, 'Der Entherrschungsvertrag im Aktienrecht', ibid. 314; P. Hommelhoff, 'Praktische Erfahrungen mit dem Abhängigkeitsbericht', ibid. 295; 'Probleme des Konzernrechts', ibid., Beiheft; K. Schmidt, 'Gleichordnung im Konzern, Terra Incognita?', 155 *ZHR* (1991), 417; H. P. Westermann, 'Umwelthaftung im Konzern', ibid. 223; W. Stimpel, 'Haftung im qualifizierten, faktischen Konzern', 20 *ZGR* (1991), 144; G. Teubner, 'Unitas Multiplex', ibid. 189; F. Rittner, 'Gesellschaftsrecht und Unternehmenskonzentration', 19 *ZGR* (1991), 203; See the comparative law overviews in 20 *ZGR* (1991), vols. 2 and 3.

[72] T. Baums, 'Die Auswirkung der Verschmelzung von Kapitalgesellschaften auf die Anstellungsverhälnisse der Gesellschafter', 156 *ZHR* (1992), 248; M. Paschke, 'Der

IN BELGIUM

In Belgium, too, the debate relating to corporate governance issues is not an explicit one. Issues that deal with governance are discussed in an unorganized way, without much view on the overall setting and mainly from the standpoint of interest groups. So, for example, there is little discussion on the issues of the one-tier or two-tier board, or on co-determination—as distinct from employee participation. The silence on the latter may be part of an implicit industrial agreement between the unions and the industry, and very much belongs to the southern European tradition rejecting co-determination.

The role and function of the auditors has been reviewed in 1985, at the time of the implementation of the Eighth EC Directive, and is not discussed anymore.

Case law reflects some '*de facto*' acceptance of the business judgement rule, although some decisions would tend to go further: in reviewing the 'reasonableness' of the board's decision by declaring it compatible or not to the company's 'own interest' as perceived by the tribunal.

Belgian company law, as re-stated in 1935, had not changed until the 1980s, when it was overhauled several times to conform to the EC directives. Exhaustive parallel legislation has been worked out dealing with accounting[73] and the professional organization of the auditors.[74] Recently, however, some very fundamental changes have been introduced in the system, mainly as a consequence of the shock wave that went through the country as a consequence of the takeover of the Société Générale de Belgique, attempted by the Italian businessman de Benedetti, but finally resulting in the French Compagnie de Suez acquiring the majority of the shares.

Extensive legislation was enacted, first on disclosure of significant shareholding, and on takeover bids,[75] later on remodeling substantial parts of the company law.

The former law led to more transparency in the corporate scene and revealed that most Belgian stock-exchange listed companies are more or less firmly controlled. In the takeover regulation, the most conspicuous rules deal with the mandatory takeover bid—framed in terms of acquisition of a controlling share at a price above market—and the rule prohibiting the

Zusammenschluszbegriff des Fusionskontrollrechts', ibid., Beiheft; B. Knobbe-Keuk, 'Umzug von Gesellschaften in Europa', 154 *ZHR* (1990), 325; 'Die Reform von Umwandlung und Fusion', 20 *ZGR* (1991), *Heft* 3.

[73] L. 17 July 1975 and RD 8 Oct. 1976; a RD of 6 Mar. 1990 deals with consolidation of annual accounts.

[74] These are the changes to the L. 22 July 1953 on professional auditors.

[75] L. 2 Mar. 1989 and its implementing decrees of 10 May, 1989 and 8 Nov. 1989; for comments see: A. Bruyneel, 'Les offres publiques d'acquisition—réforme de 1989', *JT* (1990) 141 ff; more generally, id., 'La réforme financière de 1990', *JT* (1991), 549; K. Geens *et al.* (n. 3 above); E. Wymeersch, 'Cession de controfóle et offres publiques obligatoires', *Revue pratique de sociétés* (1991), no. 6,575, p. 151.

board of directors to put into force defensive mechanisms once the bid has been disclosed. The mandatory bid rule especially resulted in important case law in the matter of *Wagon Lits*, the Brussels Court deciding on 6 August 1992 that, due to the existence of undisclosed agreements relating to the transfer of shares, French Accor acquired 'control' without disclosing it to the Banking Commission, and hence without bringing the obligatory bid. Plaintiffs would be allowed in substance to tender their shares at the same—very high—price at which Accor had bought.[76]

One should also mention the increasing concern about the predominance of foreign, especially French, interests in the Belgian economy. This concern led to proposals for better linking the leading enterprises to local ownership, including institutional investors and indirect state ownership.[77]

Among the more technical questions raised by the enactment of the 18 July 1991 change of the companies law[78] one could refer especially to the rules on 'conflicts of interest', as the rule has been framed in such broad wording that any personal interest, including moral or functional interests, are encompassed. Interlocking directorships also give rise to a conflict of interest, subject to the new legislation. Paralysis is the consequence.

Although rules on directors' liability were already quite incisive, they lacked teeth as no action could not be brought except after a majority vote at the general meeting. This requirement has been abolished, as any 1 per cent minority shareholder can bring a class action. It is feared that this remedy will often be abused in litigation within smaller, family-dominated businesses.

Among the more specific issues of the Belgian enterprise scene, one should mention the important position occupied by the holding companies, many dating back to the last century, some even before the foundation of the kingdom. These holding companies have been subjected to the supervision of the Banking Commission, acting mainly on the field of disclosure and conflict of interest. A quite interesting body of administrative case law has been developed by the Banking Commission, that could be described as a set of rules dealing with groups of companies.[79] The 1991 law has added legally binding regulation on cross shareholding, including cross shareholdings between parent and subsidiary.[80]

[76] See Brussels, 6 Aug. 1992, DAOR, no. 25 (1992) 63, and Trib. Comm. Brussels, 3, Sept. 1992, DAOR, no. 25 (1992) 93 in the so-called *Wagon Lits* case.

[77] See the report by the King Baldwin Foundation—Koning Boudewijnstichting, *Onze Welvaart: zelf beslissen, mee beslissen?* (1992).

[78] See e.g. CDVA, *Le Nouveau droit des sociétés* (SA et SPRL) (Coll. Fac. Liège, 1992); *Réforme du droit des sociétés*, Patrimoine, Bruylant, 1992, 193; J. Lievens, *De nieuwe vennootschapswet* (W. 18 juli 1991); F. Bouckaert *N.V. en B.V.B.A. na de wet van 18 juli 1991* (Biblo, Kalmthout, 1991); H. Braeckmans and E. Wymeersch eds., *Het gewijzigde vennootschapsrecht 1991* (Maklu, 1992).

[79] For an overview, see E. Wymeersch, 'La Commission bancaire belge et le droit des groupes de sociétés', *Riv. Società* (1986), 207

[80] Art. 52quinquies and sexies, Companies Law.

In the Netherlands

The Netherlands' company law has been substantially re-regulated as part of the overall reform of the Civil Code. At present it is part of Book 2 of the Code, relating to 'legal persons', Book 1 dealing with 'physical persons'.

The governance issue was much debated in the early 1970s, when the above-mentioned *structuurvennootschap* was introduced. Although in the beginning a not very popular institution, it seems more and more that the reform was an essential and rather successful part of Dutch industrial relations, while affording protection against unfriendly takeover bids.

This widening of the company interests to the enterprise interests is very characteristic of Dutch law. It is accepted that company decisions have to take into account the wider range of interests such as the interests of the employees and of the creditors. Hence, the regulation of takeovers and mergers results from a self-regulatory instrument, enacted by the Social-Economic Council, composed of representatives of the employers, employees, and of the Crown.[81] Aggressive takeovers are not favoured: these would first have to be submitted to the board of the target company.

These last few years the discussion has centered on the rules applicable to stock-exchange listed companies, especially the protective techniques of which Dutch companies have made such ample use.[82] The stock exchange favoured abolition, or at least reduction, of these protections, while the listed enterprises fiercely fought back. In the present stage of development[83]—an armistice rather than a peace treaty—allowance is made for protections that under certain conditions could be lifted

Another controversial issue relating to the same companies has been the obligation, effective only in 1992, to declare shareholdings exceeding the 5 per cent threshold.[84] Group law has received ample attention, both in case law and in legal writing. Some fine analyses have to be mentioned.[85] Finally,

---

[81] In fact the Merger Commission (Commissie voor fusicaangelegenheden). See Raaijmakers *et al.*, *De toekomst van de fusiegedragsregels* (Tjeenk Willink, 1992)

[82] For an overview of the protections, see esp. R. P. Voogd, *Statutaire beschermingsmiddelen bij beursvennootschappen* (Kluwer, 1989) BTM. Steins Bisschop, *De beperkte houdbaarheid van beschermingsmaatregelen bij beursvennootschappen* (Kluwer, 1991); R. P. Voogd, 'Statutaire beschermingsmiddelen bij beursvennootschappen' N. V. (1990), 202 ff.; also: Bosse, '1 per cent regelingen', TVVS (1991), 141.

[83] See, for the text of regulation X; Dortmond, NV (1992), 215. For commentary: Buijs, 'De beursregeling van beschermingsconstructies herzien', TVVS (1992), 247.

[84] See Willemsen, 'Inzicht in zeggenschapsverhoudingen', TVVS (1991), 81; C. P. Bierhuize, 'Het voorstel van wet melding zeggenschap in ter beuze genoteerde vennootschappen', 68 NV (1990), 145; Ho, 'Wetsontwerp melding; een gemiste kans', ibid. 137; P. Roos, 'Het wetsvoorstel melding zeggenschap in ter beurze genoteerde vennootschappen', WPNR (1991), no. 6015, 533; E. E. Canneman, in *Financieel Dagblad*, 25–7 Jan. 1992; van der Grinten, 'Illusies rond het wetsvoorstel Melding Zeggenschap', NV (1991), 133. The first lists of important shareholders have been disclosed: Beursplein 5, 7 Mar. 1992, p. 8.

[85] See van Achterberg, *De juridische definitie van het economische verschijnsel concern in het ondernemingsrecht* (Kluwer, 1991) S. M. Bartman and A. F. M. Dorresteijn, *Van het concern* (Gouda Quint, 1991).

important new legislation has attempted to prevent unscrupulous business-men making improper use of the company form.[86]

Conclusion

Corporate governance is debated in varying degrees in the different European countries compared. The discussion is mostly indirect and relating to specific issues that may be considered to have an impact on governance, but are not at the centre of the governance discussion. Also, the recent takeover movement, its rules and applications (including defensive techniques), has received much attention in these jurisdictions. Monitoring of corporate conduct, including the role of institutional investors, is an issue which is still not a major concern. One could attribute this limited interest to the structure of shareholdings: monitoring has always been strongly organized and assumed, whether by the banks (Germany) or by the controlling shareholders (France, Belgium, the Netherlands). However, it would not be correct to lump these systems together: in each company, governance is different and depends often on particular situations or even individual relationships. One difference from the Anglo-Saxon system could be safely stated: examples of the 'Berle and Means' type of corporation would be rather rare on the European Continent.

[86] See recently the requirement to transfer shares in unlisted companies by notarial deed: Ophof, 'Overdracht van aandelen op naam'. TVVS (1991), 277; for an overview: L. Timmerman, 'Aansprakelijkheid van bestuurders van nv.'s en bv's; een overzicht van enige recente rechtspraak', TVVS (1991), 197.

2

SOME ASPECTS OF THE CORPORATE GOVERNANCE DEBATE

D. D. Prentice

Introduction

The purpose of this paper is to provide an overview of the corporate governance debate. This debate at its broadest level involves the issue of the relationship between the stakeholders in a company and those who manage its affairs (the board of directors).[1] As regards the role of the board,[2] the major concerns have related to the establishing of mechanisms of accountability to ensure: (i) honesty and integrity on the part of the board; (ii) that directors do not pursue their own economic self-interest at the expense of the interests of others who have a stake in the company; and (iii) that there are in place effective structures for monitoring and evaluating the stewardship of directors. The role and responsibilities of the stakeholders in a company, and the protection to be accorded to their interests, has also been the subject of debate. There is the initial question of who is a stakeholder. It obviously includes the shareholders, but should there be a wider conception of the stakeholder class, for example, employees, creditors, or in some broad sense the community?[3] The last issue—corporate social responsibility—is particularly controversial where corporate action is clearly at the expense of the shareholder, since not all acts of corporate social responsibility are necessarily at the shareholders' expense in that they can often enure to the shareholders' long-term benefit.[4] In the USA the recent anti-takeover statutes clearly recognize the interests of stakeholders in this broader sense,[5] and in the UK, Section 309 of the Companies Act 1985 expressly imposes an obligation on corporate management to consider the interests of employees

---

[1] The latter will also be referred to as professional management, although it will be necessary on occasions to distinguish these.

[2] In this context we are normally dealing with sub-optimum performance, and not crass negligence which can be controlled by the disciplines of the market; but this, alas, is normally too late.

[3] See Handy, 'Priorities and Purpose at the Heart of Capitalism', *Financial Times*, 12 May 1992.

[4] Herman, *Corporate Control, Corporate Power* (Cambridge, 1981), 251–64.

[5] See Lipton and Panner, ch. 8 below, p. 115; Johnson and Millon, 'Missing the Point about State Takeover Statutes' (1989) 87 *Mich.L.Rev.* 846; see also *Paramount Communications, Inc.* v. *Time Inc.* 571 A 2d 1140 (Del 1989).

in discharging their functions. In addition, in other contexts there has been explicit recognition of a broad social responsibility on the part of companies.[6] One must concede, however, that these statements have often appeared aspirational in their thrust and have not provided a detailed blueprint for concrete action. Also, there have been powerful voices urging that the only proper role of companies is the pursuit of profit.[7]

The issue is not solely whether the interests of these stakeholders should (and if so, how) be factored into the corporate decision-making process, but conversely the question has been posed as to what, if any, are the obligations of the stakeholders. For example, does the concept of 'management accountability' carry with it some corollary obligation on the part of shareholders? Does 'accountability', as Jonathan Charkham states, imply 'a willingness to receive information and to react to it. It is a two way process.'[8] This aspect of the debate focusing on the duties and responsibilities of shareholders has gained greater prominence recently in the corporate governance debate. It will be returned to later.

Background to the Debate

This is not a new debate; concerns about corporate governance have existed almost since the foundation of the joint-stock company in its present form. Adam Smith did not have a great deal of good to say about the joint-stock company, which in his day was established either by act of parliament or royal charter. He had two principal criticisms of it. The first was directed towards investors in joint-stock companies, and although his criticisms of them were muted, he obviously did not hold them in particularly high esteem. These 'proprietors', as he called them,

seldom pretend to understand any thing of the business of the company; and when

---

[6] See e.g. City Code on Take-overs and Mergers, General Principle 9: 'It is the shareholders' interests taken as a whole, together with those of employees and creditors, which should be considered when directors [of an offeror or offeree company] are giving advice to shareholders.' See also *The Responsibilities of the British Public Company* (CBI, 1973), ch. 5 ('The Company and its Employees'); ch. 6 ('The Company and Society at Large').

[7] Fredman, *Capitalism and Freedom* (Univ. of Chicago Press 1962), 133: 'In such an economy [i.e. a free-market economy] there is one and only one social responsibility of business—to use its resources and engage in activities designed to increase its profits so long as it stays within the rules of the game, which is to say, engages in open and free competition, without deception or fraud.'

[8] Charkham, *Are shares just commodities?* in National Association of Pension Funds, *Creative Tension?* (London, 1990), 34 at 36; see also Charkham, *Corporate Governance and the Market for Companies: Aspects of the Shareholders' Role* (Bank of England Discussion Paper, 1989), No. 44, p. 7: 'Even so, shares are not just gaming chips and if they are treated as if they were, and if both institutional and private shareholders continue to neglect the introduction of ways of performing the limited duties the Companies Act confer upon them, the industrial system will continue to underperform and that may in time cast a shadow on the Companies Acts themselves. To argue that shareholders cannot realistically be expected to play their part is to invite a reconsideration of alternative structures such as the two-tier board which would facilitate their participation, and open the possibility of participation of others.'

the spirit of faction happens not to avail among them, give themselves no trouble about it, but receive contentedly such half yearly or yearly dividend, as the directors think proper to make to them.[9]

His criticisms of directors were more explicit and caustic:

The directors of such companies, however, being the managers of other people's money than of their own, it cannot well be expected, that they should watch over it with the same anxious vigilance with which the partners in a private co-partnery frequently watch over their own.... Negligence and profusion, therefore, must always prevail more or less, in the management of the affairs of such a company.[10]

The themes identified by Adam Smith have been developed and refined over the last two hundred years or so. One contribution merits special mention, and remains a classic of twentieth-century literature on the structure of the modern corporation: Berle and Means, *The Modern Corporation and Private Property*.[11] The Berle and Means argument has now become part of our intellectual luggage. The argument has an elegant simplicity. Because shareholders in the large listed company are dispersed, relatively ignorant, and individually hold a small percentage of the total issued shares of a company, they exercise little control over corporate management. There was a divergence between ownership and control—ownership being vested in the shareholders and control in the directors, with the latter being for all intents and purposes a self-perpetuating oligarchy. This separation of ownership and control had a potential, according to Berle and Means, for causing a divergence between the interests of the owners and managers without there being any effective check on the power of the latter. This inherent powerlessness of the shareholders has been exacerbated rather than reduced by the proxy-voting system, at least so far as the UK is concerned, because proxies tend to be exercised pro-management and are granted before any shareholder meeting is actually held.[12] The intellectual insights of Berle and Means have provided the point of departure for most contemporary writing on the corporate governance debate.

In the current literature (which is vast) on the debate, three major themes predominate: (i) the first deals with the costs, both explicit and covert, of carrying on business in collective form; (ii) the second addresses the issue of the appropriate role of shareholders in exercising control over, or in ensuring the accountability of, the board of directors; and (iii) the third deals with board function and board structure. The first theme sets out the nature

[9] *The Wealth of Nations* (Random House edn, New York, 1937), 699.

[10] Ibid. 700. Smith did not have a particularly high regard for academics either. This was because they were paid out of endowment and not, for example, by fees paid by students—performance-related payments as it were: see p. 718: 'In the University of Oxford, the greater part of the public professors have, for these many years, given up even the pretence of teaching.'

[11] First published in 1932.

[12] Gower, *Principles of Modern Company Law* (5th edn. 1992), 512–14.

of the problem, and the second and third themes address the question of a solution. I propose briefly to look at these matters seriatim.

Costs[13]

The costs of carrying on business in corporate form are often referred to as 'agency costs'. As economists point out, the firm (for which we can read company) and markets are alternative methods of organizing economic activity. As it becomes progressively more costly for entrepreneurs to negotiate separately with respect to each service or input needed for the conduct of their business, it becomes more cost-effective for them to integrate their activities within a single firm[14] and the corporate form of the firm is conveniently made available for this purpose. The corporate form also provides machinery for amassing capital under the collective control of professional management, which is beneficial in the sense that it permits specialization of function and clear differentiation between the task of management and that of risk-bearing.[15] However, this process of carrying on business in collective form gives rise to various types of cost. There are the obvious costs of setting up the arrangement for the carrying on of the collective activity of the firm and the costs of complying with any relevant legislation. In addition, there are the costs of monitoring how management is discharging its stewardship and, in particular, the costs flowing from the fact that management may pursue courses of conduct that are self-serving and that do not maximize the interests of a company's residual claimants, namely the shareholders. It has also been claimed that: (i) managers will be more risk-averse than is otherwise in the interests of shareholders since they have more to lose from failure, because unlike shareholders they cannot diversify their risk across a range of investments; (ii) that managers will satisfice (that is, reach decisions that are acceptable to the organizational group) rather than profit-maximize; or (iii) that managers may simply pursue policies of growth *per se* which, *inter alia*, to some extent will act as a barrier to a takeover.[16] Given these agency costs, the search has been for techniques to ensure that there is a congruence between the interests of management and the other corporate stakeholders, and this has been a central theme of the corporate-governance debate.

Role of Shareholders

The second theme in the corporate governance literature relates to the role of shareholders in monitoring and rendering accountable those who manage

[13] See Jensen and Meckling, 'The Theory of the Firm: Managerial Behaviour, Agency Costs and Ownership Structure' (1976) 3 *Econ.Jr.Fin.* 305.

[14] See Williamson, 'The Modern Corporation: Origins, Evolution, Attributes' (1981) 19 *Jr.Econ.Lit.* 1537.

[15] Fama and Jensen, 'Separation of Ownership and Control' (1983) 26 *Jr.L. Econ.* 301.

[16] Herman (n. 4 above), 257.

the affairs of a company. At one extreme is the position that shareholders as owners are free to exercise their ownership rights so as to maximize their own economic self-interest and are subject to no other countervailing responsibilities.[17] This view, fashionable in the 1970s and early 1980s, has been more recently called into question. Some have argued that it is too narrow a perspective to treat shareholders as the sole owners of a company, since there are others who have interests in the company, not least the company's management itself, and that these interests will not be considered adequately if the interests of shareholders with a 'betting-slip mentality' are allowed to prevail.[18] It has been argued that the interests of management must be considered so that they can be afforded an opportunity to take a long-term view of the company's commercial needs rather than be compelled by extraneous pressures to adopt a short-term strategy to maximize shareholder value. This concern about short-termism has led to proposals for curbing shareholder rights. One example is that of Lipton and Rosenblum, that elections to the board should be held every five years, thus to all intents and purposes disenfranchising shareholders during the five-year period.[19] This would be coupled with a five-year report which would comprehensively review the company's performance and set out its business strategy, and on which there would be comment by an independent expert. Less drastic proposals along these lines have been that shareholders should not be entitled to vote their shares unless they have held them for at least twelve months, a reform designed *inter alia* to curtail short-term profit-making from takeovers.[20] Other proposals have taken what appears to be a virtually diametrically opposed position. These have argued for greater shareholder involvement; for example, that institutional shareholders should play a more active role in corporate governance.[21] As we shall see later, these stances may not be as contradictory as they appear, since the former cluster of policies is designed to restrict 'exit', that is, shareholders voting with their feet and selling their shares, whereas the latter are intended to enhance (if not compel) 'voice', that is, active participation in corporate affairs.[22] Lastly, there are those who argue that shareholder passivity is

[17] This is the view of the law: see *North-West Transportation* v. *Beatty* (1887) 12 App. Cas. 589.

[18] See Lipton and Rosenblum, 'A New System of Corporate, Governance': *The Quinquennial Election of Directors* (1991) 58 *Chi.L.Rev.* 187 at 224 *et seq*. The distinction has also been drawn between 'punter-capitalists' of the UK and the US and 'proprietor-capitalists' of Germany and Japan: see Karmel, 'Is it Time for a Federal Corporation Law? (1991) 57 *Brook.L.Rev.* 55 at 65.

[19] Lipton and Rosenblum, n. 18 above (the proposal is much more richly textured than the brief description in the text).

[20] Sir Hector Laing, 'The Balance of Responsibilities', in *Creative Tension?* (n. 8 above), 59 at 66. There are analogues for this—a shareholder may not present a petition for the winding-up of a company unless he has been registered as such for six months: see Insolvency Act 1986, s. 124.

[21] This was one of the themes of *Creative Tension?*, ibid.

[22] See Professor Sir James Ball, 'Financial Institutions and their role as shareholders' in

inevitable since it is rational for a shareholder to remain passive. Given the costs[23] of making himself informed so as to vote intelligently, the minimal impact of his vote, the possibility that other shareholders may simply take a free ride on his efforts, and the *de minimis* incremental gain that will flow to a shareholder even should the action he supports be successful, it is rational for a shareholder to be apathetic.[24] This picture of shareholder apathy is one that is being called into question by the growth of holding of institutional shareholders, a topic addressed below by Paul Davies (Chapter 5).

BOARD STRUCTURE

The third theme of the contemporary debate on corporate governance has related to board structure. There have been a range of proposals (which have on the whole been treated as complementary rather than as alternatives): the split between chief executive and chairman; an enhanced role for non-executive directors; a schematic subcommittee structure of the board involving audit committees to deal with accounts and matters pertaining to the auditors, remuneration committees to deal with compensation of the executive directors, and composition committees to deal with the recruitment and appointment of non-executive directors. There has been little enthusiasm shown for a formally structured two-tier board, but some have felt that a subcommittee structure where the subcommittees are composed of at least a majority of non-executive directors will produce this effect.[25] There have also been proposals for a clearer perception of the role of the main board: English company law still clings to the outmoded principle that the board 'manages' the affairs of a company, whereas it is generally accepted that in reality, given the constraints of time, composition, and information, the role of the board is a supervisory one involving the monitoring of the performance of executive directors and senior management.

Two assumptions underly these proposals for board restructuring. The first, which is virtually explicit, is that there is a relationship between board

---

Creative Tension? (n. 8 above) at 18, where exit and voice are contrasted. This is based on Hirschman, *Exit, Voice and Loyalty: Responses to Decline in Firms, Organisations, and States* (1970).

[23] For the nature of the costs, see Rock, 'The Logic and (Uncertain) Significance of Institutional Shareholder Activism' (1991) 79 *Geo.L.Rev.* 445 at 460.

[24] See Black, 'Shareholder Passivity Reexamined' (1990) 89 *Mich.L.Rev.* 520. Older empirical studies support this picture of shareholder ignorance and passivity in the UK. Lee and Tweedie, *The Private Shareholder and the Corporate Report* (1971) found a low level of comprehension of the annual report on the part of the private shareholder; Midgley, *Companies And Their Shareholders—The Uneasy Relationship* (1975), reported that proxies were not exercised frequently and that shareholders never put forward any types of resolution. The fact that shareholders, particularly institutional shareholders, do not appear to exercise their votes does not entail that they are not actively monitoring corporate management, since institutional shareholders have other ways of making their views known and their influence felt. See p. 4, where this point is developed.

[25] See Sir Owen Green, 'Why Cadbury leaves a bitter taste', *Financial Times*, 9 June 1992 at 19.

structure and managerial performance. There have, to my knowledge, been no empirical studies on this (does board structure make a difference to a company's performance?) but it is a proposition which is capable of testing. There has been one study relating to compensation committees which showed that in companies with compensation committees composed in whole or in part of non-executive directors, executive directors were 18 per cent better paid than those in companies without such committees.[26] The second assumption underlying the proposals for restructuring the board is more implicit, and that is that shareholders will play a muted role in the governance of companies. No doubt shareholders will still have to elect the board, but in most cases this is a mere formality and there is little evidence, at least in the UK, of widespread shareholder activism with respect to the election or removal of directors. Thus non-executive directors will operate in lieu of shareholders voice.

The Context of the Corporate Governance Debate

Martin Lipton has stated that 'each generation must conduct the corporate governance debate within the parameters set by the prevailing manifestation of corporatism'.[27] What I propose to do in this part is to evaluate what are some of the more salient features of the UK context within which the debate needs to be conducted. This assessment is to be evaluated against a generalized concern, whether or not properly founded, that the present system of corporate governance is biased towards short-term results, and more generally that it has failed to deliver adequate industrial and economic performance.[28] If expenditure on R & D is a measure of blinkered horizons, this figure would bear out this conclusion. The top ten British companies in terms of R & D expenditure 'only just squeezed into the table of the top 100 international spenders'. Our largest spender on R & D research, ICI, was thirty-fifth in a world league table.[29] There are a number of broad

[26] Main and Johnston, 'Deciding on Top Pay by Committee', *Personnel Management* (July 1992), 32. They go on to hold that these committees 'seem to do little more than legitimise relatively generous pay awards' (p. 35). But size of salary (relative or absolute) is not an indication that such committees are not effective in getting value for money, since (somewhat paradoxically) the more successful a company the higher the salary where (as many recommend) it is to some extent performance-related: see Jensen and Murphy, 'CEO Incentives—It's Not How Much You Pay, But How', *Harv.Bus.Rev.* (1990), 138. Studies have shown a faster increase in directors' salaries than earnings per share or shareholder value (share-price increase plus dividends): see the *Independent on Sunday* (Business Review), 21 May 1990, p. 10; *Sunday Times* (Business), 12 July 1992, p. 6.

[27] Lipton, 'Corporate Governance in the Age of Finance Corporatism' (1987) 136 *Penn.L.Rev.* 1 at 3.

[28] In a survey conducted by 31 of 215 finance directors drawn from 740 of the largest UK quoted companies most were found to be of this view: see *The Times*, 13 Apr. 1992, p. 18. On the role of the banks and for an up-to-date discussion of the short-termism, see Capie and Collins, *Have the Banks Failed British Industry?* (IEA, 1992).

[29] See *The Independent*, 9 June 1992, p. 18.

institutional factors present in the UK which provide the backdrop for the contemporary corporate governance debate.

Finance Capitalism

A dominant feature of contemporary capitalism has been the separation of 'the decision of how to invest from the decision to supply capital for investment'.[30] In other words, the decision in what to invest is being made by persons other than those providing the funds for investment and who will enjoy the fruits of the investment. Coupled with this, the decision to invest (for example, as regards pensions) is one with respect to which many have no option.[31] Some of the implications of this are spelt out in later chapters, but one needs to be mentioned here. The prevailing public policy is to protect members of the public who supply the capital for investment against certain types of wrong-doing, which includes not only deliberate fraud but also incompetent or unsuitable advice. A major feature of this protection is the creation of compensation schemes which are industry-financed and operated.[32] These schemes are a salient feature of the regulation of markets selling financial products and services in general.[33] The setting-up of these schemes obviously requires a high degree of industry-wide co-operation and, while this has no necessary bearing on corporate governance, it does set up structures that enable the participants in the financial markets industry to co-operate. In addition, this type of industry-based regulation enables the government to harness it for the purpose of carrying out regulatory functions. An example of this would be 'whistle-blowing' responsibilities that could be imposed on a company's professional advisors.

Growth of Institutional Shareholders

Related to the above, there is the widely documented phenomenon of the growth of institutional shareholders, the figures on this are set out in Table 2.1.[34] This is the topic of a separate paper,[35] but at this juncture it suffices to point out that this arguably alters radically the landscape as regards the Berle and Means argument on the separation of ownership and control, in that there is now a body of shareholders with concentrated holdings possessing

[30] Clark, 'The Four Stages Of Capitalism: Reflections On Investment Management Treatises' (1981) 94 *Harv.L.Rev.* 561 at 564.

[31] A process that was facilitated by permitting the opting-out from state-provided pensions: see Goodman, *Social Security in the United Kingdom—Contracting Out of the System* (American Enterprise Institute, 1981); see also Davies, Chap. 5.

[32] See e.g. The Financial Services (Compensation of Investors) Rules 1992, Annex 2.

[33] They are also characteristic of other areas of consumer protection: see Borri, 'Trading Malpractices and Legislative Policy' (1991) 107 *LQR* 559.

[34] See *The Ownership of Company Shares—Share Register Survey Report at the end of 1989* (CSO, 1991). The statistics also indicate that individuals have relatively small holdings: see Table C7.

[35] See Chap. 5 below, by Paul Davies.

TABLE 2.1. *Distribution of shareholding between category of beneficial owner, 1963–1989* ($^o/_o$)

Sector of beneficial holder	1963	1969	1975	1981	1989
Persons	54.0	47.4	37.5	28.2	21.3
Charities	2.1	2.1	2.3	2.2	2.0
Public	1.5	2.6	3.6	3.0	2.0
Banks	1.3	1.7	0.7	0.3	0.9
Insurance	10.0	12.2	15.9	20.5	18.4
Pension funds	6.4	9.1	16.8	26.7	30.4
Unit trusts	1.3	2.9	4.1	3.6	5.9
Investments trusts/other financial institutions	11.3	10.1	10.5	6.8	3.2*
Industrial and commercial companies	5.1	5.4	3.0	5.1	3.6
Overseas	7.0	6.6	5.6	3.6	12.4
TOTAL	100.0	100.0	100.0	100.0	100.0

Note: *Includes SEPON ($0.5^o/_o$) the Stock Exchange account into which shares are placed while in transit between seller and buyer.

the expertise to exercise control over corporate management. In addition, shareholder passivity may no longer be the rational option. Selling an investment in an under-performing company could, because of the size of an institutions's holding, be self-defeating, and if exit is ruled out taking action to improve matters remains the only sensible option.[36]

PATTERNS OF CORPORATE FINANCE

The third issue relevant to the topography of the corporate governance debate is the structure and composition of corporate finance. The patterns of financing companies in industrialized countries show a considerable variation.[37] It has been argued that this dictates, or at least has a significant formative affect on, the structure of corporate governance. It is a commonplace to contrast the differences in the structure of corporate finance in Japan with that of the United States and the UK, although the implications of these differences are not always clear. A brief comment would be appropriate here on the position in Japan, which has similarities to that in Germany (the latter, however, will be dealt with by Professor

[36] It is interesting to note that of 215 finance directors drawn from 740 of the largest quoted companies who were surveyed by 3i, most appeared to be against giving an enhanced role to institutional investors: see *The Times*, 13 Apr. 1992, p. 18.

[37] See e.g. Baums, 'Should Banks own Industrial Firms', *Revue de la Banque* (1992), 249.

Baums).[38] Prowse gives statistics for the US and Japan as regards the percentages of corporate debt and equity held by various sectors. The statistic of interest is the percentage of equity and debt held by the banks which are set out in Table 2.2.[39]

TABLE 2.2. *Oustanding corporate equity and corporate debt held by various sectors in the US and Japan, 1984* (%)

	Equity		Debt	
	US	Japan	US	Japan
Commercial banks	0.0	20.5	45	65
Life insurance companies	3.0	13.3	18	25
Casualty insurance companies	2.2	4.4	2	na
Private and public pensions funds	14.5	5.3	17	na
Other corporations	11.1	24.0	2	na
Households	59.9	24.0		na
Foreign	5.0	5.0	5	na

Also, as has often been pointed out, Japanese business is carried on in group form (the *keiretsu*), and the provision of finance within this structure will involve a lead bank that organizes the activities of other banks.[40] It is claimed that these features of corporate finance have the following consequences: (i) Japanese firms have to compensate bond-holders less because the conflict between shareholders and bond-holders is greatly reduced, since investors as shareholders can prevent sub-optimal risk policies that affect them as bond-holders;[41] (ii) the fact that major creditors may also be major shareholders results in them being less willing to dispose of their securities, but rather than exit, they will want to remain within the company to protect themselves as creditors by retaining some influence over the affairs of the company; (iii) because of their position as debt financiers, banks as portfolio investors are better informed than their counterparts in

---

[38] See Chap. 10 below.

[39] 'Institutional Investment Patterns and Corporate Financial Behavior in the United States and Japan' (1990) 27 *Jr.Fin.Econ.* 43 at 45.

[40] Japanese banks, like their American counterparts, are forbidden to carry on investment banking and the percentage of stock that they can hold in domestic corporations is restricted to 5 per cent: see Coffee, 'Liquidity Versus Control—The Institutional Investor As Corporate Manager' (1991) 91 *Col.L.Rev.* 1,277 at 1,294. But this does not prevent them from forming consortia that own a healthy percentage of a company's equity: See Eolei, 'Toward an Economic Model of the Japanese Firm' (1990) 28 *Jr.Econ.Lit.* 1 at 14. It has been estimated that more than 65 per cent of all equity quoted on the Tokyo Stock Exchange is held by *Keiretsu* trusts: see Viner, *Inside Japan's Financial Markets* (1987), 46.

[41] Prowse (n. 39 above), 98.

the UK and US, and arguably will be in a better position to detect crisis earlier than would a straightforward investor;[42] and (iv) lastly (a point that has been documented by many), the group holding makes it virtually impossible to mount a hostile bid.

As regards the UK, as well as the growth of institutional holdings, the financing of companies would appear to involve a greater use of equity than debt as compared with other European countries,[43] and UK companies are to a larger extent quoted on the stock exchange than their European counterparts. Thus, for example, combining first-tier and second-tier markets, approximately 560 companies are quoted on the German stock exchanges, 640 on the French, 190 on the Brussels stock exchange, and over 2,000 in London.[44] For us, what are the implications of the patterns of corporate finance for the corporate governance debate? A number of questions can be posed. Institutionally, have we simply got the wrong design so that we will inherently be at a competitive disadvantage? Does the use of equity inherently produce an unstable and potentially disloyal shareholder body? And if one technique for penetrating a foreign market is acquisition (for example, the acquisition of a distribution network), does this mean that we are inherently at a competitive disadvantage since hostile acquisitions are possible within the UK market but not in many other jurisdictions?

TRANSPARENCY

The fourth factor relevant to the framework of the corporate governance debate is the transparency of the share register under English company law. It is a feature of English company law that there is a high degree of accurate information on the identity of the beneficial owners of a company's shares.[45] The fact that the share register is public, centrally located, and that copies are available on the payment of a modest fee,[46] entails that the directors cannot control access to the register. Coupled with this, there are provisions

[42] Cf. Artus, 'Tension to continue', in *Creative Tension?* (n. 8 above), 12 at 14: 'share ownership unaccompanied by the additional involvement in providing finance and other services will never provide the depth of knowledge and commitment that arises with the combination of banking and proprietary interests.' At the time of writing, Mr Artus was chief investment manager of Prudential Corp. PLC, which controls 3.5 per cent of the entire UK equity market.

[43] Coopers and Lybrand, *Barriers to Takeovers in the European Community* (1989, H.M.S.O.) (hereafter '*Barriers*') p. 15.

[44] Hopt, *European Takeover Regulation: Barriers to And Problems of Harmonizing Takeover Law in the European Community* in *European Takeovers–Law and Practice* (London, 1992). Of course the London listings will include overseas companies. See also Baums (Ch. 10 below), p. 151; Wymeersch (Ch. 1 above), p. 3.

[45] This is not to deny that there are problems with nominee holdings. Nevertheless, compared with other jurisdictions there is considerable transparency to the share register under English law.

[46] See Companies Act 1985, s. 356 (as amended). In other jurisdictions access to shareholder lists presents problems for those trying to mount an action against incumbent directors: see Black, 'Shareholder Passivity Reexamined' (1990) 89 *Mich.L.Rev.* 520 at 542; *Barriers to Takeovers In the European Community* (DTI, 1990), 16–17.

requiring disclosure of interests in shares which assist in identifying who are beneficial owners of a company's shares.[47] Also, in the UK bearer shares are not common. Although the primary motivation for these provisions was to provide the company with the means of discovering who are the beneficial owners of its shares, it also permits others to discover the identity of the owners of a company's shares for whatever purpose.

Takeovers—the Market for Corporate Control[48]

This is the topic of separate papers, but in the context of an overview of the corporate governance issue a number of points need to be made.

The first point is that, in European terms, the hostile bid is virtually a UK phenomenon. The statistics on this are set out in Table 2.3.

TABLE 2.3. *Number and value of contested acquisitions within each EC country, 1988*

Country	Number	Value (million)
France	1	765.4
Italy	1	na
Netherlands	1	93.0
UK	23	6,483.7
		7,342.1

Source: *Acquisitions Monthly* AMDATA.

Secondly, given the recent spate of statutes in the US and court decisions which enable the incumbent management[49] to defend against hostile bids, the UK may be one of a few major economies in which the hostile bid is free to flourish.

Thirdly, the theory of the role of takeovers with respect to corporate governance is straightforward and brutal—it is the *threat* of a bid which provides management with an incentive to maximize shareholder-return since (if successful) this will make their company bid-proof because they have ensured shareholder loyalty. A number of points need to be made with respect

---

[47] See Part VI, of the Companies Act 1985 ('Disclosure of Interest in Shares').

[48] See Alan Paul (Ch. 9 below), p. 135; Lipton and Panner (Ch. 8 below), p. 115. The statistics in Table 2.3 are taken from Coopers and Lybrand, *Barriers*, at 4.

[49] See Lipton and Panner (Ch. 8 below), p. 115. There is an unreported decision of Megarry V. C. which recognizes a wider power in directors to frustrate a bid than is normally accepted: see *Cayne* v. *Global Natural Resources PLC* (12 Aug. 1982).

to this issue. The first relates to the assumption that it is sub-optimally managed companies that are the target of takeovers. We have no clear evidence that it is only inadequately managed companies that are the targets, or potential targets, of hostile bids, and the question has to be raised as to whether in fact the bid is a device for taking over relatively well-managed companies, particularly those that are just being turned around after a lack-lustre period.[50] Also, to the extent that acquisitions are fee-driven (and there is some anecdotal evidence that this is the case),[51] there is no guarantee that takeovers will be exclusively motivated by considerations relating to their commercial benefits. Rather, the target company may (to some extent) have been put in play simply as a means of earning fees for the professional advisers. Secondly, both mounting a takeover or defending against one involves substantial costs, as is illustrated in Table 2.4.[52] These costs, particularly where the bid is unsuccessful, may simply be dead-weight costs to the respective companies that do not produce any countervailing advantages.

TABLE 2.4. *Defence costs*

Company	£ million	% of bid
JA Devenish	2.34	1.84
API	1.00	3.05
Invergordon	4.00	1.40
Magnetic Materials	0.43	4.34
Etam	1.17	0.97
Frogmore Estates	1.18	1.32
Torday & Carlisle	0.65	4.77
Ambrit	0.42	11.63

Source: TOI Corporate Services.

Fourthly, the theory is that it is the *threat* of a bid which is supposed to produce the beneficial results attributed to takeovers. But the possibility of the *reality* of a bid must also loom large if takeovers are to perform their disciplinary function—if a bid is a remote prospect then the threat of one is a remote threat. Where the benefits to a potential bidder from taking over a sub-optimally managed company do not justify the costs of a bid, no bid will materialize. As was stated by one commentator in the context of the US: 'Takeovers have their place, but they are a costly and imperfect way to discipline wayward managers. Only a badly managed target can justify the

---

[50] The theory of the role of takeovers also requires an acceptance of the principle that the market accurately values a company's shares. This is an issue that cannot be gone into here.
[51] See Blackman, 'Market forces put the lid on fees' (1992) *Acquisitions Monthly* (Mar.), 22.
[52] The *Observer*, 26 May 1992, p. 26.

typical 50 per cent takeover premium.'[53] The 50 per cent figure also appears to approximate the premium in the UK as regards contested bids. Table 2.5 sets out bid premiums for agreed and contested bids at different time periods before the bid or talks announced. The higher figure is probably the more accurate gauge of the premium since the bid obviously moves the market price towards the offer price.[54] Lastly, the threat of a takeover is irrelevant where the company is, to all intents and purposes, bid-proof (for example, with a weighted voting structure), or where the first indication of trouble wipes out the value of the company.[55]

TABLE 2.5. *Share-price premiums in UK public takeovers*
(%)

Period	Premium one day before offer	Premium one month before offer
Whole 1986	29	46
Whole 1987	28	39
Whole 1988	26	38
1989		
1st quarter	37	43
2nd quarter	26	39
3rd quarter	25	31
4th quarter	29	34
Whole 1989	29	36
1990		
1st quarter	19	20
2nd quarter	43	54
3rd quarter	27	33
4th quarter	30	26
Whole 1990	29	32

Source: *Acquisitions Monthly*/AMDATA (1991 March, at 24).

THE REGULATORY FRAMEWORK

The regulatory framework within which companies operate will manifestly affect the way in which the corporate governance issue is addressed. By regulatory framework I mean simply the prevailing legal and regulatory

---

[53] Black (n. 46 above), 520 at 522.

[54] Even this figure may be too conservative since the market normally moves before a bid is formally announced.

[55] See *Employee Participation and Company Structure*, Bulletin of the European Communities, Supp. 8/75, p. 32.

structure relating to the relationship of the board to the stakeholders. The regulatory framework provides a number of mechanisms that have a bearing on the question of corporate governance. These are: (a) litigation, (b) shareholder voice, and (c) government surveillance. Added to these, there are: (d) the role of auditors in ensuring compliance with a statutory system of mandatory financial disclosure, and (e) the regulation of takeovers; these latter two topics are the subject of other later chapters.[56]

LITIGATION

Litigation plays a relatively minor, if not non-existent, role in the UK in ensuring that directors comply with whatever legal duties are imposed on them; for example, in the last decade or so there have only been two reported cases of any significance involving a derivative action (that is, an action on behalf of the company commenced by shareholders).[57] In one of these, brought by the Prudential Insurance Company alleging wrongdoing by directors,[58] it was argued that the public spirit of the plaintiffs should be recognized and that the law should assist the process of self-regulation. The court's response to this appeal was distinctly frosty:

We were invited to give judicial approval to the public spirit of the plaintiffs who, it was said, are pioneering a method of controlling companies in the public interest without involving regulation by a statutory body. In our view voluntary regulation of companies is a matter for the City. The compulsory regulation of companies is a matter for Parliament.[59]

This, as Professor Gower rightly comments, is not likely to encourage institutional investors to take up the cudgels on behalf of their fellow private investors as they are constantly exhorted to do.[60]

The relative absence in the UK of litigation against directors is in contrast with the US, where litigation against allegedly wrongdoing directors is more widespread. There are a number of reasons for these significant differences. The *Prudential* decision already referred to is one. But the most important is unquestionably the existence of the contingent fee in the US, whereby the costs of the successful parties' lawyers can be recouped from any court-ordered award in favour of the successful party. Coupled with this, the courts have been willing to award attorney fees in a derivative action out of any amount recovered by the company.[61] The lawyer can also agree that this will be the sole source to which he will look for compensation—no win, no fee. Under such a system a certain amount of litigation will be commenced not for

[56] See below, Sir Adrian Cadbury (Ch. 3); Paul Reuteman (Ch. 4); Alan Paul (Ch. 9).
[57] *Prudential Assurance Co. Ltd.* v. *Newman Industries Ltd. (No. 2)* [1982] Ch. 204; *Smith* v. *Croft (No. 3)* [1987] BCLC 355. See also Stapledon (Ch. 11 below), p. 000
[58] *Prudential* etc. (ibid.); for a critique of this case see Gower (n. 12 above), 647–54.
[59] [1982] 1 Ch. 204 at 224.
[60] Gower (n. 12 above), p. 654, n. 67.
[61] Clark, *Corporate Law* at 659–62.

the purpose of obtaining legal redress but as a means of enhancing lawyers' incomes, in other word it will be fee-driven.[62] It is interesting to speculate whether takeovers in the UK are, as has been suggested, in reality fee-driven, and that this, as it were, is the UK analogue to the contingent fee.[63] Coupled with the absence of the contingent fee, the English rule of costs, whereby the loser pays the costs of the winning party, deters litigation unless there is a high probability of success.[64] Lastly, there are considerable technical legal impediments in the way of a shareholders bringing an action against directors. While such an action may be possible with respect to the plundering of corporate assets (which, despite recent events, does not appear to be a widespread phenomenon), it is virtually impossible for technical reasons to bring one with respect to sub-optimum performance involving negligence.[65]

VOICE

The regulatory framework also provides machinery for shareholders to exercise their 'voice' in order to bring pressure to bear on directors. For example, this can be done by meetings, proxy contests or votes to remove directors from office. It is simply not a part of the UK scene for these to be invoked in a co-ordinated manner as a means of ensuring accountability on the part of corporate management. For example, Midgley, in a somewhat dated survey carried out in 1975 to assess the extent of use of proxies and shareholder activism at meetings, found:

Even if a reply-paid card or form is provided the return for A. G. M. resolutions and most extraordinary general meeting resolutions rarely exceeds 15 per cent. If a form is provided but is not reply-paid the level of response dwindles considerably, and if no form is provided it seems that barely a handful of shareholders trouble to appoint a proxy. Where there are a few very large shareholders the votes which the proxy cards represent may amount to a high proportion of total possible votes. For most companies the potential votes in favour of resolutions submitted by proxy forms do not exceed 20 percent of total possible votes . . .

Companies were questioned as to whether during the last ten years any shareholders had attempted to exercise control by requisitioning any meetings, proposing or amending resolutions (other than formal votes of thanks etc.) taking any legal proceedings concerning the company, initiating any enquiry. A negative answer was given in all cases, except that one company recorded an unsuccessful

---

[62] See Coffee, 'The Unfaithful Champion: The Plaintiff As Monitor In Shareholder Litigation' (1985) 48 *Law & Contemp. Probs.* 5.

[63] See Morgan and Morgan, *The Stock Market And Mergers In The United Kingdom* (David Hume Institute, Edinburgh, Occasional Paper No. 24, 1990), 38 (professionals who act as advisers in takeovers have an incentive to seek out potential targets and encourage companies to make and persist in bids).

[64] For the effect of these and other aspects of English rules as to costs on the mature and incidence of litigation in the UK, see Prichard, 'A Systematic Approach to Comparative Law: The Effect of Cost, Fee, and Financing Rules on the Development of the Substantive Law', (1988) 17 *Jr.L.Stud.* 451.

[65] See Gower (n. 12 above), ch. 24.

attempt to amend a resolution and another the unsuccessful attempt by a ginger group to defeat the re-election of directors and propose the election of directors of their own choice.[66]

There is no evidence that much has changed. It is not clear why there is a lack of *overt* shareholder activity with respect to the exercise of ownership rights. In dealing with this apparent quiescence on the part of shareholders it is necessary to distinguish one-off complaints from systemic weaknesses in the corporate governance structure of a company. Whereas voice may be appropriate for the former it is to be doubted if it is appropriate for the latter, which requires the type of systematic restructuring which it is simply not possible to expect from the exercise of general meeting powers. Unless the shareholders, or a group of shareholders, have an ongoing relationship with the board, it is to be doubted if shareholders are in a position to ensure systematic reform. More importantly (and this may provide the explanation for shareholder inactivity), it may be that the failure to exercise formal rights at shareholders' meetings does not have any great significance where alternative, more appropriate avenues of influence are available, particularly to institutional shareholders. Failure to exercise votes does not necessarily betoken indifference if these alternatives are available.

There is some evidence that institutional shareholders do exercise pressure, but in a covert way.[67] As a starting-point, it runs contrary to human nature to assume that persons are indifferent with regard to their wealth and there is no good reason why this should not hold for institutional shareholders—after all, they are judged by their performance. The Institutional Shareholders' Committee urges a policy of persuasion rather than confrontation, and recommends that where an institutional shareholder proposes to vote against a management proposal it should, whenever possible, make representations to the board 'in time for the problem to be considered and for consultation to take place with a view to achieving a satisfactory solution'.[68] Also, with respect to a number of issues—pre-emption rights and employee share-option incentive schemes—the institutions have agreed policies with which listed companies with institutions widely represented on their share register have but little option but to comply. Because such influence is often covert, it is both difficult to measure quantitatively or to evaluate in terms of effect. As was stated by Professor Sir James Ball:

As presently conducted, there is more VOICE being exercised than is commonly supposed, and this has certainly increased in the 1980s. Nevertheless, the nature of

---

[66] *Companies and Their Shareholders—The Uneasy Relationship*, at pp. 52 and 54 respectively. This was a survey of 121 major companies in which fifty five of the companies approached agreed to participate: see p. 29. On the modern practice relating to proxies see Gower (n. 12 above), 512–5.

[67] And sometimes not so covert: see e.g. *The Role and Duties of Directors—A Statement of Best Practice* (Institutional Shareholders' Committee, 1991).

[68] *The Responsibilities of Institutional Shareholders in the UK* (Institutional Shareholders' Committee, 1991), 2.

this VOICE is unsatisfactory. It is not systematic. It takes place behind closed doors. The process itself is not subject to any serious kind of monitoring. Moreover, in the absence of the serious possibility of collective action by shareholders (however esteemed), there remains relatively little in the form of sanctions that can be applied other than a resort to EXIT—which presumably we are trying to avoid.[69]

GOVERNMENT SURVEILLANCE

I do not propose to deal with this in any great detail. There are provisions for the appointment of inspectors to investigate the affairs of companies, obtain information, and disqualify persons from acting as directors of companies. But these are *ad hoc* and have not led to the systematic examination of corporate governance by the regulatory authorities. In this debate the government has been very much a spectator, content to leave it to the City to sort out its problems.

Conclusion

The inevitable question is what form this debate will take in the future. This, of course, is the question which will be addressed in this book. As pointed out earlier, we may become one of few jurisdictions where the takeover can operate unhindered by regulation. Although the government appears now to be less convinced than it previously was on the merits of bids,[70] no official action has been taken to make them more difficult to mount.[71] The rhetoric against them appears to be gaining momentum. The future will probably concentrate on board restructuring coupled with institutional shareholders adopting collective strategies with respect to certain specific matters corporate governance which are of concern to them.[72] The attractions of this approach are obvious. Given that all investors benefit from collective action which affects all companies, the most appropriate strategy is to attempt to improve the corporate governance system rather than to improve the performance of individual companies. The central issue is whether the present 'self-help system', not involving any direct statutory intervention, will be effective or will be nothing more than a cosmetic exercise. If the latter proves to be the case then some type of government regulatory involvement seems inevitable.

[69] In *Creative Tension?* (n. 8 above), 24.

[70] See DTI press notice, 7 Dec., 1990, Mr John Redmond (the then Corporate Affairs Minister): 'Evidence is rising that, except in the very short-term, takeovers can all too often damage the wealth of shareholders of the bidding company rather than improving it. Only a limited number of British companies have been adept at taking over others, and taking the businesses on to better success.'

[71] See Panel Statement on the Report of a Panel Working Party on Takeover Rules and Practices, 1989/10; *The UK Panel On Takeovers And Mergers: An Appraisal*, Hume Occasional Paper No 21 (David Hume Institute, Edinburgh.).

[72] e.g the NAPF initiative in uncoupling executive stock option schemes from earnings per share: see the *Financial Times*, 6 July 1991, p. 1; *Share Schemes—A Consultative Approach* (NAPF).

Part II
The Role of Financial Disclosure

The Cadbury Report was published on 1 December 1992, and at the time this essay was written Sir Adrian Cadbury was addressing the Draft Report which had been published on 27 May 1992. It is important to note, as Sir Adrian points out, that the committee's terms of reference were restricted to the issue of corporate financial reporting and how the process might be improved. This, however, is an issue of considerable importance. Mandatory disclosure has been a central feature of company law for the last fifty years, and the objectivity, comprehensiveness, and comparability of a company's financial reports is central to the effective implementation of this policy. As Paul Rutteman points out, an essential ingredient for an effective disclosure policy is standardized accounting principles which do not allow alternative accounting treatments of similar subject-matter. This aspect of corporate disclosure must also be examined, as Paul Rutteman states, in the light of the accounting reforms introduced by the Companies Act 1989, which are intended to create a greater uniformity in corporate accounts and enhanced compliance with agreed accounting standards.

3

HIGHLIGHTS OF THE PROPOSALS OF THE COMMITTEE ON FINANCIAL ASPECTS OF CORPORATE GOVERNANCE

Sir Adrian Cadbury

The Committee on the Financial Aspects of Corporate Governance was set up in May 1991 by the Financial Reporting Council, the London Stock Exchange, and the accountancy profession. Its sponsors were concerned about the perceived low level of confidence in financial reporting and in the value of audits. The underlying factors were seen as the absence of a clear framework for ensuring that directors kept under review the controls in their business, together with the looseness of accounting standards and the competitive pressures on companies and on auditors which made it difficult for auditors to stand up to demanding boards.

These concerns were heightened by some well-publicized failures of companies, whose accounts did not seem to have given any warning of the true state of their affairs. In addition, there were criticisms over the apparent lack of board accountability for such matters as directors' pay.

Terms of Reference

The committee was given a relatively narrow remit and it was envisaged that it might be in a position to report by the end of the year. This point is worth making because it emphasizes how quickly corporate governance, in itself an infelicitous phrase, has moved from being largely a matter of debate between those directly involved to becoming a public issue. The committee found itself the centre of unanticipated public attention, as boardroom pay made the headlines and as the BCCI and Maxwell sagas unfolded. It also became a convenient parking place for new problems in the governance field as they arose.

As the public debate widened from issues arising from financial reporting and control to the whole question of the effectiveness and accountability of boards of directors, the limitations of the committee's terms of reference were often lost sight of and it was assumed that it was dealing with corporate governance and not simply with its financial aspects. This misunderstanding is still apparent in the responses which the committee has received to its draft report. For example, the committee has been chided for not examining alternative methods of corporate governance, as practised in other countries.

Corporate Governance

Corporate governance in its broadest sense takes in the whole framework within which companies operate. That framework is partly set by the law, partly by the participants themselves, and more widely by society. While the legal requirements on companies are relatively predictable, the boundaries to corporate behaviour set by the participants and by society are continually shifting. On the whole, the shift is in an upward direction; the standards expected of companies tend to rise and the interests which they are expected to take into account tend to broaden.

Corporate governance in terms of the committee's remit is the system by which companies are run. At the centre of that system stands the board of directors whose actions are subject to laws, regulations, the disciplines of the market-place, and the shareholders in general meeting. The shareholders in turn are responsible for appointing the directors and the auditors, and it is to them that the board reports on its stewardship at the Annual General Meeting.

The link between the board and the shareholders is the reporting system through which the board accounts to them for the progress of the company. The role of the auditors is to provide the shareholders with an external and objective check on the directors' financial statements, which form the basis of that reporting system. Although the reports of the directors are addressed to the shareholders, they are important to a wider audience, not least to employees, whose interests boards have a statutory duty to take into account.

Basis of Report

The committee's terms of reference require it to consider a number of issues relating to financial reporting and accountability and to make recommendations on good practice. The report, therefore, opens by reviewing the structure and responsibilities of boards of directors and deriving from that review a Code of Best Practice.

As a result, the committee has focused on the control function of the board and has not dealt with its literally vital role of providing the company with leadership and drive. This has led to the misunderstanding that we see boards as brakes rather than as accelerators, when in fact we appreciate only too clearly that they are both, and that the art of direction could be said to turn on judging when to apply the one or the other.

We have, as a committee, been conscious throughout that the national interest lies in fostering enterprise and entrepreneurial drive. But the pursuit of these qualities must be balanced by acceptable safeguards for those who are investing their money or their livelihood in the companies concerned. The encouragement to take risks has to be matched by the building in of sufficient checks and balances to retain the confidence of those on whom the efficient working of the system depends.

Report Principles

This leads on to what I would suggest are some of the principles underlying the committee's approach to its task. These are that:

- there is no inherent conflict between the demands of efficiency and control; more often than not they go hand in hand, and a business where the control system is weak is unlikely to continue to be efficient;

- there is a basic requirement for disclosure, for boards to be as open as is commercially feasible about their actions and their plans; the accountability of boards depends on the provision of timely and relevant information, as does confidence in the governance system;

- the responsibilities for financial reporting and control have to be unambiguously clear; this is against a background of undoubted confusion over the respective responsibilities of directors and auditors;

- the necessary checks and balances have to be built into the operating structure of companies if the governance system is to remain largely self-regulating within the legal framework.

The committee took the governance system as it was, partly because its terms of reference only addressed certain aspects of the system, but also because the way in which the majority of companies are run in this country does not appear to call for a basic change in the framework within which they operate.

This approach has been supported by the evidence which the committee has received. This has been almost wholly directed at improving the working of the present system of governance and not at changing it. What the committee felt was called for was a tightening-up of the existing system and the establishment of yardsticks against which standards of corporate behaviour could be judged. Here, the committee's proposals need to be considered alongside the programme which the Financial Reporting Council, the Auditing Practices Board, and the Accounting Standards Board have in hand for strengthening the accounting framework.

Code of Best Practice

At the heart of the committee's recommendations is the Code of Best Practice which is to apply to all listed companies registered in the UK. The committee expects companies to be required under the London Stock Exchange's listing agreement to state how far they comply with the Code.

The Code itself is based on the need for openness, integrity, and accountability. It starts with the nature, task, and composition of the board of directors, because a company's standards are set from the top and the board is responsible for all that goes out in its name. Boards should be in full control of their businesses and should combine the expert knowledge of executive directors with the outside experience of non-executive directors. It is the responsibility of chairmen to hold their board teams together and to get the best out of them. It is also for chairmen to ensure that the interests of those whom the company is there to serve are unfailingly taken into account and balanced.

Given the primary importance of their task, chairmen should not in principle double up as chief executives, a quite different and separate role. There should also be a clearly accepted division of responsibilities at the head of a company, so that no one individual has unfettered power. If the chairman is the chief executive, it is essential that there should be a strong, independent element on the board to ensure that the interests of the company prevail at all times.

Non-Executive Directors

Non-executive directors and executive directors carry the same legal responsibilities and the same duty to provide the leadership which companies look to from their boards. Non-executive directors, however, are well placed to exercise an independent judgement over the particular aspects of corporate governance with which the committee was concerned, such as financial reporting and control, because they stand back from the day-to-day management of the business.

In addition, boards may have, from time to time, to face perfectly proper conflicts of interest. These can arise as a result of takeover bids, management buy-outs, top-level succession, and the determination of directors' pay. Here again the independent judgement of the outside directors can be invaluable to the board as a whole in coming to its collective decisions.

The committee's recommendations on non-executive directors include that their calibre and number should be such as to ensure that their views carry significant weight with the board, that the majority should be independent of the company apart from their fees and their shareholding, that they should be nominated by the board or by a nominating committee of the board (to avoid any suggestion of patronage), and that they should be appointed for fixed terms with no automatic expectation of reappointment.

Independence

A basic issue which arises in discussing the role of non-executive directors is what is meant by the term 'independent'. This is a point which the committee may wish to consider further, so my view on the matter is at this stage only a personal one.

The simple distinction is between directors whose involvement with a company is limited to their seat on its board and those who have some further link with the company, such as former employees or members of firms which may supply services to the company. The second group will have been appointed to the board because of the contribution which they can make to it, and referring to them as not being independent carries no implication that their board standing is different from that of their fellow non-executive directors.

Non-executive directors who have no business or financial connection with a company apart from their fees and their shareholding are in the best position to take the lead on those committees of the board, such as the audit, remuneration, and nomination committees, where potential conflicts of interest could arise. This provides an assurance to everyone concerned that the final decisions taken by boards are taken in the light of advice from those best placed to make an objective assessment of where the interests of the company lie.

A misunderstanding to which the distinction between independent directors and their board colleagues seems to have given rise is that this is all a matter of trust, with the implication that only the former group is to be trusted. This is to miss the point. The aim is that all members of a board should contribute from their own particular standpoint, and just as executive directors will take the lead over matters where knowledge of the business is of paramount importance, so will independent directors where the balancing of interests is the prime concern.

There is, however, a need to go further than the simple distinction with which I started. If the fees were high or the shareholding large, could a non-executive director still be considered to be independent? Alternatively, if non-executive directors either use the services of the companies on whose boards they sit or have some other business relationship with them, does this debar them from being considered independent?

In my view it is all a question of degree. I like the approach of the New York Stock Exchange to the question of membership of audit committees: 'an Audit Committee comprised solely of directors independent of management and free from any relationship that, in the opinion of its Board of Directors, would interfere with the exercise of independent judgment as a committee member.' That puts the responsibility where I consider that it belongs, on to the directors individually and collectively to determine who is in a position to exercise independent judgement. The test which they would apply is that of materiality. There is no reason to suppose that if bank directors have accounts at their own bank, that this would affect their independence of judgement.

Materiality, however, is an individual matter and cannot be reduced to objective rules. Even when it comes to fees or shareholdings, for example, what could be immaterial to one director, could be material to another. Thus we are left with broad guide-lines, within which there is a need for directors to determine individually and collectively where they stand.

There remains the important issue of how the outside world is to know on what the determination of independence has been based. Here we need to rely on disclosure. Provided that directors declare their interests in full, then shareholders and others can judge for themselves the degree of independence which those directors bring to the board.

Board Control

The aim of the committee's proposals on the composition of boards is to ensure that boards have an appropriate balance of external non-executive directors and internal executive directors, and that there are enough independent non-executive directors to give a lead on those matters where an outside, objective view is looked for. A board made up in that way is in a position to exercise full control over a business.

If, however, board members are to control their company to the degree expected of them, they must have the means to do so. The Code requires boards to report on the effectiveness of their companies' system of internal financial control and to appoint audit committees of the board made up of non-executive directors, the majority of whom should be independent in the terms which have been already discussed. An issue which has been raised in response to the draft report, and which the committee will want to address, is whether executive directors do not also have a useful part to play as members of audit committees.

Board Structure

While there is a wide degree of agreement over the importance of effective audit committees to sound governance, there is a tendency in this country to be somewhat dismissive of organizational orthodoxy. This is on the basis that, provided the right people are on the board, any governance system can be made to work.

The converse to that proposition is clearly true, but it would be misguided to underrate the role of structures in governance. Audit committees, for example, give non-executive directors the opportunity to become involved in a key area of the board's work and to extend their knowledge of the business, without treading on management's toes. At the same time they give the board the reassurance that financial reporting and control systems have been reviewed in more detail than would normally have been possible for the board as a whole. Audit committees are committees of the board, and so the board abdicates no part of its responsibilities by setting them up; they are there to assist the board in the discharge of its duties.

Disclosure

The Code's approach to board accountability is to require the highest level of disclosure by boards consonant with the competitive position of their companies. The principles of disclosure are that financial reporting should meet the traditional test of being true and fair, and that boards should present a balanced and understandable assessment of the state of their companies. The committee supports the aim of including with that assessment an explanation of the factors likely to influence the company's future progress.

On the much-discussed question of directors' pay, the committee proposes a higher level of disclosure than is at present required, so that not only the amount but also the basis of the remuneration of those heading the business are openly declared. The Code also proposes that the pay of the executive directors should be subject to the recommendations of a remuneration committee made up wholly or mainly of non-executive directors.

The committee considered thoroughly various proposals for putting directors' pay to the vote at the AGM, but the difficulty with such an approach lies in the nature of a general meeting. A resolution can only be supported or defeated, but not modified, the course which shareholders dissenting over remuneration would be most likely to wish to take. If shareholders voted against a particular remuneration package, the board would still have to decide how the director concerned was to be paid. In addition, the pay of new directors has to be agreed at the time of their appointment and cannot be left until an AGM.

Auditing

Before returning to the role of shareholders, I will comment briefly on the question of auditing. The committee considered the audit process in detail, since its perceived value was a particular concern of its sponsors. The committee concluded that the annual audit was one of the corner-stones of corporate governance and an essential element in the corporate system of checks and balances.

The two issues which the committee addressed were how to ensure that audits were objective and effective. Maintaining the necessary degree of objectivity is the joint responsibility of auditors and of boards of directors. The committee proposes that it should be reinforced by a periodic change of audit partners and by disclosure of the total fees earned by auditing firms for non-audit work.

To increase audit effectiveness, the committee recommended that the audit coverage should be extended to include the internal system of financial control and the ability of companies to continue as going concerns.

The auditor's role is to report to the shareholders on whether a company's financial statements give a true and fair view, and the audit process is designed to provide a reasonable assurance that they are free of material misstatements. There is a degree of confusion over the respective responsibilities of directors and auditors for financial statements. The committee, therefore, recommends that a brief description of directors' responsibilities for the accounts should appear in the Directors' Report as a counterpart to a statement by the auditors about their reporting responsibilities.

Caparo

The *Caparo*[1] judgement is clearly of considerable consequence to all preparers and users of accounts. The committee did not recommend that the legal position with regard to civil liability laid down by *Caparo* should be altered by statute, but did point out that auditors are fully liable in negligence to the companies they audit and to their shareholders collectively.

Caparo can perhaps best be considered as unfinished business, both in the sense that the case continues and in the sense that the present judgement seems unlikely to be the last word on the matter of reliance on audited accounts.

Role of Shareholders

The final section of the committee's report considers the role of shareholders and how their influence could be strengthened in the interests of board effectiveness and board accountability. A number of proposals were made to the committee based on the formation of shareholder committees, to act on behalf of all shareholders as a direct link with boards of directors. The problems over shareholder committees are practical and constitutional; they include how to ensure that they are truly representative, how they would keep in touch with all their constituents, and how they would balance the interests of institutional and individual investors.

It was because the committee found it difficult to see how shareholders

[1] [1990] 2 AC 605.

could act collectively that it recommended that both shareholders and boards of directors should consider how the effectiveness of general meetings could be increased. Too often AGMs are an opportunity missed, and the committee has put forward suggestions for making them more useful occasions for boards and for shareholders. A more fundamental suggestion which has been put to the committee is that the Companies Act should be altered to make it easier for shareholders to submit resolutions to general meetings.

The institutions are the shareholder group which is best placed to influence the standards of corporate governance. It is in their collective interest to raise the level of company performance, since speaking generally they can only sell the shares of a company with which they are dissatisfied to each other. They have the resources to monitor the major listed companies, if they shared the burden between them. They are, however, on the whole acting as agents for others, and their willingness to take an active interest in the governance of companies turns on the degree to which they see it as their responsibility as owners to do so and the extent to which it will be of advantage to those whose money they are investing.

The Committee, therefore, warmly welcomed the positive approach towards governance put forward by the Institutional Shareholders Committee in their publication on the *Responsibilities of Institutional Shareholders in the UK*. This proposes that there should be regular contact between institutional investors and senior executives, that institutions should use their voting rights, and that they should take a positive interest in the composition of boards of directors.

An important point about the institutions as shareholders is that many of them, like the pension funds, work to long time horizons. They have, therefore, every incentive to encourage boards of directors to adopt the same time-frame in running their companies. This alignment on the aim of the consistent creation of shareholder value into the future would do much to counteract the insistent criticism that UK shareholders and directors focus on short-term results at the expense of longer-term growth, in contrast to our more successful competitors.

The Unitary Board

Before considering how the committee's draft proposals are to be turned into action, there is one issue which needs to be flagged up. The committee's recommendations are addressed, as I said at the outset, to the present pattern of governance in this country. They do not take into account governance systems in the rest of Europe—keeping in mind that they themselves vary considerably—nor whether there will be some movement towards convergence in this field as the Single European Market becomes a reality.

Hence, the role which the committee sees non-executive directors playing in corporate governance does not represent a move towards a two-tier board structure. What is proposed is a distribution of responsibilities within a unitary board without detracting from the overall authority of the board itself. All directors have equal legal responsibilities and all share the same duty to the company. It is up to chairmen and their fellow directors to make the best use of the individual capacities of board members. Non-executive directors have a particular contribution to make within the board, which is of special relevance to the issues which the committee was set up to consider. They do so, however, as part of the board, not as a separate group within it. The responsibility for retaining the essential unity of the board is, in my view, squarely that of the chairman.

Action on the Report

This brings me to the matter of how the committee's final proposals, (given that this is a draft report) will be put into effect. The committee is looking for broad support for them from the three main constituencies which it is addressing: boards of directors, shareholders, and the accountancy profession. That support is necessary to establish the Code of Best Practice and thus to set the standard which the great majority of companies will then wish to be seen to meet. Force of example will, therefore, have its place in bringing about compliance with the committee's proposals.

More specifically, the London Stock Exchange is expected to require listed companies registered in the UK to state how far they comply with the Code and to give reasons for any areas of non-compliance. This will make public the extent to which companies are in line with the Code and so where they stand in relation to those aspects of corporate governance covered by the committee's proposals.

It will then be up to shareholders to press their boards to comply, or to be convinced that their boards are justified in taking a different stance. Either way, the information on a company's approach to governance will be available to shareholders and to financial commentators. In effect, the committee has provided them with an agenda for a dialogue with boards of directors. This will encourage shareholders to focus on the committee's recommendations and so will assist in their implementation.

A strong incentive for boards of directors to implement the Code's proposals lies in the knowledge that they will be followed up. The committee has proposed that the Financial Reporting Council should convene a new group in May 1994 to monitor progress and to consider whether the Code needs updating; this would be the first stage in an ongoing process.

The ultimate, if negative, argument for compliance with the committee's proposals is that failure to do so could well lead to a greater degree of regulation. The problem about regulation in this particular field is that it is difficult to frame statues which will raise standards of conduct and improve the quality of governance. Many of the committee's proposals are qualitative in nature and are proper subjects for the judgement of shareholders rather than for the rule of law.

Throughout, the committee has recognized the diversity of companies and of those responsible for running them. It has not attempted to impose a single pattern of governance, but rather to state the principles on which it considers good governance should be based, leaving it to those responsible to decide how best to implement them.

When the committee's recommendations appear in their final form, I believe that they will be broadly supported, because they go with the grain of promoting a competitive and efficient company sector and because boards will consider it to be in the interests of the market-standing of their companies to do so.

4

CORPORATE GOVERNANCE AND THE AUDITOR

Paul Rutteman

Introduction

The Cadbury Committee was set up by the Financial Reporting Council, the London Stock Exchange, and the accounting bodies in response to mounting criticism of the quality of financial reporting and the effectiveness of the audit. The context was some well-publicized major scandals involving fraud and the sudden collapse of a number of companies shortly after receiving clean audit opinions. The accounting profession took the initiative in order to deal with the much discussed but ill-defined 'expectations gap'.

In this paper I propose to review the Cadbury recommendations as they affect the auditor, question some of the conclusions, and put forward some views of my own as to what can and cannot be done to meet the criticism and to bridge the expectations gap.

Code of Best Practice

The starting-point for a response to the criticism is to make it clear just who is responsible for financial reporting and financial controls of a public-interest company. The focus must be primarily on the directors rather than the auditors. Auditors may be somewhat over-sensitive on this point, but they feel that whenever a scandal occurs or a company fails the auditors seem to be attacked rather more than the directors, and are certainly much more likely to be sued. The *Caparo*[1] decision may change that perception, but auditors and their professional indemnity insurers have yet to be convinced. However, the terms of reference of the Cadbury Committee appear, therefore, to be primarily concerned with directors' responsibilities and only secondarily with those of the auditors.

The principal recommendation of the Cadbury report is a Code of Best Practice which listed companies would be expected to follow. It would not be a statutory requirement but, more in keeping with City tradition, would be called voluntary. A recommendation that companies state in their annual report that they comply with the Code of Best Practice would not be worth much in the absence of both a monitoring mechanism and sanctions. The sanctions would be applied by the London Stock Exchange, which would

---
[1] *Caparo Industries plc* v. *Dickman* [1990] 2 A.C. 605.

make it a requirement of continued listing that companies include a compliance statement in their annual report. The CBI is unhappy with this proposal, arguing that its mandatory nature will make it inflexible and less open to development and that the sanctions are unworkable anyway because removal of listing would be too draconian a measure. While there is some merit to that argument, the alternative of no sanctions and a truly voluntary system would deprive the Code of its usefulness—those who were already complying would continue to do so, others might choose not to. It is a pity, therefore, that the London Stock Exchange has already announced that it will not make it a requirement of the Listing Agreement that companies state their compliance with the Code of Best Practice.

It is in the area of monitoring compliance with the Code that the greater difficulties arise. Cadbury suggests that auditors would endorse the directors' statement of compliance, but the Code of Best Practice is broadly drawn and covers a number of areas on which it would be difficult for an auditor to express an opinion. For example, without actually attending board meetings how can an auditor opine on whether the calibre and number of non-executive directors are such that their views carry significant weight in the board's decisions, and whether they really do bring an independent judgement to bear on issues of strategy and financial performance? A blanket endorsement of the directors' statement of compliance with the Code of Best Practice cannot be lightly given, and if routinely appended would certainly not narrow the expectations gap—it would widen it. Perhaps the solution lies in a limited endorsement which makes it clear that the auditor confirms that the formal parts of the Code have been complied with but does not express a view on the quality of management.

Internal Control

In addition to a statement of compliance with the Code of Best Practice, directors would be expected to set out a statement in the annual report on the effectiveness of their system of internal financial control. Again the auditors would be expected to report on that statement. This follows the lines of a submission by the Institute of Chartered Accountants to Cadbury and is based on developing practice in the US. A typical report on internal controls in the US would contain a statement by management as to the nature of the audit control system it had put in place and the roles of its internal auditors, its external independent auditors, and any audit committee in overseeing and in evaluating these controls. There would also be a statement from the company's independent auditors on the adequacy of the company's financial statements and its accounting principles.

I support the proposal but recognize the practical difficulties involved, not the least of which is determining what is meant by a system of internal control. Clearly we are talking about more than a system of proper bookkeeping. There needs to be a management information system whereby top management receives financial information on a timely basis in a form that enables it to take decisions. The control system needs to ensure the safeguarding of the company's assets. But how much further does it need to go?

At present the accounting bodies are working out, together with representatives from industry, some guidance on the controls concerned, how to assess their effectiveness and the form of report to be given. It is not proving as easy as might be expected. Should the controls simply extend to the provision of up-to-date and accurate financial information, or should controls over efficiency be included? And how should the directors and auditors report?

At present auditors normally provide directors with a management letter following the annual audit in which they report any weakness in the systems which came to their attention in the course of their audit. It is standard practice to point out that the auditors have not carried out a comprehensive review of the system of internal control so that there may be other weaknesses not referred to in the letter. Will the auditors have to carry out a complete systems review in future in order to report on the directors statement? And if some weaknesses are found, will they have to qualify their report in significant detail if the management letter is to contain worthwhile points? In the US the directors often include a statement of responsibility for the controls, but the auditors do not report on it formally. Clearly, if the statement were inconsistent with the facts the auditors would feel compelled to act. That is a possible solution in the UK also.

Audit Committee

The recommendations of Cadbury that all listed companies should have an effective audit committee is welcome. However, the emphasis needs to be on *effective*. Many companies already have audit committees, but the quality and effectiveness of such committees is variable. I have worked with very good audit committees and have come across others less good. In one, the chairman of the audit committee, although a non-executive director, was a close relation of the chairman of the company. The key to the effectiveness of such a committee lies in the quality of the non-executive directors, and too often companies with strong chairmen have had weak non-executive directors. Cadbury clearly recognizes the danger and therefore proposes that non-executive directors should be nominated by the board as a whole (good in theory, but a strong chairman will still secure the appointment of his candidates in practice). A better idea is to have a nomination committee comprising a majority of non-executive directors. Cadbury appears to accept that the chairman should chair the nominating committee, but it seems preferable to have a non-executive director chair it.

Expanded Interim Financial Information

Cadbury recommended that the half-yearly interim reports of listed companies should contain more information about the balance-sheet position and that this information should be reviewed by the auditors. Although interim statements are usually headed up 'UNAUDITED', it is normal practice for the auditors to review the results, enquire about the consistency of accounting policies, and perform analytical review tasks to highlight any unexpected trends. However, the expansion of the information about the balance sheet is new and reflects the present economic climate, where solvency is as important as earnings.

Surprisingly Cadbury does not recommend quarterly financial reporting. In the US listed companies have to report quarterly. It does involve extra costs for companies but reveals some imperfections to the market. Cadbury records that shareholder bodies in the UK have not recommended quarterly reporting; they are content with the present pattern of reporting. The intention is made of speeding up financial reporting. Surely all Annual Reports by listed companies could be available within ninety days of the end of the financial period as in the US.

Auditing

Cadbury analysed the problems surrounding the auditors role very well—recognizing that the question is not whether there should be an audit but how to ensure its objectivity and effectiveness. The committee points out that the framework in which auditors operate is not well designed in certain respects to provide the objectivity expected; the reason for this being:

- accounting standards provide too much scope for presenting figures in a variety of ways;
- the auditors may be formally appointed by the shareholders, but continuing relationships are between auditor and management—there is no practical way of providing a continuing direct link between shareholders and auditors;
- the competition between audit firms is intense, and in so far as the competition is based on price and on meeting the needs of clients, this may be at the expense of meeting the needs of shareholders;
- companies are putting pressure on auditors to reduce audit costs.

ACCOUNTING PRINCIPLES

Whilst recognizing that an essential first step must be the development of more effective accounting standards that do not allow alternative accounting treatments, Cadbury fails to analyse the problem any further. Cadbury acknowledges the work of the Accounting Standards Board and offers full support. However, it is the very weakness of our standards and practices that gives rise to the expectation gap.

In the UK there is more pressure on management to show strong financial performance than in competing countries. This is because an under-performing company can relatively easily be taken over. In Holland this would not be possible because companies are permitted to have defence mechanisms which prevent hostile takeovers. In Germany hostile takeovers are virtually unknown. In those countries accounting policies tend to be less aggressive than in the UK. It is true that there are similar pressures on management to perform in other countries with strong stock markets such as the USA, Canada, and Australia. Both the USA and Canada have strong accounting standards with a tight regulatory system that limits the opportunity of interpretation of standards in the way that happens in the UK and Australia. One can hardly blame management for choosing the interpretation that produces the highest earnings per share. The problem lies in the standards and the standard-setting process.

In the late 1980s there was a tremendous growth in acquisition activity. Companies with the strongest earnings became the acquirers; those with the weakest performance the targets. This encouraged not only aggressive accounting practices but the taking on of additional debt obligations. When the recession years of the 1990s arrived the reversal of fortunes was made more obvious—property values declined but companies were slower to reflect the decline in values than they had been to recognize their growth in value in the 1980s. It is understandable that there is a loss in confidence in financial reporting in these circumstances.

The question, therefore, is how effective will the Accounting Standards Board (ASB) be in imposing tougher standards. There is no doubt that the ASB has a much greater chance of success than its predecessor body. Equally, there is no doubt that it is led by a very competent chairman and technical director. However, its handicap is that it has to work within a framework of consensus standards. If industry does not like an exposure draft, the ASB would find it difficult, if not impossible, to impose it. In the USA the SEC has the influence to ensure tough standards are introduced when necessary.

The ASB has been going for two years now and has produced two standards—on cash-flow statements and consolidated accounts—neither of them particularly controversial subjects. It has produced many other discussion papers, exposure drafts, and papers on statements of principles. It has not produced any standards on subjects where the differences in accounting are known to be the greatest and where the UK is most out of line with practice in other countries—such as accounting for goodwill, brands, depreciation (or rather non-depreciation), and off-balance-sheet finance. That is not intended as a criticism of the work of the ASB. From the very start it recognized that these subjects were controversial and that it would not be possible to obtain an early consensus. At present the issues may appear to be less urgent because without acquisitions there are no new goodwill problems and in present market conditions not too many companies are keen to revalue their brands. Experience with the predecessor body—the Accounting Standards Committee—showed that over the years pressure groups learned how to lobby to best effect; it will be no easier to obtain consensus in the future. The ASB must be given the support it needs to be able to introduce standards that deal effectively with such subjects without having to obtain consensus agreement. To ensure that confidence in UK financial reporting is maintained (or restored, depending on your point of view), the ASB must be able to act in this area soon. If the power of the pressure groups becomes too great, the very future of the ASB will be in question. Would a UK form of SEC then not become inevitable?

QUARANTINING AUDIT FROM OTHER SERVICES

Turning now to other recommendations on audit, the accounting profession heaved a sigh of relief that Cadbury did not recommend any prohibition on auditors providing other, non-audit, services to audit clients. Such a prohibition had been suggested by some as being necessary to ensure independence and to avoid firms taking on audits at uneconomic fees in the hope and/or expectation of making good the loss on the audit from more profitable non-audit work. The Cadbury Committee was not convinced by that argument. However, it did consider it important that the accounts should disclose fees paid to the auditors for audit and non-audit services. A similar requirement introduced by the SEC in the USA some years ago was withdrawn as being of little benefit.

ROTATION OF AUDITORS

Similarly the profession was pleased that suggestions of some form of compulsory rotation of audit firms was rejected. Rotation of auditors is not only costly but inefficient. Audit problems are less common when the auditor is familiar with the client systems than when he is not. The first year of a new audit, therefore, requires additional learning time. A system of rotation does exist in Italy but it is not generally regarded as a great success.

While rejecting rotation of audit firms, Cadbury sees merit in a periodic rotation of audit partners and recommends that the accounting bodies should draw up a guide-line to this effect. This is a much less onerous requirement.

Auditors' Reports

Part of the expectation gap is that many people believe auditors are responsible for preparing the accounts and choosing the accounting policies used in those accounts. Cadbury picks up this point and acknowledges that it is not the auditor's role to prepare accounts, nor to provide absolute assurance that the figures in the financial statements are correct, nor to provide a guarantee that the company will continue in existence. Indeed, Cadbury recommends that the directors' report should include a brief description of the directors' responsibilities for the accounts and that the auditors' report should include a statement about the auditors' responsibilities. The Auditing Practices Board has already put forward proposals to this effect. The resultant report is lengthy and defensive in style. Instead of the current short (normally four-line) audit report, the standard clean opinion report would run to ten paragraphs, and while designed to fit on one page, will only do so if the print size is small. This will not encourage shareholders to read it and the expectation gap will remain. Moreover, it would be more logical to have one statement setting out the directors' and auditors' responsibility rather than two in separate sections of the financial statements.

Cadbury recommends that the directors should report on the effectiveness of the company's system of internal financial control. It further recommends that the auditors should report on that statement. Thus the standard clean audit opinion will have to be expanded to accommodate this. The difficulty in giving a simple endorsement has already been referred to. While I would prefer a simple statement, it is quite likely that the audit report would have to describe the extent of an auditor's responsibility in relation to that endorsement.

Perhaps the most significant factor in the expectations gap is the perception that a clean audit opinion means a clean bill of financial health. In the present recessionary climate companies may fail within months of receiving a clean opinion. Cadbury, therefore, recommends that the directors should state in their report that the business is a going concern with supporting assumptions or qualifications as necessary. This is intended to mean that the directors have a reasonable expectation that the company will continue in operation for a time-period defined by guide-lines to be drawn up. The auditors would then be expected to comment on the directors' statement.

At present, if auditors have reason to suspect the validity of the going-concern basis, they will carry out procedures designed to test that basis normally for a period of six months following the date of the audit report or one year after the balance-sheet date. Recently, however, the Auditing Practices Board has published an exposure draft on the 'going concern' in which it proposes that auditors should, as a matter of course, test the going-concern basis and obtain from the directors a written statement confirming their considered view that the company is a going concern. The directors would be expected to look at least one year ahead from the date on which they approve the financial statements and to any circumstance they know will occur thereafter. The directors would be expected to provide auditors with the necessary evidence supporting their statement.

This is where matters become difficult. Typically, the auditor looks for a comfort letter from the company's bankers that the present credit facilities will remain in place over the next twelve months or a longer period as appropriate in reviewing future cash-flows. A number of banks are regretting having given such letters in the past and are reluctant to make such commitments for the future.

Of course, the auditors' position becomes most difficult when they have worries about the going-concern basis but the directors are confident they can get the necessary statement. The directors will regard the banks' unwillingness to give a commitment on facilities as being routine. The auditor will have to take a view, but clashes between confident directors and cautious auditors can be foreseen, with complaints that even a qualification by the auditors couched in the mildest terms will damage the confidence of customers, suppliers, and other creditors in the company.

Fraud

Another aspect of the expectation gap is that it appears to be widely assumed that if a company is found to have suffered material fraud the prime responsibility for preventing and detecting it lies with the auditor. Cadbury rightly points out that the prime responsibility for prevention and detection lies with the directors. Nevertheless, auditors do have a responsibility to carry out their audit in such a way as to have a reasonable expectation of detecting material mis-statements in the financial statements.

Where there is a collusion, or where management itself overrides the controls, the auditors will find it very difficult to detect the fraud. Cadbury, therefore, acknowledges that it is not practical simply to place a duty on the auditor to detect material fraud. Further checks could be made by extending audit procedures, but in the absence of suspicion of fraud it is questionable whether the additional cost involved is justified.

Cadbury, therefore, merely recommends that legislation should be introduced to provide auditors with statutory protection so that they can report reasonable suspicion of fraud to the authorities. This is hardly a major measure. Auditors have in the past found ways of dealing with such matters without statutory protection, so this cannot be expected to have a major impact. Nevertheless, it is a welcome move.

Caparo

The *Caparo* decision has proved controversial within the accounting profession and outside it. Generally auditors have welcomed it, bankers dislike it intensely, and many commentators have called for a change in the law. Basically, as I understand it, the decision reaffirmed that auditors do not have a duty of care to prevent loss to anyone relying on their report other than: (a) the company; and (b) the shareholders as a body.

Auditors welcomed the decision because they thought that this would significantly reduce the number of claims brought against auditors. Others wondered if this did not narrow the duty of care too much. Some believe that a statutory audit only has value if anyone who relies on the audit report can sue the auditor.

It is understandable that people believe the court's interpretation is too narrow and that it disregards commercial practice. In Holland, for example, audit reports are not addressed to the shareholders as in the UK. It is assumed there that the auditors' report is to be more widely used and relied upon. In the UK, however, there has been much more litigation seeking to recover losses on investments from the auditors. Claims have become more numerous and in some cases very large. Since directors would not be able to pay such sums they are seldom brought into the action. This is clearly inequitable. The accountancy profession has considered a number of ways of making the system fairer. I favour the proportional-liability route whereby, if auditors are found to be only partially responsible for the loss, they should not be required to make good 100 per cent at loss but only that proportion for which they are to blame. It would not be easy to introduce such a system because it would involve much wider changes to the framework of law. As such *Caparo* may be regarded as a practical interim solution.

Conclusion

The Cadbury report came as a pleasant surprise. I had not expected much of it, but the report is well argued and for the most part contains sensible recommendations. However, as regards financial reporting I was disappointed that, having identified the 'looseness of accounting standards' as an underlying factor in the perceived low level of confidence in financial reporting, Cadbury had so little to say about it. Certainly the accounting profession is working hard to put the auditing recommendations into practice. It is not easy and will take time, but at last there is a will to do so.

Part III
The Role of the Institutional Investor

One of the most debated topics is the role of the institutional investors in exercising their rights as the dominant owners of the shares of public companies. Paul Davies traces the growth and significance of this role, and one of the points he develops in his essay is the question as to how institutional activism can be encouraged and developed. The other two papers are intended to provide much-needed information on how institutions actually do exercise their rights as owners. Lord Alexander speaks as a banker, and of course banks perform the dual roles of providing finance and managing its portfolio of investments in shares. Paddy Linaker speaks from the perspective of a major unit-trust group. His paper refers to what is one of the more intractable problems relating to institutional shareholder involvement with the management of companies in which they invest, namely, the risk that this involvement will make them insiders with all that this entails with respect to the management of their investment in the company of which they have become 'insiders', perhaps unwittingly.

5

INSTITUTIONAL INVESTORS IN THE UNITED KINGDOM

Paul L. Davies

Introduction

The purpose of this paper is to assess the role currently and potentially performed by institutional investors in the United Kingdom. In some ways this is part of a very old debate concerning the separation of ownership and control in large companies in the UK. However, the growth of institutional shareholdings does give that old debate a new twist. In the past discussion has revolved around the question of what the significance of that separation was for the governance of companies, whereas the growth of institutional shareholding has raised the question of whether we need to contemplate a future in which separation will continue to be a significant feature of the corporate scene. Of course, the two aspects are intimately linked: whether one welcomes the prospect of ending the separation must be influenced by one's view of the consequences of the divorce of ownership and control.

Moreover, the role of the institutional shareholder is also part of two more recent debates which are linked to, but distinct from, the separation issue. The first of these concerns the desirability of reliance upon the takeover as the prime means of removing under-performing management, and the second the role and responsibilities of the trustees of occupational pension funds. Should monitoring of management by institutional shareholders be seen as an alternative to the takeover as the prime method of disciplining management? Does the shareholder interest acquire a new legitimacy if it represents the long-term savings against retirement of millions of working people? A positive or even semi-positive answer to either of these questions would suggest a more active role for the institutional shareholders in the management of their portfolio companies. But are there any adverse consequences likely to flow from more activism on the part of the institutions? In any event, is greater institutional involvement likely to be seen by the institutions themselves as in their own best interest and, if not, are there feasible regulatory strategies that could be pursued that would encourage greater involvement on their part?

These are some of the questions this paper will seek to address, beginning with an analysis of the instruments of long-term saving in the UK and the reasons for their post-war growth.

The Instruments of Long-Term Saving

The dominance by the financial institutions of the market in the ordinary (equity) shares of UK companies is a well-established fact. In 1963 the institutions owned 22.1 per cent of the ordinary shares of listed UK companies; in 1975 the figure was 42.9 per cent; in 1985 it was 59.5 per cent; and in 1990, 61.3 per cent.[1] Within the overall category of financial institution two types of institution were, in turn, dominant. These were the pension funds (which alone held 31.4 per cent of the ordinary shares of listed companies in 1990) and the insurance companies (20.4 per cent). Given the relative unimportance of unit trusts (open-ended mutual funds) at 6.1 per cent, banks (0.7 per cent), and 'other financial institutions'—including investment companies, that is, closed end mutual funds—at 2.7 per cent, this paper will concentrate on the position of pension funds and insurance companies as shareholders in UK companies.

Pension funds and insurance companies have acquired their strong positions as owners of equity securities because they are both instruments for long-term saving. As far as insurance companies are concerned, this result flows mainly from their activities as providers of life insurance (rather than other classes of insurance business). Although life insurers were traditionally concerned to provide an income to dependants after the death of the insured, today life insurance is often used as an instrument for pure saving over long periods (say ten, twenty, or twenty-five years). Although the contract between the policy-holder and the company may be a simple one in which a fixed sum is promised at a future date in exchange for premiums payable over a period of time, savings policies tend to be more sophisticated. In such 'with profits' or 'investment linked' policies the sum eventually payable depends upon the investment success of the insurance company, though the nature of the link varies from one type of policy to another.[2]

Pension funds are clearly instruments of long-term saving. The typical 'occupational' pension scheme consists of a fund to which both the employer

---

[1] Confederation of British Industry, *Investing for Britain's Future: Report of the CBI City/Industry Task Force* (London, 1987), 18; Central Statistical Office, *Economic Trends* (Oct. 1991), 153. The significance of the high percentage of UK equities held by UK institutions is reinforced by the fact that a high percentage of the assets of UK institutions is invested in UK equities, the figure for pension funds being 54 per cent at the end of 1989 and that for long-term, non-pension assets probably little different. See The WM Company, *WM UK Pension Fund Service Annual Review 1990* (London, 1991), 2.

[2] The policy-holder's return may depend upon the performance of a particular fund run by the company or upon the company's general investment success; and success may be judged wholly at the point of maturity of the policy or the return may be influenced in part by judgements made during the course of the policy.

and its employees make defined contributions. The fund is established as a legal entity separate from the employing enterprise, usually as a trust, although some or all of the trustees of the pension fund may be senior executives of the company (the 'sponsor') which established and contributes to the pension scheme. The distinct nature of the legal obligations placed upon pension trustees, even if they are also directors of the company, seems clearly established in law, even if not always sufficiently recognized in practice.[3] The typical occupational scheme exists to pay defined benefits to retired employees (usually a fraction—say one half or two-thirds—of their salaries in the years immediately before retirement, with some element of adjustment for inflation). The contributions required of employer and employee are usually fixed in the contract of employment and the entitlements of the pensioners in the trust deed. Since there may be a mismatch between the contribution obligations and the pension entitlements, many trust deeds require the sponsoring company to make special additional contributions if the scheme becomes actuarially insolvent.[4]

Funded occupational schemes need to be distinguished from state pension schemes, which are normally financed on a 'pay-as-you-go' basis out of current taxation. Such schemes are of no interest for the purposes of this paper: they do not lead to the acquisition under the scheme of equity shareholdings—or indeed of any long-term assets—since these schemes are not funded. Of more interest are private pension schemes where the contributions are defined but the benefits are not. Often the funds created in these cases are identified with the individual worker. The worker, and sometimes the employer too, pays into a fund which is invested by the worker. Such 'personal pensions', which have been much encouraged by recent governments, may be invested in a number of different ways, but a common method of investment is in a plan run by a life-insurance company. Defined contribution plans obviously throw a greater financial risk upon the employee than do defined benefit plans.

Through personal pension plans the insurance companies thus become directly interested in the pensions business, and so the neat division of function between pension funds and life-insurance companies breaks down. In fact, if one goes down one level from the institutions themselves to the management of the funds they collect, the picture becomes even more complicated. Although some large pension funds do their own investment

[3] See N. Inglis-Jones, *The Law of Occupational Pension Schemes* (London, 1989), s. 4, but cf. the practical realities uncovered by investigations into the affairs of the Maxwell companies' pension funds: House of Commons, Session 1991–2, Social Security Committee, Second Report, *The Operation of Pension Funds*, HCP, 61-II, 4 Mar. 1992. See also 'Clouds on the Retirement Horizon', *Financial Times*, 7 Mar. 1992.

[4] Where this is the case the employer obviously has a stronger moral claim to take a 'pension holiday' if the fund is actuarially over-funded. For a discussion of the complex issues involved in pension-fund surpluses, see R. Nobles, 'Who is Entitled to the Pension Fund Surplus?' (1977) 16 *Industrial Law Journal* 164.

management, most delegate the investment of some or all of their funds to separate and specialist fund managers. Among the fund managers which offer their skills to pension-fund trustees are the life-insurance companies. Thus the Prudential Corporation recently reported that its portfolio management subsidiary had £35 billion under management, which figure was more than double that for the company's own life funds.[5] Moreover, both pension funds and life-insurance companies make use of fund managers such as merchant banks, and there are some large management companies which are not engaged in either banking or insurance.[6] Thus, at the fund-management level a very complex picture indeed begins to emerge.

These, then, are the main instruments for long-term, personal-sector saving in the UK. From a comparative point of view it is interesting to note the insignificant role played by banks as collectors of long-term savings, although they play a part as fund managers. However, this description of savings instruments does not explain the substantial growth of equity ownership by insurance companies and pension funds in the post-war period. This development might have been the result of a switching of assets by the institutions, for example, out of fixed-interest securities and into equities, without any overall growth in their assets. Not surprisingly, there is evidence that post-war inflation did predispose the institutions in favour of equities and against fixed-interest securities, and that this had an influence upon the composition of their portfolios.[7] Nevertheless, it seems clear that the major contributing factor has been the post-war growth in long-term saving. Thus, the value of accrued rights in occupational pension schemes rose from £50 billion in 1976 to £440 billion in 1989 and, as a percentage of personal sector wealth, increased from 11 per cent to 18 per cent. In 1988, however, state pension rights were still a bigger component of total personal-sector wealth.[8] These were high figures by international standards, as were the equivalent ones for life insurance.[9]

The determinants of long-term savings growth seem to be income growth (old-age security appears to have a large income elasticity of demand), demographic factors, and the extent of the provisions made by the state for income security in old age. In the post-war period in the UK all three factors

[5] E. V. Morgan and A. D. Morgan, *Investment Managers and Takeovers: Information and Attitudes*, Hume Occasional Paper No. 25 (David Hume Institute, Edinburgh, 1990), 11. Similar figures are given for the Norwich Union.

[6] Ibid.

[7] The share of bonds in the portfolios of UK pension funds fell from 25 per cent in 1966 to 14 per cent in 1988, and the share of equities rose in the same period from 42 per cent to 68 per cent: E. P. Davis, 'The Development of Pension Funds—An International Comparison' (1991) 31 *Bank of England Quarterly Bulletin* 380, 386–7.

[8] CSO, *Economic Trends* (Nov. 1991), 104. In 1989 state pension rights still accounted for 22 per cent of personal wealth, but that figure had *fallen* from 30 per cent in 1976.

[9] See Table 5.1.

TABLE 5.1. *Percentage of personal sector assets*

	Life insurance	Pension funds
UK	21.5	23.2
US	8.8	13.2
Germany	14.7	2.4
Japan	11.7	2.1
France	10.6	3.1

Source: E. P. Davis, *International Diversification of Institutional Investors*, Bank of England Discussion Paper, Technical Series No. 44 (London, 1991). The figures refer to 1988 and, for the UK, seem to have been compiled on a slightly different basis from that used by the *Economic Trends* statisticians.

have been favourable to long-term saving. Real incomes have risen (although not continuously), the percentage of the population over 65 is increasing (though not as rapidly as in many other countries),[10] and the state pension scheme introduced in the immediate post-war period consisted of low, flat-rate benefits in exchange for low, flat-rate contributions. This scheme was supplemented by a state earnings-related scheme only relatively late in the day, by which time private occupational pensions were well established.[11]

The retirement-driven nature of long-term saving in the UK is perhaps well illustrated by the differential performance of life-insurance companies and pension funds in recent decades. Life insurance increased its share of personal-sector wealth by about half between 1965 and 1988, while pension funds almost tripled their share in the same period.[12] In terms of the percentage of ordinary shares of listed companies held, an even more contrasting picture emerges. Insurance companies held 10 per cent of ordinary shares in 1963 and 20 per cent in 1990, while the share of pension funds increased from 6 per cent to 31 per cent in the same period.[13] Thus, one may conclude that fear of inflation for much of the post-war period, coupled with conditions favourable to long-term saving, especially for retirement, has produced, and seems likely to reinforce in the future, a situation of dominance by the insurance companies and pension funds in terms of the ownership of UK listed companies.

[10] *Economic Trends* (Nov. 1991), 6.
[11] L. Hannah, *Inventing Retirement* (Cambridge, 1986), ch. 4.
[12] Davis (n. 9 above).
[13] *Economic Trends* (Oct. 1991) 153.

The Separation of Ownership and Control

In 1932 Berle and Means[14] drew attention to the fact that in large companies in the UK the need for capital was tending to lead to a situation in which no one shareholder held a significant block of shares and that, in consequence, the costs to any one shareholder of operating the traditional internal corporate machinery for holding management accountable were increasing (because of the level of collective action required on the part of the shareholders), while the likely benefits from such action were decreasing (because of the small proportion of the equity held by any one shareholder). Sale, rather than activism, was thus the rational response by such a shareholder dissatisfied with the management's conduct of the company's affairs. A broadly similar picture of the dispersion of shareholdings was drawn by Florence[15] for the UK in work carried out in the 1950s. Most of the debate in the decades succeeding the publication of Berle and Means's book concerned, not the accuracy of their factual analysis, but the significance of the facts they had uncovered. There have been two main dividing-lines in the debates. The first is between those who think the separation of ownership and control does not give managements of companies significantly greater freedom of decision-making than they had (or have) in owner-controlled companies, and those who disagree with this proposition. The second is within the latter group, and relates to whether greater freedom of managerial decision-making is likely to be used for purposes which, in public-policy terms, are good or not.

There is not space here to review comprehensively this debate. Some comments, however, need to be made. The more extreme views of the significance of the divorce between ownership and control seem not to have carried conviction. Thus, theories that, freed from the tyranny of the shareholders, managers of companies are able to give effect to the dictates of the 'corporate conscience', a line of argument associated in his later writings with Berle himself,[16] have foundered in the face of difficulties in giving operational meaning to the vague notion of a 'corporate conscience', and in finding the mechanisms by which managers are constrained to give effect to it, assuming it can be defined.[17] However, less strong forms of the theory continue to be popular, notably those based on the idea that separation enables managers to give effect, as Lipton and Rosenblum have recently put it, to the 'interest of the corporation in its long-term success as a business enterprise'.[18] This is a more manageable approach, at least at first sight, since

[14] A. A. Berle and G. C. Means, *The Modern Corporation and Private Property* (rev. edn., New York, 1967), 110.

[15] P. Sargant Florence, *Ownership, Control and Success of Large Companies* (London, 1961).

[16] A. A. Berle, *Power Without Property* (London, 1960).

[17] George W. Dent, jr., 'Towards Unifying Ownership and Control in the Public Corporation' [1989] *Wisconsin Law Review* 881, 892–4.

[18] Martin Lipton and Steven A. Rosenblum, 'A New System of Corporate Governance: The Quinquennial Election of Directors' (1991) 58 *Chicago Law Review* 187, 189.

it confines itself to economic success and so avoids some of the more intangible elements of the 'corporate conscience'. However, it is submitted that it is, ultimately, equally difficult to operationalize.

First, the statement that 'the corporation has an independent interest in its own long-term business success' seems to be a piece of reification to which it is difficult, if not impossible, to attach a meaning. Does a paper bag have an interest in not being burned? That is not a question that can readily be answered. We can, of course, ask the question whether the owner of the bag has an interest in its not being burned, and easily answer it by looking at such factors as whether the owner wished to re-use the bag or, on the other hand, regarded it as a piece of potential litter. So with the corporation: we can sensibly ask whether individuals or groups of people have an interest in the company being managed in a particular way, but not whether the company, considered apart from the interests of such persons, has an interest in a particular decision. For example, how would one answer, without referring to such interests, the question of whether the company 'as such' has an interest in not being liquidated? The notion of the corporation having an independent interest serves to obscure the potential conflicts among the various groups of persons affected by the way the company is run, or worse, to disguise a policy of promoting the interests of one of those groups at the expense of the others.

Lipton and Rosenblum implicitly accept the force of this point in their discussion of the 'constituency statutes', that is, those amendments to corporate law passed by many state legislatures in the US which permit (but generally do not require) boards of directors to have regard to the interests of employees, suppliers, creditors, customers, and the community in which the company operates, as well as to the interests of the shareholders.[19] 'Constituency statutes', they state, 'are best understood as a means of permitting boards of directors to consider the interests of the corporation as a business enterprise.'[20] So here, as elsewhere in the article where the idea of the interest of the company is made concrete, the task is carried out by reference to the interests of those persons whose well-being may be affected by managerial decisions. This step, however, merely reveals the second difficulty, which is how to reconcile the competing interests of the various groups in the way the company is run. Lipton and Rosenblum seek to cause this difficulty to disappear by asserting that 'all [groups] prosper in the long run if the enterprise prospers in the long run'.[21] Although it is probably true to say that few people benefit if the company becomes insolvent, the benefits which are obtained from a going concern vary from group to group according to how prosperity is defined and on the methods used to achieve it.

[19] L. Herzel and R. W. Shepro, *Bidders and Targets* (Cambridge, Mass. and Oxford, 1990), 62–4.
[20] Lipton and Rosenblum (n. 18 above), 215.
[21] Ibid.

This remains true even if we confine ourselves to long-run prosperity. Does prosperity mean maximizing the company's long-term profitability or its size or the number of its employees, or is prosperity measured by some other criterion or by a mixture of these criteria and, if so, which? Often these criteria will point in the same direction, but cannot be guaranteed to do so. Where they do not coincide, the question arises as to how conflicts among them are reconciled and by whom. There is a respectable body of writing which suggests, for example, that shareholders may prefer profitability and managers size,[22] so that the question of whose view is to prevail is not without importance.

Again, where a company proposes to shift production to a green-field site in another part of the country (or another country) rather than refurbish an existing plant, that may be to the benefit of those groups whose stake in the company is relatively mobile (shareholders and, to some extent, senior management), but contrary to the interests of the employees at the current plant and of local suppliers and the local community. Of course, one might seek to avoid the force of this point by shifting from a micro-level focus on the particular decision of a particular company to a macro-level concern with decisions of this type by companies in general. It might then be said that employment opportunities and so on will be maximized by allowing company managements a free hand. This argument has some plausibility, though it still depends heavily on how one defines the group whose interests are promoted. Is it the local community, the nation as a whole, or some cross-national group? Economic history is full of examples of technological and industrial advances that resulted in the decline of particular regions or even whole countries. That process may have been inevitable or for the overall benefit of the industrialized world, but it cannot be said to have benefited the local constituencies of the industries that underwent decline. In relative terms at least, these groups would have been better off with the *status quo*. More to the point, it is difficult to see how one builds the interests of workers or suppliers as a class or communities in general (as opposed to current employees and suppliers and the community in which the company is currently located) into the mechanisms of corporate governance (though there may be other means of taking them into account).

It is perhaps not surprising, therefore, that when Lipton and Rosenblum come to a concrete proposal for corporate governance reform, the interests of the other stakeholders, so prominent in the their discussion of the corporate constituency statutes, disappear, and that what emerges is a proposal for managerial accountability to shareholders, albeit one designed to free management from short-term shareholder pressure. Their idea is 'to convert every fifth annual meeting [of the shareholders] into a meaningful referendum on essential questions of corporate strategy and control, and to

---

[22] R. Marris, *The Economic Theory of 'Managerial' Capitalism* (London, 1964).

limit severely the ability of stockholders to effect changes in control between quinquennial meetings'.[23] This task is entrusted to the shareholders because, as they put it, 'ownership and management remain separate, but the structure of stock ownership ensures the alignment of the interests of the managers and stockholders around the long-term interests of the business enterprise'.[24] This statement is in some contrast with the earlier statement, 'constituency statutes are best understood as a means of permitting boards of directors to consider the interests of the corporation as a business enterprise rather than solely the interests of the stockholders'.[25] Quinquennial elections may be a way of protecting management against short-term shareholder pressure—we discuss the issue of short-termism below—but they do not appear to be a mechanism for ensuring accountability to any group other than the shareholders.

So far we have argued that analyses of the separation of ownership and control do not carry conviction when they seek to show that it has permitted or even caused management to pursue a radically different set of objectives than was—or indeed is—the case in owner-controlled companies. The debate thus narrows to one between those who assert that separation makes no difference by itself (because other mechanisms, legal and non-legal, constrain management to pursue faithfully the shareholder interest) and those who argue that separation to some degree enhances managerial discretion. (Within this latter group there is still a division between those who welcome this enhanced discretion and those who do not.) It is important to appreciate the relatively narrow limits of this debate. As Nichols has pointed out, refering in particular to the writings of Marris and Williamson,[26] even the writers who detect an enhanced discretion for management do not assert 'that non-propertied directors pursue policies which are radically at odds with the interests of the shareholders'.[27] Even if managers prefer to maximize growth and shareholders profitability, the two are overlapping aims, so that conflict between the two is not continuous, especially as it may commonly be difficult to assess accurately whether a particular business plan will eventually contribute more to the one goal or the other.

Those who argue that the separation of ownership and control is by itself unimportant point to competition in the product and capital markets, and especially to the market in corporate control via takeovers, as sufficiently strong pressures to keep shareholder interests in the forefront of managerial concerns, even with the atrophy of the general meeting and other traditional

---

[23] Lipton and Rosenblum (n. 18 above), 224 ff.

[24] Ibid. 222.

[25] Ibid. 215.

[26] Marris (n. 22 alone); O. E. Williamson, *The Economics of Discretionary Behaviour: Managerial Objectives in a Theory of the Firm* (NJ, 1964).

[27] T. Nicholls, *Ownership, Control and Ideology* (London, 1969), 111.

methods of shareholder control. However, as Coffee[28] has pointed out in relation to takeover bids—and the argument seems applicable to the other techniques—these pressures are neither constant nor operative at an early enough stage. The company may need only occasional access to the capital markets, while takeovers run in cycles which seem to be dependent more upon the availability of finance than of inefficient or self-seeking management deserving to be bought out. Moreover, the threat of liquidation or takeover arises for such managements only after a period of under-performance.[29] On these counts there is good reason for those who wish to strengthen the shareholder interest to aim to supplement market disciplines with monitoring by shareholders: it ought to be both a more constant and (because internal to the company) more quickly acting form of supervision. If this is so, then the questions that arise are: (i) whether there are any adverse consequences that might be expected to flow from closer monitoring by shareholders and which should be taken into account against the expected advantages; and (ii) whether the mechanisms for effecting such monitoring are available. These are the topics to which we now turn.

The Institutions and Short-Termism

It is easy for corporate lawyers to assume that managerial accountability to the shareholders is an unproblematic concept. The legal structures within which we traditionally work are based on that idea. The statutory model articles of association in the UK may confer the management of the company upon the board of directors, but those same articles typically make the directors periodically electable by the shareholders, and since 1948 UK company law has enabled a simple majority of the shareholders to remove any or all the directors at any time and for any reason, even in breach of contract.[30] Thus, consistently with the growth of large bodies of shareholders, the traditional model does not call upon the shareholders to manage the company, but it does make the lines of accountability run from management through the board to the shareholders, and thus gives the latter a crucial role in the function of monitoring management's performance. If there is a worry about the development by management of an element of unaccountable discretion, one obvious starting-point for reform is to try to

---

[28] J. C. Coffee, 'Regulating the Market for Corporate Control' (1984) 84 *Columbia Law Review* 1145, 1,202–3.

[29] Of course, takeovers may be motivated by other factors, such as synergy, to which the remark in the text does not apply.

[30] Companies (Tables A to F) Regulations 1985, SI 1985/805, Table A arts. 70 and 73 and Companies Act 1985, s. 303. The dismissed director's contractual and other rights to compensation are, however, expressly preserved by the statute: s. 303(5). That even senior managers find the concept of shareholder ownership difficult to grasp, in spite of its hallowed legal pedigree, is demonstrated by the recent comments of Sir Owen Green, chairman of BTR, on the draft report of the Cadbury Committee: see 'Why Cadbury Leaves a Bitter taste', *Financial Times*, 9 June 1992. On the Cadbury Committee, see n. 78 below.

make the traditional model work. Whether, in view of the dispersion of shareholdings, such a course of action is feasible is, of course, one of the major questions raised by Berle and Means. But the traditional model of corporate law tends to lead one to suppose that doubts lie only in the area of feasibility, whereas there are at least two broad areas of debate about the desirability of a restoration of the traditional model.

The first and major area of debate today revolves around the proposition that, in essence, a degree of managerial unaccountability is preferable to enhanced monitoring by shareholders. This is the debate about short-termism. It is said that enhancing shareholder pressure causes corporate management to take decisions that increase the company's revenues in the short-term, but at the expense of its long-term profitability and competitiveness. The first thing to be said is that it is in many ways odd that this particular charge should be levelled against a shareholder community like the one in the UK that is so dominated by institutional shareholders. Both pension funds and insurance companies have to meet long-term liabilities, and in principle would seem to have only a limited interest in the short-term performance of any asset in which they invest. Both institutions face only small liquidity risks, arising from early surrenders and demand for policy loans in the case of insurance companies, and transfers and optings-out in the case of pension funds, though in most cases these options are not attractive from the individual investor's point of view. It is often said in response that the tendency towards short-termism lies not with the institutions themselves, but with their investment managers whose investment performance is assessed on a quarterly basis, and who therefore would be likely to pressurize management to take short-term decisions. However, the evidence is that performance statistics of managers may be collected on a quarterly basis, but that performance is assessed over much longer periods of time.[31] Indeed, it would hardly be rational for institutions with long-term interests in the performance of their investments to take a different view. In any case, it is not entirely clear how pressurizing management to take short-term decisions helps a fund manager's performance measured against the market index or the performance of other funds. There is certainly a free-rider problem here which we shall examine further below. As Marsh has put it: 'The only way [a manager] can outperform is to identify undervalued shares and buy them, and/or overvalued shares and sell them. This, however, can be achieved only through careful investment analysis of a company's short and longer-term prospects—something widely held to be a good thing.'[32]

Indeed, the fundamental basis of the short-term criticism of the

---

[31] P. Marsh, *Short-termism on Trial* (London, 1990), 32. A three-year 'period is now commonly used in assessing pension fund performance': WM Company (n. 1 above) 5.
[32] Marsh (n. 31 above).

institutions seems to rest on the proposition that stock-market prices do not accurately reflect the company's value and especially not the value of its long-term investments. Since institutions must make their primary investment judgements on the basis of these prices, this is a serious issue. However, a City/Industry Task Force, organized by the CBI, reported in 1987 that it was a 'myth' to think that investment managers placed too much weight on current profit announcements, or that they applied inappropriate discount rates to future profits and so encouraged short-term investment.[33] It was an 'uncomfortable reality' that the problem with the British economy lay more in the lack of profitable investment opportunities, because of industrial weaknesses, than in failure by the financial community properly to value those that were pursued.[34] Although unlikely to be the last word on this topic, the report is significant because it was a joint effort by financial and industrial interests in the UK to achieve a common view on this contentious topic, and the consensus arrived at was one which located most of the difficulties in the industrial rather than the financial area. So the case that closer shareholder monitoring would lead to a distortion of management investment decisions seems not (or not yet) to be made.

The second argument is of a more fundamental character and builds on the fact that the shareholders are not the only group whose well-being is affected by corporate decisions. Would a strengthening of the shareholder interest mean a concomitant downgrading of the interests of these other groups? Indeed, it is sometimes suggested that other groups, especially the employees, have a greater stake in the company than shareholders whose only risk is financial. To this latter argument the dominance by the institutions of the equity markets is again relevant. The institutions invest, typically, not the funds of speculators or the incomes of *rentiers*, but the earnings of workers, albeit the better-off workers, who aim to save against loss of income in old age.[35] Insurance companies and pension funds represent a form of employee interest in the enterprise, although not, of course, the whole of the employee interest, nor are they a very transparent form of representation.[36] This argument, by itself, does not do more than place the shareholders' interest on a plane with the interests of other groups. One can still ask why these other groups are not represented in the

---

[33] CBI (n. 1 above) 18 ff.

[34] Ibid. 17 and Marsh (n. 31 above), 63 ff.

[35] The Social Security Committee (n. 3 above) found that: 'Almost half the adult population, nearly 25 million people in the UK, are members or beneficiaries of non-state pension schemes. Nineteen million belong to occupational pension schemes organized by their employers while the remaining 4.6 million have taken out personal pension plans' (para. 15). See also the statistics on the proportion of personal-sector wealth represented by pension schemes, quoted above, p. 72.

[36] See the discussion of accountability below, and in general, R. Buxbaum, 'Institutional Owners and Corporate Managers; a Comparative Perspective' (1991) 57 *Brooklyn Law Review* 1.

mechanisms of corporate governance. The answer probably is that there exist, or ought to exist, protective mechanisms for these other groups too, but that there is only limited scope for using the board in this way. Employee interests have been successfully institutionalized at board level in some countries,[37] and, without committing oneself to the view that only shareholder interests can appropriately be represented at board level, it is nevertheless probably true that the more groups to whom management is accountable within corporate law, the easier it will be for management to escape control by anybody.[38] It may not be too cynical to suppose that one of the main attractions to directors in the US of the constituency statutes, which do not even *require* management to take into account non-shareholder constituencies, is the freedom thereby conferred upon them, rather than any new form of accountability that is engendered.[39] Consequently, one may conclude that more effective monitoring by shareholders need neither distort managerial decisions nor be inconsistent with proper accountability to other groups through non-board mechanisms.

The Feasibility of Institutional Monitoring

Berle and Means attributed the growth of managerial power at the expense of shareholders to the dispersion of shareholdings among a very large number of small holders. The growth of institutional shareholdings offers to challenge the factual basis of the Berle and Means analysis, thus throwing the debate back to an earlier stage when the facts, rather than the significance of the facts, were at issue. Briefly, the argument is that the concentration of holdings in institutional hands makes possible a resurgence of shareholder monitoring along the lines the traditional corporate law model aims to provide. Some caution is immediately called for. The institutions are, indeed, a way of collectivizing the savings of small savers, but for prudential reasons, legally required in the case of pension funds,[40] any one institution will restrict the size of its holding in any one company. However, this is not a fatal counter-argument. Thirty years ago Florence pointed out that Berle and Means had probably overestimated the degree of managerial control in US companies by concentrating on the holdings of the largest two or three shareholders, whereas co-ordinated action was possible among a rather larger group of people. He suggested the largest feasible size for collective

[37] Notably, of course, in Germany.

[38] City Company Law Committee, *A Reply to Bullock* (London, 1977), para. 35; O. Williamson, 'Corporate Governance' (1984) 93 *Yale Law Journal* 1,197, 1,198. This will be especially likely in a legal system, like that in England, which assesses directors' duties subjectively: did they act in what they believed to be in the company's best interest, not in what the court believed to be in that interest?

[39] cf. R. Romano, 'The Future of Hostile Takeovers: Legislation and Public Opinion' (1988) 57 *University of Cincinnati Law Review* 457.

[40] Trustee Investments Act 1961, s. 6.

action was normally about twenty people.[41] This work has been built on more recently by Scott,[42] who has drawn attention to the fact that shareholdings in UK companies often taper off quickly after the the first twenty or so holdings, thus reinforcing Florence's point. More importantly, he points out the extent to which the same names reappear in the lists of the twenty largest holders of the biggest UK companies. In an examination of 100 of the largest 250 financial and non-financial companies in 1977, he found that eight names appeared in what he terms the 'controlling constellations' of these companies in more than fifty cases.[43] In no case did the largest twenty shareholders in the companies examined hold more than 50 per cent of the equity, but equally in no case did they hold less than 10 per cent. Thus, the picture that emerges is not, typically, one of domination of any one UK company by a single institution, but of the potential of control by a group of institutions, these being normally also members of the potential controlling groups of other large companies.

However, it is one thing to point to the potential for control and another to define the conditions under which it is likely to be turned into reality. Indeed, if Florence was correct about the possibility of group action in the 1950s, then the issue is not a new one, although the subsequent growth of institutional shareholdings must have enlarged the potential for institutional shareholder control. It may be that the present concern with the possibilities of shareholder activism is the result of disappointment with alternative mechanisms for shareholder accountability, notably the takeover bid, rather than any significantly greater chance that institutional potential will be turned into greater actual control. Of course, there has always been a degree of shareholder activism on the part of the institutions. The question is whether conditions have changed to such a degree that a higher level of activism can be expected in the future. The answer must depend in part on whether the traditional alternative course of action to intervention in the management of the company—sale of the shares, either in the market or to a bidder—is becoming more difficult for the institutions and/or whether intervention is becoming easier.

In this connection it is worth pointing out an ambiguity to be found in

---

[41] P. Sargant Florence, *The Logic of British and American Industry* (rev. ed. edn., London, 1961), 187. See also 192, n. 2.

[42] J. P. Scott, *Capitalist Property and Financial Power* (Hassocks, 1986) and 'Corporate Control and Corporate Rule: Britain in an International Perspective' (1990) 41 *British Journal of Sociology* 351.

[43] These were: Prudential Assurance (88); National Coal Board Pension Fund (75); Co-operative Insurance Group (64); Legal and General Assurance (64); Norwich Union Insurance (64); Pearl Assurance (64); Barclays Bank (60); Hill Samuel (55); and Robert Fleming (52). In addition, Prudential Assurance was the largest shareholder in 43 of the companies (ibid. 100 and 103). Given the changes in fund management since the 'Big Bang' of 1986, it is not necessarily the case that the same names would appear or would appear in the same rank order today—though the domination of the Prudential Corporation continues—but there is no reason to suppose that the pattern of shareholdings would be very different.

writings about institutional activism. In some cases such activism is predicted as something that will occur (or is already occurring) as an automatic consequence of changes in the market environment in which the institutions operate. The institutions will (or have) come to see that intervention rather than sale is in their best interests, and so no legislative or regulatory effort is needed to bring this change of behaviour on their part about. In other cases the argument seems to be the less strong one that intervention has become a realistic possibility for the institutions, but that this course of action still has to compete with others, especially sale, for adoption in any particular instance. In public policy terms, one might be content to leave the decision to the free choice of the institutions or one might want to influence that choice in favour of intervention, and the issue that then arises concerns the appropriate instrument by which to exercise that influence. That discussion might cover methods ranging from semi-official exhortation to statutory compulsion.

In favour of the automatic theory of intervention, it is sometimes said that the institutions are locked into their shareholdings, or at least cannot sell them without causing an unacceptably adverse movement in the price of the securities. It is clear that such situations do exist, especially in relation to institutional investment in medium-sized companies, for example those quoted on the Unlisted Securities Market (USM). In such companies the investment of an amount of money that an institution would regard as worthwhile might easily lead to the building up of a stake in the 20–30 per cent range to which the 'locked in' argument would seem applicable. It would seem to be no accident that some of the clearest recent examples of institutional intervention on grounds of dissatisfaction with substantive business policy have concerned medium-sized companies.[44] What is less clear is whether the typical institutional stake in the larger listed companies is of such a size as to give the automatic theory credibility. Here, not surprisingly, stakes tend to be much smaller.[45] Certainly, even 2 per cent is a large investment in a major UK company and might well be thought big enough to repay some expenditure on monitoring, but such stakes can usually be placed at a reasonable discount to the market or liquidated over a reasonable period of time. Either way, it would not seem to be the case that the institution cannot move except at an unattractive price. It may be, too, that the institutions will be able to keep to their policy of restricting the size of their stakes in any one company if the expansion pressures on them slacken somewhat in the future as pension funds reach maturity and as the working population grows more slowly.[46] In any event the removal of

[44] 4 'Tougher at the Top', *Financial Times*, 28 September 1991, citing TACE, Bunzl and Budgen.

[45] The British Rail Pension Fund reports that it has holdings that exceed 5 per cent in seventeen companies and holdings exceeding 3 per cent in companies, suggesting a much lower level of significance.

[46] Cf. the comment in WM Company (n. 1, above) 16: 'The trend of negative contributions

exchange-control barriers at the beginning of the 1980s has given the institutions some headroom for growth in equities through overseas investment.[47] But perhaps the most important point about this discussion is that it fails to demonstrate that the institutions are normally locked into their investments in the stronger sense indicated above.

At this point in the discussion an alternative and less strong form of the locked-in theory usually makes its appearance. This says that, in spite of the possibilities for overseas investment, the institutions are to some large degree locked into the UK economy and therefore have an interest in the efficient functioning of its major components, that is, the large companies.[48] This is a plausible argument and an attractive one, but the differences between it and the previous version of the 'locked-in' theory need to be recognized. The argument no longer relates to the position of an individual institution and its stake in an individual company, but to the position of the institutions collectively and their stake in the economy as a whole. This approach puts the emphasis on *collective* action by the institutions and thus raises interesting questions as to how such action could be organized among firms that are also in many respects competitors with one another. Secondly, the argument is no longer so much that the institutions have no option but to intervene, but rather that such intervention would be in their economic best interests. Put this way, the argument implicitly recognizes that the institutions have a choice in the matter of intervention and might in fact choose not to intervene or (probably more realistically) to intervene at less than the optimal level. Consequently, the issue of regulatory pressure to encourage intervention is placed on the agenda. Finally, the less strong version of the 'locked-in' theory perhaps reveals more clearly the public interest in this issue. To be sure, the argument is that the institutions' economic well-being will be furthered by more interventionist policies, but so, of course, will the well-being of all those other groups whose interests depend on the UK economy. In other words, this is a task which is being allocated to the institutions partly in their own interest and partly in the broader public interest.

At this point it is perhaps worth trying to describe what forms of intervention on the part of the institutions seem already to be well

continued for the fourth consecutive year, reflecting not only contribution holidays and the maturity of pension funds, but also the increased use of personal pensions.'

[47] Life insurers had some 10 per cent of their assets abroad in 1988 and pension funds 14 per cent. Overseas investment enables managers to protect themselves to some extent against a poor performance by the UK economy, though there is a prudential argument that investment ought to be largely in assets denominated in the same currency as the fund's liabilities. In the case of insurance companies this is formalized in regulations which, in effect, mean that 80 per cent of assets must be in sterling. E. P. Davis, *International Diversification of Institutional Investors*, Bank of England Discussion Paper, Technical Series, No. 44 (London, 1991) 17, 18, and 23.

[48] J. Charkham, *Corporate Governance and the Market for Companies: Aspects of the Shareholders' Role*, Bank of England Discussion Paper, No. 44 (London, 1989).

established, in order to see what additional activities might be involved in a more-activist policy. The first point to make is that some form of institutional intervention is not new.[49] Given Florence's arguments about the feasibility of group action among twenty or so people, and given the steady growth of institutional shareholdings over the post-war period, this should be no surprise. Thus, Knight[50] links a change of attitude on the part of company management in the 1950s with the growth of institutional investment, while stressing the role of the takeover threat in aiding the institutions to make their presence felt. The second point, however, is that intervention on the part of the institutions has traditionally covered a relatively narrow range of matters. Institutional action was most likely on financial matters, on issues of executive compensation (especially where this took a novel form), on issues relating directly to the shareholders' influence within the company, and on proposals for fundamental corporate change. In these areas the institutions could be said to have the necessary expertise to evaluate management's plans (unlike in the general business areas), and the incentive to intervene because the shareholders' powers were at stake or because management was subject to a severe conflict of interest. Furthermore, the costs of intervention on these issues were not necessarily high. It was not expensive, for example, for an institution to develop a policy on non-voting shares and, once developed, it could be applied to all portfolio companies as the need arose. Moreover, the instruments of intervention were already in existence, the Investment Protection Committee of the British Insurance Association (to which most British insurance companies belong) having been set up in the 1930s, for example, though at that time its main function was to scrutinize the terms of debt issues.[51]

The forms of established institutional intervention can be classified under four headings.

· SHAREHOLDER RIGHTS

The purpose of intervention here is to maintain the potential for institutional influence over management by safeguarding the shareholders' basic rights. Thus, the institutions have long run a campaign against non-voting shares. In spite of a legislative refusal to take steps to prohibit such

[49] See e.g. R. H. Mundheim, 'Institutions as Shareholders—The British Experience' *Institutional Investor* (Jan. 1968), 36.

[50] J. Knight, 'The Role of the Shareholders and the Institutions', in Corporate Policy Group, *Control of the Corporation* (1980), 13: 'In the 1950s it was still customary to speak of the company as if it belonged to the directors. The attitudes of directors in matters involving company property and the use of privileged information were on the whole less sensitive than they are today, to say, the least ... shareholders were treated in a fairly cavalier way.'

[51] The counterpart to the ABI for the pension funds is the National Association of Pension Funds, Ltd. and they, together with other representatives of institutional shareholder groups, co-ordinate policy through the Institutional Shareholders' Committee.

issues,[52] the campaign has had some success. Weinberg reports that 'a number of proposals to make capitalization issues to ordinary shareholders in non-voting shares have been dropped following institutional objections' and, perhaps more important, 'there are no instances in recent years of a company seeking a listing for any class of non-voting equity capital'.[53] Opposition to 'the creation of equity shares which do not carry full voting rights' still appears as the third point in the Institutional Shareholders' Committee's recent code of practice,[54] and the Institutional Fund Managers' Association has recently carried the same message, though without obvious immediate success, to continental stock exchanges as well.[55]

An equally long-running saga has been institutional insistence on pre-emption rights for existing shareholders when a company makes an equity issue for cash.[56] Here, institutional pressure did achieve a legislative result, though one primarily due to the UK's obligation to implement the Second Community Directive.[57] But the institutions continue to insist with some success on more restrictive rules than the statute imposes. Consequently, whereas the statute allows the shareholders to disapply the pre-emption requirement for periods of up to five years at a time, the Stock Exchange's rules, under institutional shareholder influence, limit the period, in effect, to that between the annual general meetings,[58] and the National Association of Pension Funds and the Association of British Insurers try to impose an even more rigorous policy. This policy, embodied in informal guide-lines issued by the Stock Exchange, commits the institutions to voting for disapplication, even on an annual basis, only where the company in question undertakes to limit any non-rights issue to 5 per cent of the issued capital of the company in any one year and to 7.5 per cent in any rolling period of three years.[59] Interestingly, these guide-lines, unlike the statute, cover vendor placings which, technically, do not involve the issue of shares for cash, but which in economic terms achieve a similar result.[60] Thus, the institutions, operating through the mechanism of the Stock Exchange, have been able to

---

[52] Report of the Company Law Committee, Cmnd 1749, 1962, paras. 123–40 and the Note of Dissent at p. 207.

[53] *Weinberg and Blank on Take-overs and Mergers* (London, 1989), paras. 3–805.

[54] ISC, *The Responsibilities of Institutional Shareholders in the UK* (London, 1991), 5.

[55] 'Investors Seek More European Rights', *Financial Times*, 15 July 1992.

[56] Knight (n. 50 above), regarded this institutional policy as 'the first signal that the old relationship was going to be altered'.

[57] Directive 77/91/EEC. See now Companies Act 1985, s. 89–95.

[58] Council of the Stock Exchange, *Admission of Securities to Listing*, s. 5, ch. 2, para. 37.1. This provision is buttressed by the requirement of s. 3, ch. 2, part 3, para. 3.5 that, when an issue is proposed and 10 per cent or more of the voting capital of the company is likely to remain unissued, the directors must undertake in the listing particulars to make no further material issue of shares within the following year, except on a pre-emptive basis, unless the shareholders in general meeting approve the specific issue.

[59] 'Pre-emption Rights' (1987) 27 *Bank of England Quarterly Bulletin* 545.

[60] In a vendor placing the issuer allots the shares to the vendor of the asset the issuer wishes to acquire and the vendor immediately places the shares with investors in exchange for cash.

achieve (though not without controversy) a distinctly tougher regime for listed companies than general company law requires, and this is a measure of their influence.[61]

A policy of opposing the issue of non-voting shares helps to preserve the shareholders' position of ultimate control, and insistence on pre-emption rights does both this and protects the shareholders' equity interest from dilution. Both policies also make it indirectly more difficult for management to take pre-bid defensive measures against takeover bids. Although the City Code prohibits defensive tactics once a bid is imminent, before that point is reached the Code does not apply. One may look to the general law in this situation, but that, on analysis, provides considerable scope for defensive action. That such opportunities are exploited relatively rarely seems attributable in large part to the influence of the institutions, operating either directly or through the Stock Exchange rules.[62] Thus, decisions on changes of control via takeovers are placed in the hands of the shareholders, and the Stock Exchange rules aim to achieve a similar result in cases of radical changes in the nature of the company by other means. Those rules require shareholder consent to substantial acquisitions and disposals and reverse takeovers, whether or not such consent is demanded by the company's articles or the general company law.[63]

STRUCTURE AND COMPOSITION OF THE BOARD

A more recent, but certainly not new, concern of the institutional shareholders has been the structure and composition of boards of directors of portfolio companies. The Institutional Shareholders' Committee's code of practice, while not specifically calling for a split in the roles of the chairman of the board and the chief executive of the company, nevertheless refers to the need to avoid 'concentrations of decision-making power not formally constrained by checks and balances appropriate to the particular company'. It also calls for the appointment of a 'core' of appropriately qualified non-executive directors and the appointment of compensation and audit committees of the board.[64] These precepts clearly had a strong

[61] A somewhat similar picture emerges in relation to repurchases of shares by companies, where the Stock Exchange and the Association of British Insurers impose tougher requirements than the statute requires. See 'Share Repurchases by Quoted Companies' (1988) 28 *Bank of England Quarterly Bulletin* 382, 385.

[62] P. L. Davies, 'The Regulation of Defensive Tactics in the United Kingdom and the United States', in E. Wymeersch and K. Hopt (eds.), *European Takeovers-Law and Practice* (London 1992).

[63] *Admission of Securities to Listing* (n.58 above), s. 6, ch. 1. A 'Super Class 1 Transaction', requiring shareholder approval, is defined as one involving the acquisition or disposal of assets amounting to 25 per cent or more of the assets of the company effecting the transaction, or assets carrying 25 per cent or more of the company's net profits, or involving a consideration amounting to 25 per cent or more of the company's assets, or requiring the issue of equity capital amounting to 25 per cent or more of the company's existing capital: para. 3.1.

[64] ISC (n. 54 above), 5.

influence on the report of the Cadbury Committee, where these suggestions appear in a somewhat stronger form, but coupled with an express endorsement of the ISC code.[65] How much influence the institutions have had in this area is more difficult to judge. A report of research carried out by Pensions Investment Research Consultants suggested that a quarter of large companies still combine the chairmanship and the position of chief executive and that one-third of companies fall short of the Cadbury Committee's guidelines on non-executive directors.[66] More important from the present point of view is the fact that this form of intervention is essentially procedural; it avoids head-on confrontation over substantive issues of business policy and, as a general policy, requires no detailed investigation of the circumstances of individual companies.

EXECUTIVE REMUNERATION

Institutional concern at the potential conflicts of interest involved in the setting of executive remuneration is, again, not new, and that concern again finds expression in the statement in the ISC code that 'institutional investors support the disclosure of the principles upon which directors' emoluments are determined'.[67] Again, the influence of these views upon the recommendations of the Cadbury Committee does not need stressing. When the company is doing well, there is no doubt a tendency to let these matters slide, but institutional disquiet has understandably been expressed at the size of the pay-offs received by the some departing chiefs of companies whose businesses have been run with a conspicuous lack of success.[68] What these cases perhaps revealed to the institutions was their lack of control over, or even knowledge of, the way compensation was determined in portfolio companies.

INTERVENTION TO CHANGE BUSINESS POLICY

None of the above forms of intervention, however, really gets to the heart of what is probably in the minds of those who advocate monitoring of management by the institutions. The acid test seems to me to be whether the institutions are prepared to intervene to change business policy, either by devising and imposing on the existing, unsuccessful management a new strategy or, more likely, by giving their support to those, whether within or

---

[65] See n. 78 below at pp. 35–6.
[66] *Guardian*, 13 June 1992; *Financial Times*, 5 February 1993, p. 10.
[67] ISC (n. 54 above).
[68] 'The History of Handshakes', *Financial Times*, 1 Nov. 1991, quoting as examples the Burton Group, Berisford, Ferranti, and British Aerospace. See also 'Shareholders Wage War', *Financial Times*, 6 Nov. 1991, and the recent guide-lines produced by the National Association of Pension Funds, Ltd., *Share Schemes—A Consultative Approach* (London, 1992), attempting to ensure that executive share option schemes give rise to rights which are exercisable only where there has been a genuine improvement in the performance of the management.

without the company, who have an alternative strategy on offer. Such interventions involve not only the likelihood of a bruising confrontation with the existing management, but also much greater commitments of time and energy in analysing the company's problems and in helping to devise a solution. How much of such intervention currently takes place?

In attempting to answer this question, it is necessary to put on one side two types of intervention which, at first sight, look very much like what we are searching for, but which turn out on analysis to be of only limited significance. The first is the situation discussed above where the institution is truly locked in because of the size of its shareholding as, for example, with substantial institutional shareholdings in medium-sized companies. The second is where an unsuccessful company has recourse to a rights issue to repair the ravages of its balance sheet. It has long been clear that when a company needs to make use of the capital markets, an opportunity for shareholder influence presents itself. Indeed, an important feature of recent examples of this influence is that the initiative for managerial changes seems to have come from the company itself, rather than from the shareholders. The companies, or their advisers, seem to have become convinced that an appeal to the capital markets via a rights issue would not succeed if it was the same unsuccessful management that was putting itself forward as the people to whom the new money should also be entrusted.[69]

So what one is looking for are examples of institutional initiatives, on a group basis, to secure changes in business policy where the lever of a rights issue was not available. That such interventions do occur is clear; the difficulty lies in making some accurate estimate of the scale of this activity. Although changes in management, at least at board level, are publicly recorded, the pressure that produces such changes, or *a fortiori* changes in policy not entailing board replacements, is applied behind closed doors rather than in, say, the general meeting.[70] The evidence from insiders is that intervention is increasing,[71] but that is from a low base and there must be a doubt whether greater activism will survive the reappearance of circumstances in which the alternative of sale of the shares, either in the market or to a bidder, becomes an available and attractive option.

The reasons for the traditionally low level of institutional intervention in the business policy of portfolio companies are too well known to need elaborate rehearsal here. For a variety of liquidity and prudential reasons the institutions have spread their investments widely, so that a typical

---

[69] See 'The Institutions get Militant', *Financial Times*, 11 June 1991, citing the examples of Asda, Granada, and Brent Walker, and 'Tougher at the Top', 28 Sept. 1991, adding the case of British Aerospace.

[70] See House of Commons, Session 1990–1, Trade and Industry Committee, Minutes of Evidence, 8 May 1991, HC 226-x, para. 928 ff (questions to Mr Sandland, Chief Investment Manager, Norwich Union Fund Managers, Ltd.).

[71] Ibid.

institution has acquired a range of portfolio companies that far exceeds its ability to engage in effective monitoring, especially given the modest size of in-house staff. Some of the costs of intervention, which in the case of business policy are potentially quite high, can be spread through collective institutional action, which is probably in any event necessary in order to bring enough pressure to bear upon management. However, collective action among potential competitors brings its own problems, and there is always the temptation to free-ride, which reduces collective solidarity. Finally, it would be wise not to underestimate the practical problems of forming and maintaining against the best efforts of the management of the portfolio company an effective and solid coalition of institutional investors with perhaps rather diverse interests and views as to the merits and demerits of the incumbents.[72]

Possibilities for Reform

It thus seems reasonable to preserve considerable caution about the chances of extensive institutional intervention in the business policies of large UK companies coming about of its own accord. Given the problems mentioned above, of competence and of organizing effective collective action, which face an institution dissatisfied with the performance of one of its portfolio companies, it is not likely that mere exhortation will encourage the institutions to be more interventionist, even when such exhortation is coupled with dire predictions of unwelcome political developments if the institutions do not show greater 'responsibility', or with inducements to the effect that the public good will be furthered if British companies become better governed.[73] Such political threats, if there is no intervention and/or the prospect of benefit to the intervening institutions, would have to become a great deal more immediate than they currently are to outweigh the immediate costs and difficulties of intervention. Indeed, it is not difficult to see that intervention might bring its own rather different political risks with it, involving a questioning of the legitimacy of the power sought to be exercised by the institutions. The 'constituency statutes' in the US[74] are a remarkable example of the mobilizing of political power by management against, *inter alia*, institutional shareholders who opposed the adoption of poison pills.

The spate of institutional interventions to replace unsuccessful manage-

---

[72] Cf. 'A Coalition versus a Dictator', *Financial Times*, 27 May 1992. The story of institutional intervention in the affairs of the Savage Group is interesting from this point of view. The institutions maintained solidarity over the removal of the incumbent management but lost it over the issue of whom to install instead, allowing the non-executive directors to take control: 'When Men in Grey Suits Choose to Apply Savage Pressure', *Financial Times*, 20 Dec. 1990.

[73] See e.g. Charkham (n. 48 above).

[74] See text at n. 19 above.

ments—which occurred in 1990[75], but has tailed off somewhat since—might seem to contradict this pessimistic view, but this is probably not so. The deep recession simultaneously revealed the managerial misjudgements of the preceding boom, made it unattractive to shareholders to sell their holdings in the market, and removed any realistic prospect of a takeover bid to get the shareholders out of their difficulties. What this episode suggests, rather, is that institutional activism is unlikely on any consistent basis unless either the institutions come to perceive it to be in their own self-interest to intervene more extensively, or legal or regulatory controls require such intervention on the part of the institutions.

The essence of the problem, if one wants to encourage more institutional activism, is how to shift the balance of advantage for institutions somewhat away from sale (either through the market or to a bidder) and somewhat towards intervention in cases of under-performing companies. In principle, this might be expected to happen without regulatory action when sale becomes more difficult. Thus, we have suggested above that the greater institutional intervention detectable in the current recession is in part attributable to reduced opportunities for sale, either in the market or to a bidder. But the economic conditions that have lowered the possibilities of exit cannot be expected—or desired!—to be permanent. In more normal conditions, sale over a period of time or acceptance of a takeover offer are likely to be serious competitors against an interventionist strategy. It might be thought that index-tracking funds, which are becoming more popular, constitute an exception to this analysis, since the operators of such funds have in effect abandoned exit and chosen to lock themselves into the market. However, the attraction of tracking and the basis on which the managers of such funds compete is the low cost of running the funds. The managers and users of such funds are thus not likely to be attracted by a strategy which involves the expenditure of substantial resources on monitoring.

In fact, the index fund draws our attention to a larger truth, which is that, no matter how much the attractiveness of sale declines, an institution still has to be convinced that a cost–benefit analysis favours intervention as opposed to an often forgotten but always available strategy of doing nothing. Since there are other pressures on management to perform, arising from, for example, competition in the product market, institutional passivity is not an entirely irrational strategy. What role might regulation play in inducing a somewhat greater disposition on the part of the institutions towards intervention? It seems inconceivable that regulation could ever tell the institutions when the balance of advantage favoured intervention and when it did not. That would be a business/financial judgement to be taken by the institutions on a case-by-case basis. What regulation might do is to require

[75] See e.g. 'Life at the Top Gets Riskier as Institutions Make their Mark', *Financial Times*, 15 Nov. 1990.

the institutions to put themselves in a position *vis-à-vis* their portfolio companies such that action could be taken in appropriate cases and, perhaps most important of all, by placing all institutions under common require-ments to do something to reduce the free-rider problem. These are essentially modest goals, but they do amount to proposals to go beyond mere exhortation of the institutions to keep themselves better informed about their portfolio companies.

A starting-point might be to require the institutions actually to vote their shares. A recent survey found that voting by fund managers as a matter of course was uncommon,[76] in spite of the long-standing institutional insistence on companies not issuing non-voting shares. Of course, it can be said that the value of votes lies in the threat of their use rather than their actual use, but it would be a useful discipline to monitoring if institutions were obliged to formulate and express a view on all issues put to a vote at shareholder meetings. The Institutional Shareholders' Committee comes close to accepting this principle,[77] and the ISC's Code has been endorsed in the Report of the Cadbury Committee.[78] However, a bare obligation to vote would have little impact. It would have to be accompanied by an obligation to ensure that the vote was informed, that is, based upon reasonable independent investigation and consideration of the matters at stake and not, for example, the result of a policy of always voting for the incumbent management. Such a rule would not necessarily prevent the institution from delegating voting decisions to the fund managers, but the institution would retain a responsibility to monitor the managers' discharge of their voting obligations.[79] The actual research necessary for effective voting could be carried out either by the institution/manager itself (though the in-house research staffs of these bodies tend to be modest),[80] or by brokers or the newly emerging breed of institutional advisers, such as Pensions Investment Research Consultants Ltd.,[81] which now offers a corporate governance service.

Beyond mandatory voting, the challenge would be to link up the

---

[76] 'Management of UK Equity Portfolios' (1987) 27 *Bank of England Quarterly Bulletin* 253, 257.

[77] Institutional Shareholders' Committee, *The Responsibilities of Institutional Shareholders in the UK* (1991): '[Institutional] shareholders should register their votes wherever possible on a regular basis.' See also British Rail Pension Trustee Company Ltd., *Corporate Governance: Policy Statement*: 'BRPTC accepts the following general policies: A—voting on resolutions placed before company meetings.'

[78] Report of the Committee on the Financial Aspects of Corporate Governance (London, December 1992), 50–51.

[79] The rules on voting developed by the US Department of Labor under ERISA would repay study in this context.

[80] Morgan and Morgan (n. 5 above), ch. 2.

[81] PIRC offers a 'corporate governance service' and the National Association of Pension Funds offers a 'proxy voting service', both of which provide information and, to some extent, advice on issues arising at forthcoming company meetings.

institutional shareholders with the non-executive directors of the portfolio companies. As the Trade and Industry Committee of the House of Commons perceptively noted in its report on takeovers and mergers,[82] 'there are two key elements in [corporate governance] and they are not always connected: the institutional shareholders who own the majority of all UK shares and the non-executive directors'. Professors Gilson and Kraakman put the same point in this way: proposed reforms too often aim at making 'outside directors independent of management rather than dependent on shareholders'.[83] This criticism, it is submitted, can be made of the Draft Report of the Cadbury Committee and of the activities of PRONED.[84] The point is not simply that making non-executives independent of management is only half the task, but rather that independence of management *can only be achieved* in a reliable way by making the non-executives dependent on another powerful group within the company. Study after study[85] has shown that non-executive directors are at present ineffective except in rare times of complete breakdown in senior management. This is not because they lack independence of judgement or business acumen or because they have financial interests in the company other than as non-executive directors, but because they owe their positions on the board to the existing executive management of the company, and because they share that management's view of how exacting or rather unexacting their scrutiny of the company's affairs ought to be. The Cadbury Committee's recommendations seem unlikely to do much to alter this situation. The nomination of non-executive directors by the board as a whole[86] will not be a significant thing if that board is dominated (not necessarily in numerical terms) by executive management, and the non-executives' access to outside sources of advice[87] becomes important only if they conceive of a need to take such advice. All the external indices of independence, business experience, and sagacity, laid down in the

---

[82] House of Commons, Session 1991–2, Trade and Industry Committee, First Report, Take-overs and Mergers, HC 90, para. 209.

[83] R. J. Gilson and R. Kraakman, 'Reinventing the Outside Director: An Agenda for Institutional Investors' (1991) 43 *Stanford Law Review* 863, 881.

[84] PRONED is a body sponsored by a number of leading financial bodies, including the Bank of England and the Institutional Shareholders' Committee, and by the Confederation of British Industry, which aims to promote the greater use of non-executive directors by British companies. It has produced a Code of Practice, which is set out in the CBI/City Task Force Report (n. 1 above), 36.

[85] See esp. MACE, *Directors: Myth and Reality* (1971) and J. Lorsch, *Pawns or Potentates: the Reality of America's Corporate Boards* (1989). See also the recent research in the UK conducted by PRONED, which found that current appointment processes for non-executive directors were typically informal and embarked upon when the chairman or CEO already had a candidate in mind, and that the decision was often in effect delegated to the chairman. Not surprisingly, the same survey found that only 3 per cent of institutional shareholders thought non-executive directors were effective: PRONED, *Research into the Role of the Non-executive Director* (London, 1992). See also 'Cadbury Attacks Old-Boy Network', *Financial Times* 28 Sept. 1992, and 'Clique of Senior Directors Studied', 29 Sept. 1992.

[86] Cadbury (n. 78 above), para. 4.15.

[87] Ibid., para. 4.18.

Cadbury Report, could be satisfied and yet the chosen non-executives could still take the traditional limited view of their function, no doubt in part because they may often be executive directors of other large companies with their own non-executives to cope with.[88]

In short, Cadbury and its many predecessors can be said to have given insufficient attention to the dynamics of change. How does one get from the typical situation presently obtaining, where the non-executive is chosen by the management and shares its culture of limited monitoring, to one where the non-executive sees him- or herself as dependent upon shareholder choice, as the traditional legal model of corporate governance assumes? This is indeed a very difficult problem and it is a criticism of Cadbury made at the very highest level that it failed to solve it. Nevertheless, it is the crucial problem if significant change in corporate governance is to be made. As the Trade and Industry Committee put it, one must link up the non-executives and the shareholders, meaning in particular the institutional shareholders. As Gilson and Kraakman have pointed out, this might lead to the development of a new breed of professional, full-time, non-executive director, acting for the institutions on a number of company boards.[89] Several legal reforms might be made to encourage such a development, but short of Coffee's draconian proposal[90] to limit the number of holdings of any one institution so as truly to lock it into its portfolio companies, it is difficult to see what reform might be made which would guarantee that the institutions would make the, or some of the, non-executive directors their nominees in fact as well as in name. If institutional control remains a matter of collective action by shareholders whose individual stakes are relatively small, then the prospect of determined management opposition to a fragile coalition is likely to make intervention an unattractive alternative in many cases to sale in the market or to a bidder.

Thus, possible and appropriate regulatory reforms seem to be modest and focus essentially upon an obligation to vote. An important question then arising is what the available legal mechanisms are to effect the voting requirement or, indeed, more substantial reforms that might emerge. In relation to pension funds, the mechanism and the opportunity for reform seem both to exist at the moment. At least under the funded occupational pension scheme model, trust law already gives embryonic recognition to

---

[88] The recent ousting of the chairman and chief executive of BP by the non-executive directors may seem to be the exception that proves the rule, but there a newly appointed chief executive fell foul of the existing non-executives, who thus had not been appointed by him, before he had established himself. He seems also to have alienated the executive directors and thus to have placed himself in an isolated position in a company whose *modus operandi* was more consensual, and even bureaucratic, than many companies. See *Financial Times*, 26 June, 1992, pp. 1 and 19.

[89] Gilson and Kraakman (n. 83 above.)

[90] J. C. Coffee, Liquidity versus Control: the Institutional Investor as Corporate Monitor (1991) 91 *Columbia Law Review* 1,277, 1,355–7.

the notion that the trustees do not have a free discretion in the exercise of their powers, but rather must exercise them in the best interests of the beneficiaries of the scheme. The current regime for pension funds also gives some substance to the notion that the trustees are accountable to the beneficiaries for their stewardship of the fund. This latter element will be extremely important if pension funds are to be more active in monitoring corporate management, for the legitimacy of such activity must depend heavily upon its being seen to be carried on in the interests of the contributors to the fund.[91] It is, of course, necessary to stress the incipient nature of the recognition given to these issues by the current regime for occupational pensions. The nature and extent of the duties of pension fund trustees are vexed legal issues,[92] and on the matter of accountability the more imaginative ideas from the 1970s for compulsory employee representation among the trustees of pension funds were not enacted.[93] However, in the wake of the scandals connected with the pension funds of Mirror Group Newspapers and Maxwell Communications Corporation, an irresistible head of steam seems to have built up for a general review of pension law, which would not be confined to the issue of the security of fund assets, the point most directly raised by the Maxwell affair.[94] The issues raised above should be an integral part of the considerations of the committee whose task it will be to produce recommendations for reform.[95]

[91] Cf in this context the remark of the Vice-Chancellor in *Harries* v. *The Church Commissioners for England* [1992] 1 WLR 1241, 1247 that the otherwise rather restrictive legal duties on trustees, requiring them to maximise the financial return on their investment assets, do not prevent them from acting as 'responsible shareholders'. This remark was made in relation to charity trustees, but seems equally applicable to pension trustees (see at p 1248A-B). Thus, pension trustees would seem legally free fully to participate in a developing practice as to the proper role for trustees in relation to their portfolio companies, though they might face some legal obstacles if they were to take the lead in that process and such lead were to impose a significant penalty on the trust's return on its investments.

[92] See R. L. Nobles, The Exercise of Trustees' Discretion under a Pension Scheme [1992] *Journal of Business Law* 261.

[93] See *Occupational Pension Schemes: The Role of Members in the Running of Schemes*, Cmnd. 6514, 1976, ch. 3; cf. Occupational Pensions Board, *Solvency, Disclosure of Information and Member Participation in Occupational Pension Schemes*, Cmnd. 5904, 1974, paras. 105–25. See generally P. L. Davies, 'Institutional Investors: a UK View' (1991) 57 *Brooklyn Law Review* 129, 140–2.

[94] See Social Security Committee (n. 3 above, which recommended that an enquiry be established for the purpose of bringing forward proposals for a Pension Act to replace the common law of trusts, which Act the Committee described as needing to be a 'major piece of legislation'. On 8 June the government announced the establishment of an independent commission under the chairmanship of Professor Roy Goode to make recommendations for the reform of pensions legislation: *Financial Times*, 9 June 1992, p. 10.

[95] It is much more difficult to build the suggested reforms into the existing structure of life-insurance contracts, whether these are used as a way of providing personal pensions or as simple instruments of long-term saving. The contract of insurance imposes no fiduciary duties upon the insurance company analogous to those imposed upon pension-fund trustees, and it provides no ready mechanism for accountability on the part of the insurance company to the savers as a group.

Conclusion

The conclusion of this paper is a modest one. There is probably some scope for regulatory changes that would induce the institutions to be somewhat more active monitors of the companies they invest in. Such a development is to be welcomed. The counter-arguments based on shareholder short-termism and the desirability of managerial freedom from accountability have been overplayed. But, so long as the primary responsibility of the institutions and their managers is to maximize the performance of the funds for which they are responsible (even on a long-term basis) rather than to promote the health of the British economy in general, monitoring will continue to be judged by the institutions as only one possible way of maximizing performance and it will continue to have to compete with the alternative strategies of sale, whether in the market or to a bidder, or of passivity, that is, of waiting for the other pressures on unsuccessful management to have their effect. Of course, the institutions have a strong general interest in the health of the British economy in which, despite exchange-control relaxation, they will continue to be heavily invested. However, no one has yet demonstrated that the returns to the institutions from active monitoring are higher than those from using intervention as just one possible tool for the maximization of the fund's value. In the absence of such a demonstration it would be competitively unsound, and perhaps illegal, for an institution to place all its eggs in the basket of monitoring. The question, then, is how far one wishes to go in shifting the emphasis to a degree in favour of intervention. A limited proposal to this end has been made above and perhaps some more-imaginative steps in this direction could be envisaged. However, in the absence of a wholesale restructuring of the UK's financial system, it seems unlikely that institutional monitoring will achieve the levels traditionally associated with (but perhaps no longer typical of) banks in Germany. Perhaps the final word should be given to the group chief investment manager of the single biggest institution in the UK, the Prudential Corporation:

My guess is that any conceivable increase in [monitoring] activity will not amount to a major new element of accountability in our system matching that of bank-based economies, since share ownership unaccompanied by the additional involvement in providing finance and other services will never provide the depth of knowledge and commitment that arises with the combination of banking and proprietary interests.[96]

---

[96] National Association of Pension Funds, *Creative Tension?* (London, 1990), 14.

6

CORPORATE GOVERNANCE— THE ROLE OF THE BANKS

Lord Alexander of Weedon

An American industrialist once designed his own epitaph: 'Here lies a man whose skill was in gathering around him men and women much cleverer than himself.' I feel a little that way this morning as I look at the list of distinguished experts who are to follow me. But what I would do is simply trail in general terms a few themes and thoughts which other speakers, in their greater knowledge, may wish to pick up on as the Colloquim develops.

I would like to start by stressing some of the basic strengths of our system. One of the undoubted strengths of UK industry is its ability to tap the City's very liquid capital and equity markets. The openness of these markets and the information freely available in the UK on both companies and markets assist capital-raising and investment. This is in marked contrast to the markets in mainland Europe. They are considerably less liquid and open. This has sometimes been a complaint of captains of UK industry. They have felt vulnerable to hostile bids launched from the continent. In mainland Europe many companies which are listed operate under the protection of technical and statutory barriers which no longer exist in Britain. Even more pertinent is the fact that there are many fewer listed companies in Europe than in the UK. This is highlighted by the fact that only 665 domestic companies were quoted on the German exchanges at the beginning of this year, 551 in Paris and 224 in Milan. In the UK 1,915 domestic companies were quoted. In Germany the market value at the end of last year of their domestic equities was around £210 billion. This represented only 36 per cent of the total funds raised from domestic fixed interest securities like bonds. By comparison, in the UK the market value of domestic equities was £541 billion, over two-and-a-half times greater than in Germany.

I do not think that anybody would call into question the need to preserve open and efficient markets in the UK. If change is desirable, it is in bringing the European norm up to the practices that pertain in the UK. There is no doubt that as we approach the single-market deadline this already is occurring. Indeed, the banking industry is developing a fairly good record in providing a level playing-field as a framework for competitive activity. The European Second Banking Directive[1] provides banks from one country with

---

[1] Council Directive 89/646/EEC, OJ L386/1 of 30 Dec. 1989.

a licence to establish operations throughout the Community. The proposed Investment Services Directive[2] establishes a framework for equal competition within the securities market. Its aim is to open up markets which are currently closed to foreign competition and, as such, it is clearly important. Similarly, the draft Capital Adequacy Directive[3] provides a minimum-capital adequacy regime for authorized investment firms and banks operating in the securities market. This is another significant step towards creating a single European securities market, much as the BIS Capital Adequacy Standard[4] has underpinned the strength and stability of a more unified banking system. The breaking down of exchange-control barriers also bodes well for a more liberal and competitive market.

Nevertheless, the efficiency and liquidity of the UK market does, in turn, raise other questions. For example, is J. M. Keynes right when he likened the Stock Exchange to a casino, where, as David Ricardo, the nineteenth-century economist put it: 'The members of the Stock Exchange consider more the immediate effects of passing events, rather than their distant consequences'? To what extent does our system not only permit but encourage short-termism? Is management's expectation that the City's vision only extends to the next dividend payment becoming a self-fulfilling prophecy? Similarly, do directors focus on the rewards to shareholders to the detriment of a more balanced view of all constituents; of their staff and customers, the business partners, such as suppliers? Finally, are the recent endeavours to improve corporate governance enough, or should we be examining a wider picture than was contained in the brief of the Cadbury Committee?

Some of these problems tend to be more acute during times of stock-market and economic boom. As we all know, hostile bids, approved bids, management buy-outs, mergers and acquisitions, and highly leveraged transactions became an increasingly lucrative business for merchant bankers and sport for arbitrageurs during the 1980s. This has been followed by a period of introspection and calmer reflection. But this does not mean that the issues have gone away for ever. Other problems become more acute in times of recession. The cracks in some over-geared companies appear. Management failings are not concealed by profitability which rises with the economic tide. Some spectacular collapses highlight the danger of control of a company by one dominant individual. This emphasizes the need for good corporate government and checks and balances at the top.

So some of the problems emerge in the dynamic of economic growth, and

---

[2] Amended Commission Proposal for a Council Directive on Investment Services in the Securities Field, OJ C42/7 of 22 Feb. 1990.

[3] Commission Proposal for a Council Directive on the Capital Adequacy of Investment Firms and Credit Institutions, Council of Ministers' Common Position, 27 July 1992 (7943/1/92).

[4] 'International Convergence of Capital Measurement and Capital Standards', by the Basle Committee on Banking Regulations and Supervisory Practices, July 1988.

some in the decline of recession. Clearly it is right that we should seek to learn the lessons of the past and to improve upon our corporate systems and philosophies.

Perhaps any analysis should begin with recognizing where ownership of companies lies. Nowadays our stock market is dominated by major institutional investors. In the late 1950s two-thirds of British industry was owned by private individuals; now less than one-fifth of domestic equities is held by individual shareholders. While the number of individuals holding shares has been increasing over recent years, largely due to privatizations, the percentage of shares held by private investors as a whole has still been declining.

I think we must recognize that the trend from private investor to institutional investor ownership will be a difficult one to reverse. For example, the wider share ownership movement, now known as Pro Share (United Kingdom) Ltd., has had only limited success in trying to encourage greater private shareholding. De-regulation of the market has created some disincentive for small shareholders by driving up charges. But both fiscal incentives and the need for expertise tend to go against the small shareholder. Along with others, I feel that this is a pity. But without practical action by way of tax incentives, it would seem that numbers will continue to dwindle. The reality today is that fewer than one hundred fund-management businesses effectively control institutional investment in this country. It is their actions which determine the ownership of a listed company and, to some extent, their wishes which influence a company's approach to issues such as dividend policy.

The debate on the role of institutional investors has been well aired. Should they be active or, indeed, pro-active and take greater interest in the companies in which they have shareholdings, even to the extent of replacing the government of a company where there is evidence of mismanagement? Or should they manage the portfolios of those whom they represent, simply making 'buy' and 'sell' decisions?

Shareholders are generally a form of remote control in the background. Where institutional investors do become involved in the government of a company, matters tend already to have gone badly wrong and so action is dramatic. We have seen this action in the case of the change of management of a number of companies recently. But it is desirable that the problems of a company should be grasped and improved before matters go so badly wrong. This is why the improvement of corporate governance is so pertinent. It is a much better, steadier form of monitoring and improving a company's performance than if, as a last resort, shareholders have to be more active in disciplining the management.

Corporate governance is not just about form; it is about substance. The ultimate aim of corporate government goes well beyond systems, control, transparency, and integrity. These are important parts of its function, but are there ultimately to secure efficient and proper management of resources and profitability. So the equality of the participants is crucial. So, too, is the brief which they are given. For this the chairman must carry a large part of the responsibility. He or she must make sure that the board debates the right issues; that it has enough information on which to have an informed debate; the opportunity to question management; and that it is alerted early to any incipient difficulty which a company confronts.

The media sometimes point out, generally in the context of pay, that there are a large number of inter-related directorships in corporate Britain. This is, in fact, inevitable if the executive directors of one company are to give valuable service by sitting as the non-executive directors of another company. But, quite apart from the general experience which they bring, the presence of experienced managers as non-executives on the board of other companies has another distinct advantage. It can stimulate the knowledge and cross-fertilization of best practice.

I would like just to tick off some of the areas which I believe are important for better governance of companies. I must own to a definite bias in favour of unitary boards. These ensure that the executive and non-executive directors alike share responsibility for policy development and implementation. Their perspectives may obviously differ. The non-executives may often rely heavily on the executives for information and experience. But each group has the same responsibility to further the interests of the company's shareholders.

Not only do the non-executive directors provide a check upon management; they have valuable outside experience to offer. They also enable the company to have an independent audit committee and remuneration committee. This ensures both a clear check on management and operations and unbiased examination on the pay of the senior management. NatWest shares the widely-held view that the membership of both such committees should consist solely of non-executive directors.

It would seem to me undesirable to suggest how many non-executive directors each company should have. This must depend on the size of the board, the number of executive members, and the size and diversity of the company. There is scope for flexibility in individual companies, but the principal is clear. We should all aspire to ensure that there is a sufficiently objective, independent, and powerfull outside view available to the organization.

The Cadbury Report suggested the extension of non-executive directors to all listed companies. Some have queried whether it will be practical to find enough non-executives of sufficient quality. Yet Pro-NED, the body that promotes the use of non-executive directors amongst UK corporates, believes that there is a good deal of talent which is currently untapped. It may also be that we should extend the catchment area from which non-executive directors are drawn. There are many solicitors, barristers, and accountants I can think of who would give real service in this area. I believe there is enough skill and aptitude available that this should not be a real problem. What is fundamental to raising quality is that the chairmen of individual companies should recognize the advantage, as so many of them already do, of securing able, experienced people with independence of mind.

Good corporate governance also depends very much on the participants themselves, particularly the personal chemistry between the chief executive and chairman. I do not wish to be dogmatic as to whether the role of chairman and chief executive should be separated. Indeed, as H. L. Mencken said: 'To every complex problem there is a solution, and it is usually simple, plausible and wrong.' But I believe that separate roles for the chairman and the chief executive will increasingly be the norm, and there are many valid and excellent reasons why this should be so—not least, because there are often two quite separate large jobs which need to be performed in close co-operation. The presence of a separate chairman may in certain situations also be necessary to give confidence to shareholders that management is, in fact, serving their interests. In some cases, however, the role of chairman and chief executive is combined and shareholders have been served effectively. I think it undesirable that this question should be governed by legislation. But I believe that these cases will become increasingly rarer.

What of the general duty of directors? This was considered recently in a decision in the commercial division of the Supreme Court of New South Wales, called *AWA Limited* v. *Daniels*.[5] The court made one observation which is undoubtedly realistic. It said that, 'of necessity as the complexities of commercial life have intensified, the community has come to expect more than formerly from directors, whose task it is to govern the affairs of companies to which large sums of money are committed by way of equity capital or loan. The affairs of a company demand an appreciable degree of diligent application by its directors if they are to attempt to do their duty.'[6] It ended its analysis of the duties of directors on a thoughtful, or provocative, note: 'the commercial reality of the matter is that, in these days of conglomerates, and perhaps trans-national conglomerates at that, the opportunity for non-executive directors to exercise meaningful control over management is as slight as the ability of ministers to control a vast bureaucracy.'[7] Fighting talk; but it emphasizes that, as Lord Hanson said recently, there will sometimes be the need for non-executive directors to be hound-dogs rather than watch-dogs. Yet they will still need to know when to bark in the night.

To whom, in governing the company, do the directors owe their duty? The ultimate duty is clearly owed to shareholders. But this, like so many

---

[5] (1992) 7 ACSR 759. See also Ch. 11 below, by G. P. Stapledon.
[6] Ibid., at 865.
[7] Ibid., at 878.

other statements, is an over-simplification. There is a clear duty to employees which is enshrined in Section 309 of the Companies Act, 1985. But in any event, the duty to shareholders cannot be fulfilled in modern conditions without regard to the interests of others who have a stake in the company. For the profitability of companies depends on the service which they give. This means that they have to focus on the interests and needs of the customer, and to do this they need trained and well-motivated staff. There may sometimes be tensions between the interests of the various stakeholders: for example, how much should be paid in dividend as opposed to wages; but there is no ultimate conflict: profitability depends on taking proper account of the interests both of customers and work-force.

I also find that the work-force brings a stimulus to the maintenance of high-standard corporate government, and responsiveness and sensitivities to the needs of societies. They do seem willing to question and critically to examine our own corporate values and cultures. This is healthy. To recruit and retain high-quality staff we will need to preserve and enhance our standards.

So I do believe that, within the framework of our company law, a company is able to take account of the interests of all those who have a stake in it. It will not always be straightforward to do so. There are inevitably tensions between the need to increase charges and the wish to serve customers. There are tensions between the reality that an efficient company cannot offer total job security and the wish to encourage better work-force motivation. There are tensions between the demands of shareholders for dividends and the need for a company to maintain its reserves.

But some see greater problems. The one most commonly raised is that the structure of our market, and the way in which institutions exercise ownership, promotes the short-term view. Over a year ago, in his maiden speech to the House of Lords, Lord Laing, formerly chairman of United Biscuits, stated that: 'Our society as a whole is shot through with short-termism.' This charge is often linked with the vulnerability of companies to contested takeovers. It is obviously not wholly easy to evaluate it. When I was chairman of the Takeover Panel, I met strong and good corporate leaders who claimed to be uninfluenced by a potential threat of takeover and felt comfortable that they could operate their company on an appropriately medium or long-term basis. If research and development expenditure plans stood up to rigorous examination and were well explained, and the company was seen to be well run, then the investment could be made. The pharmaceuticals industry is often quoted as an example. By contrast, other competent managers felt that the potential of a takeover bid was an undue restraint. A bid could be launched at a time when a company had set in train the development which would lead to fuller profitability, or had suffered an isolated misfortune and was valued more lowly in the market than management considered its prospects warranted.

Obviously one of the issues that this raises is the quality of a company's investor-relations management. I do not claim that this will provide a panacea for all ills, but it does have a significant role to play. How openly and clearly one communicates with one's shareholders, and particularly the institutional investors, will be a determining factor is how acceptable a company's investment-versus-payout ratio is perceived to be by the shareholders. If you do not try to explain your case cogently and frequently then it is surely invidious to complain when investors hold a different view of your medium-term prospects.

Institutions would also deny that they take too short-term an approach. Professor Sir James Ball, in giving the Stockton Lecture last year, gave an eloquent testimony in defence of institutional investors. He explained that the Legal and General Life Fund would hold a notional share on its portfolio for an average of ten years. Share dealing was often a matter of topping-up underweight positions in period of weakness, and top-slicing in periods of strength. As a matter of practice, they did not generally trade complete holdings above 1 per cent in their fund. Much of the same is true of NatWest Markets Investment Management. NatWest's investment style, which is reflected in the way the NatWest Pension Funds are managed, is to maintain core positions in the larger capitalization companies in the market. According to the relative merits of the company's shares in question, these positions are either added to or reduced. It is extremely rare that complete holdings will be traded.

But when it comes to takeovers a judgement has to be made by institutions as to whether to accept the price offered. It is in takeover situations more than any others that the focus is on a single interest only: the interest of the shareholders of the target company.

Let us consider for a moment what are the checks and balances in play in takeovers. The Office of Fair Trading and (if a bid is referred) the Monopolies and Mergers Commission are, with rare exceptions, only concerned with the effect of a bid upon competition. So, too, is the European Commission in a bid which qualifies for consideration at Community level. The Takeover Panel has the important and difficult role of ensuring fair play in the conduct of the takeover.[8]

The system, in my experience, works admirably but it does have a limited objective: to ensure that shareholders of the target company may fairly receive a bid for their company, while it reinforces the focus which is placed on considering the interests of those shareholders. It seems to me that it is during a takeover that least consideration is given to the interests of the widest stakeholders in the target company: the staff, customers, suppliers, and the contribution made to the community. This is illustrated by the fact that there is no need at present for the bidding company to issue a full

---

[8] See below, Ch. 9 by Alan Paul.

prospectus, detailing what are its plans for the target company if it succeeds in the bid. Indeed, it seems to me that relatively little thought is given during the course of a takeover to the impact on the work-force of the target company. Yet this work-force will ultimately become part of the staff of the merged group if the bid succeeds. Certainly, the very fact of the bid creates uncertainty. What degree of centralization will be needed in the merged corporation? What will be the new working conditions? What will be the impact on the culture of the target company? None of these factors has to be addressed during the bid itself.

Paradoxically, it has been estimated that 90 per cent of mergers fail to live up to expectations. Because of disappointing results, around one-third of all acquisitions have historically been sold off within five years. Perhaps this is, to some extent, because the management of the acquiring company does not have to make a business case to its own shareholders, or to the staff of the target company. All it has to do is show that it is prepared to pay enough for the shares in the target company. Part of the blame for the failure of mergers may well be that those who actually have to effect the merger and make a successful new organization—in other words, the work-force—are not courted for support, and are not given adequate information on the merits of the takeover, nor sufficiently encouraged to ensure successful integration. A takeover can still be an example of capitalism red in tooth and claw.

Earlier I mentioned the possibility of Europe moving towards the more open and liquid market found in the UK as we develop the free-market principles in Europe. The other side of the coin is that it may be that the British fashion for contested takeovers will become less acceptable as cross-border mergers within Europe gather momentum. Just as European fashions can move from north to south, so they could move across Channel from south to north.

In one sense, the ideal situation would be if the threat of takeover was so effective a stimulus that it never had to be put into practice. But we shall never have an ideal world. I would hope, however, that sound management and sound corporate government, as well as societal attitudes, would make contested takeovers a last resort rather than a regular form of market trading.

There is no time to touch on the role of auditors and regulators in the debate on the strengths of our corporate markets. Both are of considerable importance. But I would like to close by mentioning that banks have a very real and wide-ranging interest in this debate. Good corporate governance must be an integral part of the conduct of our own activities. But it must also be of significant comfort to banks when they come to lend money to companies. The spectacular failures of the last few years did not take place in companies which were soundly managed, with a strong board and good non-executive directors. They tended to take place where a single individual, sometimes of flawed character, became over-powerful and overrode any nominal checks and balances. So we have a very real interest in the proper government of companies, sound regulation, effective auditing, and proper reporting practices.

I am encouraged about the current development of corporate government. I believe the trend is in the right direction. The almost continuous debate we are having will raise standards. Some lessons have been learnt, and some progress is being made. Or is there a danger of the wish being father to the thought?

7

THE INSTITUTIONAL INVESTOR—INVESTMENT FROM M&G'S VIEWPOINT

Paddy Linaker

· The purpose of this paper is to present the view of an institutional investor on how we see our duties and responsibilities to our customers, be they policy-holders, unit-holders, or pensioners, and to the community at large.

If the private sector is to flourish and compete internationally, one very necessary requirement is for a situation of trust to exist between the owners (shareholders) and management (boards) of companies, and it is up to both to see that this position of mutual confidence is established and maintained. If it is to be maintained, then it has to be worked on by both. In addition to the provision of periodic statutory information, most UK companies are today making a great effort to keep their large investors in the picture through regular meetings with top management—chairmen and chief executives these days work hard to keep us informed, and most institutional investors welcome this. There has also been a change over recent years in the institutional investors's attitude to his role, and the vast majority now recognize that meeting and talking to companies is an essential element of their daily routine. This is probably the most interesting and stimulating part of an investment managers' duties: I like to see our managers out and about, away from their desks and the blandishments of brokers.

At M&G our investments are biased towards medium and smaller companies, which makes regular meetings with management even more important—in fact, essential. Of course investment managers like meeting the management of large companies, but it is important that this should not be at the expense of contact with the 'smaller fry'. Large companies are widely researched and their management is constantly under the scrutiny of the financial press and security analysis. I would go so far as to say that investment in a small company, with unknown management, is a somewhat hazardous or reckless policy for an investing institution to follow. For each company in which we hold a significant stake we designate an investment manager who has overall responsibility for that investment, and it is his job to see that regular contact is maintained. Although theoretical analysis can be valuable, it is dangerous to rely solely on it, and much is of low quality. Investment managers should realize that ultimately it is the ability and integrity of management which is what investment is all about, and upon which the success of their investments rest. I would argue that our practice of constant involvement does also tend to result in investment managers taking a somewhat longer view. It is worth adding that we encourage companies to seek our advice on matters where they feel that our views would be valuable, and we do not mind becoming 'insiders' in such circumstances. Any advice of this nature is given in the light of our position as a long-term shareholder, and has the advantage of being independent, and indeed attracts no fee. Over the past twenty years M&G has built up a high profile on issues of corporate governance (a pompous term, but what is the alternative?) We have not sought this. You may ask how has this reputation come about? I think it is due largely to an annual letter we write to the chairmen of companies in which we have a substantial investment. It is a private and informal letter which of course will often touch on topical issues. The press has, on certain occasions, gained access to this letter. Some reporters have misunderstood its nature, interpreting it as a special, unilateral statement; whereas it is in fact part of a continuous dialogue. By way of illustration the following are some of the issues we have raised over the years:

- The composition of boards and the importance we attach to independent outside directors (raised in the 1970s). All this may now seem very old hat, but if one casts one's mind back twenty five years, many large UK companies were run by boards of non-executive directors with the general manager in attendance—it is perhaps ironic that in the 1980s we had difficulty in getting some large companies to accept the presence of non-executive directors at all. To us a balanced board is the answer, but I would add it is certainly no guarantee of success—the people or the chemistry may be wrong.

- The desirability in normal circumstances of the separation of roles of chairmen and chief executives—(again mid 1970s). We have always maintained these are two separate jobs, and that each needs the other.

- The importance attached to a consistent dividend policy. The concept of dividend growth over the long term forms an important part of our investment philosophy. It is also extremely important for most of our unit-holders and the charities. It is, in fact, intrinsic to the concept of a widespread popular participation in equities.

- Our willingness to subscribe capital through rights issues for expansion, both in good times and in periods of difficult economic conditions. This must be a responsibility for the long-term investor.

- M&G's long-term commitment to companies—as long-term share-holders we support management in investing for the future, even if this is at the expense of current profitability (which normally it is not). And here I shall touch on the debate we have had over the years on 'short-termism', of which the investment institutions have been accused by both industry and governments over the years. I believe the paper published by Professor Marsh of the London Business School in 1990[1] has very effectively cleared the institutions of this charge, with the conclusion that in fact responsibility lies with industry managers themselves. This whole subject came to the boil at a time of high (contested) takeover activity, and now, with virtually no activity in this area, we hear little about it. It is, however, as important as it ever was—companies must think long term in their investment programmes, must spend on research and development, must spend on education and training, and I am quite sure no institutional investor would argue otherwise, provided the management at the top is capable of making sensible decisions in these areas. It is a prime responsibility of the investing institutions to satisfy themselves that the right long-term planning procedures are in existence. I regret to say that not all UK companies measure up here.

- With good management in place, it follows that our long-term commitment will not be overturned when a hostile bid comes along. We will normally support incumbent management.

- We have expressed general reservations on the value of contested takeover bids and the huge resources that are consumed in the process. History does not seem to bear out the success of a significant proportion of these ventures. Diversification can be carried too far, and very often leads to a lack of focus and dissipation of senior-management time. We are wary of the concept of growth through acquisition which in the 1980s became almost an end in itself. It was no doubt lucrative for many in the City, but the end-result for the UK PLC is an open question.

- In 1988 we expressed concern at the number of highly leveraged contested bids and also highly geared management buy-outs. Our worry was that sound business and work-forces could be put at risk by financially overstretched conglomerates. I am afraid that these fears proved only too well founded over the following years.

- In 1987 we raised the point of pre-emption rights and vendor placings. We value our stake in companies and do not like to be diluted, not simply because of the financial losses sometimes involved, but more fundamentally in our rights as stakeholders.

- In 1979 we touched on the subject of representation at AGMs—we are sometimes criticized for not being present at companies' AGMs, but this absence does not denote lack of interest, and in our experience we have learned that we can use our time more effectively to keep in touch with

---

[1] *Short-Terminism on Trial* (London Business School, 1990).

management—leading on from this we now seek to vote in all cases where we hold over 2.5 per cent of the share capital. Obviously we also vote on other occasions when our vote is necessary or where we particularly wish to express our support for or opposition to an issue.

From all of this it is clear what we like to see in the companies in which we invest. We like to see a consistent long-term and focused business which knows where it is trying to go and is not constantly changing direction. It should have a philosophy, and its aim should be to provide long-term growth, and of course dividend growth to its shareholders. It should have a well-structured board and above all it should have a first-class team of executive directors and a number of first-class non-executive or independent directors who are able to bring an outside perspective to the board's deliberations. Such a board would, of course, have open and honest accounting policies free from the creative financial reporting that can still exist. There should be a separation of the roles of chairman and chief executive. We like to see a remuneration committee and an audit committee, both primarily composed of suitably experienced independent directors.

Again, on the subject of contracts of employment we are unconvinced of the need for long-term contracts. In most cases one-year rolling contracts are quite sufficient. There have been too many examples of relatively unsuccessful companies which, as a result of either takeover or financial restructuring, have made very substantial payments to retiring board members, often in cases where the shareholders have done badly. I would stress that we wish to see good pay for good performance. Good management needs good basic pay, and success in terms of growth deserves to be rewarded through incentive schemes. We also like to see executive directors as shareholders and option-holders in their companies. It is a depressing experience for us institutional shareholders to see boards where virtually no shares are held by the directors. A good company must have a good management team at the top. A company that revolves around one person is taking a great risk and may well fail in the end. A board needs to have succession plans, and here the independent directors are likely to play an important part. There is also something to be said for independent directors being appointed for a fixed period, perhaps renewable once. This keeps a flow of new blood and new ideas. Often non-executive directorship are almost 'a job for life', which is no good to anyone.

The Cadbury Committee recommendations are, on the whole, very much in line with our philosophy—and for that reason we very much welcome them, as do the vast majority of investment houses. Acceptance of the Cadbury principles will, I am sure, produce a favourable framework for the relationship between industry and the city which would benefit the economy and the nation as a whole. I hope that the introduction of Cadbury will not have the effect of deterring both companies and investors from continuing to think for themselves on issues of corporate governance and investor relations generally. Fund managers and industry need to understand what they expect from the other. However, we must realise that should the Cadbury Committee proposals fail then there is no doubt in my mind that legislation will be introduced, which would be regrettable. Cadbury will require teeth, and institutional investors, through responsible use of their voting powers, may need to provide some of them.

Part IV
The Role of Takeover Bids

The takeover bid, or more accurately the threat of a takeover bid, has been seen as a major instrument for ensuring that corporate management maximize shareholder wealth. It has almost uniquely been an Anglo-Saxon phenomenon, but as Martin Lipton and Morris Panner indicate recent regulatory reforms in the United States have greatly blunted the effectiveness of the hostile bid. Hostile bids are virtually unknown in Germany because, as Professor Baums shows, of the structure of the market—his paper once again emphasizes the importance of fully appreciating the effect of market structure in conducting any comparative analysis of the corporate governance issues. Given this diversity in market structures, as Eddy Wymeersch indicated earlier, the EC harmonization programme with respect to company law and financial markets may fail to achieve anything like a uniform result in each member state. Alan Paul, in his analysis of the UK regulation of takeover bids, makes the critically important point that many of the defensive techniques common in the US, and to some extent in other EC jurisdictions, could be introduced by English companies. That this has not happened may be attributable in no small part, as he suggests, to the fact that initially shareholder approval would be needed, and shareholders (particularly institutional shareholders) may be unwilling to give the necessary approval. This is an example of institutional attitudes inhibiting particular developments within a framework that favours shareholder choice.

8

TAKEOVER BIDS AND UNITED STATES CORPORATE GOVERNANCE

Martin Lipton and Morris Panner

Introduction

During the two decades prior to 1990 the hostile takeover bid was the principal tool of corporate governance in the United States. The takeover bid was considered by Wall Street and many academics to be the most effective means by which corporate management could be held accountable for substandard performance or failure to optimize shareholder value. As the number and size of hostile bids grew in the 1970s, they ultimately evolved into the dreaded 'two-tier, front-end-loaded, bootstrap, junk-bond-financed, bust-up takeover'.

Takeover defence tactics and much of corporate law in the US for the last twenty years have been focused on dealing with hostile takeover bids. The starting point was the enactment by Congress in 1968 of the Williams Amendments to the Securities Exchange Act of 1934.[1] As a disclosure statute, the Williams Act did not regulate the form of tender offers (for example, it did not block partial bids),[2] but simply mandated specific

---

[1] Pub. L. No. 90–439, s. 2, 3, 82 Stat. 454, 455 29 July 1968 (amending 15 USC, s. 78 *m* and *n*) (the 'Williams Act'). The Williams Act added s. 13(d) to require disclosure of 10 per cent acquisitions of equity securities, s. 13(e) to regulate acquisitions of stock by the issuer, s. 14(d) and 14(e) to regulate tender offers, and s. 14(f) to regulate changes in the composition of the board of directors pursuant to substantial stock acquisitions or tender offers and without a meeting of the issuer's shareholders. Congress later amended the Williams Act to allow the Securities and Exchange Commission ('SEC') to make rules and regulations and to reduce the reporting level of stock ownership from 10 per cent to 5 per cent. Pub. L. No. 91–567, s. 1, 2, 3–5, 84 Stat. 1497 *et seq.*, 22 Dec. 1970. See Martin Lipton and Erica H. Steinberger, *Takeovers and Freezeouts* (1991), s. 2.01.

[2] Although the Williams Act does not define a 'tender offer', the legislative history to the Act describes it as a public offer to purchase for a fixed price (usually at a premium above the current market price) some or all of the securities of a publicly held corporation if certain specified conditions are met. See Hearings on H. R. 14475 and S. 510 Before the Subcomm. on Commerce & Finance of the House Comm. on Interstate and Foreign Commerce, 90th Cong., 2d Sess. 11, 14, 44 (1968). See also Note, 'The Developing Meaning of "Tender Offer" under the Securities Exchange Act of 1934' (1973) 86 *Harv. L. Rev.* 1,250, 1,251 ('tender offer has been conventionally understood to be a publicly made invitation addressed to all shareholders of a corporation to tender their shares at a specified price').

time periods during which information had to be distributed and an offer kept open for shareholder acceptance.[3] Essentially, the Williams Act did not create a level playing-field. Rather, tender-offer tactics continued to favour bidders. The Williams Act left bidders with the ability to employ a wide variety of techniques which coerced shareholders into tendering into an offer rapidly or risk being deprived of much of the value of their shares. Targets responded by attempting to find ways to gain time to manœuvre.[4]

The Takeover Era

A major turning-point for hostile takeover activity came in 1974 when Morgan Stanley & Co. arranged a tender offer for Electric Storage Battery, Inc., by the International Nickel Company of Canada.[5] This offer marked the first time that an old-line investment bank had engaged in a highly publicized, hostile takeover. Handing an ultimatum to the chief executive officer of ESB on the Friday before he was to begin his vacation—an African safari—INCO and its team of advisors began what later became known as a 'Saturday Night Special', making a $28 per share offer for ESB (ESB was

---

[3] The Williams Act did not explicitly provide for any minimum period during which a tender offer could be consummated. It did, however, require proration rights for tendering shareholders during the first ten days of a partial offer and provide for withdrawal rights during the first seven days of any offer, thus implicitly requiring that offers remain open for at least ten days in a partial offer and at least seven days in an any-and-all offer. The SEC subsequently has used its rule-making authority under Rule 14(e) of the Exchange Act to limit certain coercive elements of tender offer. Rule 14d–10 (known as the 'all holders' rule) prohibits exclusionary tender offers and provides that the consideration paid to any security holder pursuant to a tender offer must be equal to the highest consideration paid by the offeror to any other security holder during the tender offer. Rule 14d–7, as amended in 1986, also extended withdrawal rights during the entire period that the offer remains open. Rule 14d–8, adopted in 1982, requires a bidder in a partial.tender offer to accept on a *pro rata* basis all securities tendered during the life of the offer. See Lipton and Steinberger, n. 1 above, at s. 2.05. See generally Comment, 'Front-End Loaded Tender Offers: The Application of Federal and State Law to an Innovative Corporate Acquisition Technique' (1982) 131 *U. Pa. L. Rev.* 389, 410 (discussing whether SEC exceeded its authority in adopting Rule 14d–8).

[4] The first generation of state takeover statutes were designed with this end in mind. States responded to political pressure to curtail takeovers by enacting statutes that required additional notice—ranging from ten to sixty days—before the commencement of an offer and, in some cases, approval by state securities commissioners which allowed further delays. These early efforts, however, were declared unconstitutional on the grounds that they were pre-empted by the Williams Act, a federal law, or violated the Commerce Clause of the Constitution. See e.g. *Edgar* v. *Mite Corp.*, 457 US 624, 102 S. Ct. 2629, 73 L. Ed. 2d 269 (1982). More than thirty-five states had enacted laws to regulate tender offers by 1982. See n. 26 below for a more detailed discussion of state statutory efforts to restrict takeover activity in light of early judicial decisions.

[5] Subsequently, in Dec. 1974, Loews Corp., through a bid managed by Salomon Brothers, took over CNA Financial Corp. in a contested transaction. This added to the perception that hostile takeovers were to be the business of establishment investment banks and their clients.

then trading for $19.50). With the intervention of United Technologies as a white knight, a spirited bidding contest developed. Ultimately, INCO won with a $41 bid.[6] With the success of the INCO bid, investment banks that had previously deemed hostile takeovers to be a dirty business began to change their views and advise their aggressive corporate clients accordingly. Hostile takeovers and related financial and tactical innovation grew to become the major focus of Wall Street in the 1980s.

Although the INCO–ESB bid was hostile, it still resulted in the merger of two industrial companies. This was true for much of the 1970s. Most of the takeovers were strategic rather than financial. However, toward the end of the 1970s and through the 1980s many of the takeovers were by financial entrepreneurs who used the technique of the two-tier, front-end-loaded takeover bid. In this technique the bidder makes a first-step cash-tender offer for approximately 50 per cent of the target's shares, and then 'squeezes out' the remaining shareholders in a lower priced 'back-end' merger. Two-tier bids are coercive, since the two-tier aspect of the bid stampedes shareholders into tendering (in the first step) out of the fear of receiving only the lower back-end consideration in the second-step merger.[7]

The two-tiered bid was well suited to the financial entrepreneur. For example, Mesa Petroleum, led by T. Boone Pickens, in 1982 borrowed $500 million to bid $40 per share for half the shares of General American Oil Company, stating that upon gaining control it would merge with General American, issuing Mesa equity or subordinated debt (with a value of less than $40 per share) for the remaining half of the shares. Thus the commercial banks financing Mesa were assured two dollars of asset coverage for each dollar loaned to Mesa.[8] Mesa could in effect finance 100 per cent of the cost of the takeover—the ultimate bootstrap acquisition.

The ability of investment banks to sell below investment-grade, high-yield securities (known as 'junk bonds') added a new dimension to takeover

---

[6] This price was a 110 per cent premium to the market price when the offer commenced. By 1982 INCO, after losing a great deal of money, had divested itself of most of ESB and closed the remainder of the business. For a narrative account of the transaction, see VerMeulen, 'Guide to Corporate Takeovers', *Working Woman* (Feb. 1985), at 75.

[7] The partial tender offer is a similar technique. A bidder gains control of the target by purchasing a controlling stake with no promise of a second-step merger. The remaining shareholders then have limited protection from self-dealing by the raider or a later squeeze-out merger.

[8] See Lipton and Steinberger (n. 1, above), at s. 1. 08. Note that the Mesa offer was even more coercive given the prevailing rules. Under then-existing SEC rules, the proration period (the period during which shares tendered into the offer are required to be purchased on a *pro rata* basis) was ten days, while the offer would remain open for twenty days. Thus, shareholders were under great pressure to tender prior to the expiration of the proration period. The adoption of Rule 14d–8 made the offer period and the proration period co-terminous. For a case study of the Mesa bid, see Arthur Fleischer, Jr., *Tender Offers: Defenses, Responses and Planning* VI, (1990).

fights. It allowed raiders to replace the two-tier technique with a return to the all-cash bid, and the growing junk-bond market allowed financial entrepreneurs to pursue larger and larger targets previously thought to be immune to a hostile takeover. In addition, the resulting pressure to meet interest payments on junk bonds and reduce heavy debt-levels led acquirors (who were no longer typically industrial companies, but takeover entrepreneurs who pursued acquisitions solely for short-term gain) to manage an enterprise to generate cash in the short term and/or to 'bust up' the target to generate cash.

The judicial, corporate, and statutory response to the bootstrap, bust-up takeover animated the next decade of corporate law in the US. In the process, the legal effort shifted from the focus on extending the period an offer was kept open (Williams Act and early state takeover statutes) to confronting what came to be perceived as financial structural advantages inherent in the two-tiered bid. And, as the junk-bond-financed, bust-up takeover became increasingly popular, states and corporations responded to the efforts by financial entrepreneurs to profit by exploiting and dishonouring what had hitherto been unspoken commitments by the company to its employees and community.[9] Increasingly, anti-takeover measures were designed to give the board the ability to negotiate a transaction that would be substantively fair to the shareholders and the various constituencies of the corporation. Finally, these measures were designed to enable the board to 'just say no' and keep the target independent unless and until the board was ousted in a proxy fight and the new board agreed to the takeover.

Charter/By-law Shark Repellents

Initially companies tried self-help. They adopted a number of changes to their charters and by-laws which made it more difficult for an acquiror to gain control of the board. Although none of these provisions was able to defeat a determined bidder, particularly one willing to make an all-cash offer, they had the effect of giving a board of directors some leverage in its negotiation with a hostile bidder.[10] There also was significant debate over whether such provisions simply advertised the perception of vulnerability

---

[9] Many states have responded to this situation by passing corporate constituencies statutes. See n. 30 below. The courts also have provided boards of directors with a legal basis for considering other constituencies than only shareholders. See e.g. *Unocal Corp.* v. *Mesa Petroleum Co.*, 493 A.2d 946 (Del. 1985); *Paramount Communications, Inc.* v. *Time, Inc.*, 571 A.2d 1140 (Del. 1989).

[10] See generally Stephen A. Hochman and Oscar D. Folger, 'Deflecting Takeovers: Charter and By-Law Techniques' (1979) 34 *Bus. Law.* 537.

on the part of the corporation.[11] Set forth below is a partial list of provisions adopted by boards.[12]

STAGGERED BOARDS

Corporations adopted 'staggered' or 'classified' board-of-director provisions. Under this regime, a portion of the board (typically one-third) comes up for re-election each year and each director's term is extended to three years. At least two annual meetings of stockholders, instead of one, will generally be required to effect a change in a majority of the board. Staggered board provisions also were combined with cumulative voting[13] provisions limiting the number of directors and the method of their removal, as well as requiring a 'super-majority' vote for amendment of the applicable charter provisions. In addition, the corporate laws of certain states were changed to provide that if a corporation has a staggered board, directors can only be removed for cause unless the charter provides otherwise.[14] Although there were no legal problems in adopting a staggered board, the adoption of the charter amendment typically required a shareholder vote, and was subject to shareholder resistance.[15]

SUPER-MAJORITY VOTE

These provisions require a super-majority vote of shareholders to approve any business combination with a person owning a specified percentage of the target's shares. Sometimes the amendment was coupled with a provision making it inapplicable if certain pricing criteria for the transaction were met or if the transaction was approved by the 'old' directors. The courts have, in general, sustained the validity of super-majority provisions.[16]

[11] See e.g. 'Arbitrageurs Unimpressed by "Super Majority" Defenses in Takeover Bids', *Securities Week*, 26 June 1978, at p. 9: 'Corporate charter provisions designed to avert takeovers have left many of Wall Street's risk arbitrageurs unfazed, although the defenses have been adopted by dozens of companies ... But rather than dissuading companies from attempting a takeover, the provisions "telegraph with your chin" that the company believes it could be prime for an acquisition, and actually sharpen interest in the corporation, major arbitrageurs say.'
[12] Other provisions include amendments prohibiting green-mail, eliminating shareholder action by written consent in lieu of a meeting, limiting the ability of shareholders to call a special meeting, and provisions for longer notice periods for shareholder meetings.
[13] Under a cumulative voting regime, a stockholder can cast all of his votes for one director rather than dividing the votes among the slate of directors.
[14] Del. Code Gen. Ann. tit. 8, s. 141 (k)(i).
[15] Institutional shareholder resistance to such provisions has not abated. See e.g. 'Takeover Defenses: Covering the Flanks', *Mergers and Acquisitions* (May/June, 1992), at 34.
[16] *Seibert* v. *Gulton Industries, Inc.*, No. 5631. 5 Del. J. Corp. L. 514 (Del. Ch. 21 June 1979), aff'd without opinion 414 A.2d 822 (Del. 1980) (sustaining the validity, under Delaware law, of a super-majority charter provision). See also *Seibert* v. *Milton Bradley Co.*, Civ. No. 77–464 (Mass. Super. 31 Jan. 1979), aff'd 405 N.E.2d 131 (Mass. 1980) (upholding super-majority charter provision under Massachusetts law).

TAKE-OUT OF REMAINING TARGET SHAREHOLDERS; FAIR-PRICE PROVISIONS

Fair-price charter amendments also were adopted by many companies as a protection against acquisitions that utilized two-tier pricing.[17] Fair-price provisions were designed to achieve a measure of assurance that any multistep attempt to take over a company was made on terms which offered similar treatment to all stockholders. A fair-price provision requires that a super-majority (usually 80 per cent) of the voting power of the company approve any merger, or similar extraordinary transaction, with an acquiror who owns a specified (usually 5 or 10 per cent of the voting power) interest in the company, unless the transaction was approved by the 'old' directors or certain fair-price provisions were complied with.[18]

Dual Class Capitalization

Besides adopting charter amendments, companies also adopted dual-class capitalization structures to make it more difficult or impossible for anyone to gain voting control. This, however, has been the subject of considerable controversy. In July 1988 the Securities and Exchange Commission (SEC) adopted Rule 19c–4, designed to prohibit such capitalization structures.[19] The SEC's action was then invalidated by a federal court on the grounds that the SEC had exceeded its authority under the Exchange Act in adopting the rule.[20] The New York Stock Exchange, however, had, prior to the court decision, adopted its own rule (approved by the SEC) implementing Rule 19c–4, and the court's decision did not affect the validity of the NYSE's rule. Recently the NYSE has proposed for discussion a revised rule permitting dual-class capitalization in certain circumstances.[21]

[17] As of Oct. 1987, 153 of the Fortune 500 companies had adopted fair-price or related charter amendments and 225 had classified boards.

[18] See Hochman and Folger, n. 10 above, at 553–7.

[19] As adopted, Rule 19c–4 prohibited national securities exchanges and associations from listing or authorizing for quotation common stock or other equity security of a domestic company that 'issues any class of security, or takes other corporate action, with the effect of nullifying, restricting or disparately reducing the per share voting rights of holders of an outstanding class or classes of common stock'. Reg. s. 240.19c–4, Fed. Sec. L. Rep. (CCH) [¶] 26,298D at 19,317–3.

[20] *Business Roundtable* v. *SEC*, 905 F.2d 406 (D.C. Cir. 1990).

[21] The proposed NYSE rule sets general standards that must be met by companies issuing common stock with disparate voting rights or seeking to change the voting rights of outstanding common stock. These are: all shares of common stock must be freely transferable; the decision to issue shares with disparate voting rights, or to change relative voting rights, must be approved by a majority of a committee of independent directors; the decision must be approved by a majority of the board of directors; if, following the implementation of the decision, management or a control group would have the majority of the voting power, then a majority of the board of directors of the company shall be independent directors; and the decision must be approved by a vote of a majority of the outstanding shares of capital stock entitled to vote on the matter and of any class which would be adversely affected by the decision, without counting the vote of any interested shareholder. See NYSE, 'One Share—One Vote', Summary (Discussion Draft 29 May 1992).

The Poison Pill

The Poison Pill is cogently described in Fleischer, Sussman, and Lesser's *Takeover Defense* as follows:

The poison pill has evolved to become the single most widely-used takeover defense of general applicability. Although other measures may be more lethal in particular situations and a number of judicial decisions have demonstrated that it should not be viewed as the takeover target's panacea, the pill has survived repeated litigation attacks to prove its effectiveness in preventing a variety of coercive takeover tactics and in enabling target companies' boards to respond to hostile bids in a deliberative and unfrenzied manner.

Despite the controversy it has continued to generate (as epitomized by the staying power of its pejorative name), the pill has won widespread acceptance as an indispensable addition to a company's defensive arsenal.

Its proliferation became particularly rapid under the catalytic influence of the Delaware Supreme Court's 1985 decision in *Household*[22]—which confirmed both the corporate authority of a Delaware corporation's board to adopt a pill as a pre-planned defense measure and the applicability of the business judgment rule to insulate a board's decision from attack where the pill is shown (under the general *Unocal* tests for defensive measures)[23] to be a proportional response to a reasonably perceived threat to corporate policy and effectiveness—and the same court's 1986 decision in *Revlon*,[24] which upheld the adoption of a pill as a responsive defense to a hostile tender offer. As of 31 August 1990, almost 1,300 companies have adopted a pill, in one form or another, as their first line of defense and the litigation focus has shifted from attacks on the pill's adoption to challenges against the manner of its subsequent use.

During its brief history the poison pill has gone through several forms and the process of evolution is a continuing one. Nevertheless, there is today a common understanding that the term '*poison pill*' denotes a distribution to stockholders of a right which acquires significant economic value upon the occurrence of specified events involving a non-board-approved acquisition of a significant ownership position in the company. Since this economic value consists of an entitlement to receive money or property from the company or the raider, and the acquisition cannot be consummated without triggering this entitlement, the raider cannot swallow up the company without also ingesting the economic poison represented by the value that has to be delivered upon exercise of the rights.

Today, the prevalent version of the pill is the '*status flip-in/flip-over*' stockholder rights plan. Although there cannot be said to be a single uniform model of the status flip-in pill, the basic concept is the same for all variants:

- The board declares a dividend of one stock purchase right for each outstanding common share.
- The right has no economic value unless and until a raider acquires a specified percentage (typically 15 per cent or 20 per cent) of the target's voting stock

---

[22] *Moran v. Household International, Inc.*, 500 A.2d 1346 (Del. 1985).
[23] *Unocal Corp. v. Mesa Petroleum Co.*, 493 A.2d 946 (Del. 1985).
[24] *Revlon, Inc. v. MacAndrews & Forbes Holdings, Inc.*, 506 A.2d 173 (Del. 1986).

without board approval. The raider's attainment of the status of a non-board-approved owner of that level, irrespective of its intentions regarding the possible use of the stock, entitles all other stockholders to purchase additional voting stock at a 50 per cent discount to market price (this is the discriminatory '*flip-in*').

- In addition, if, after a flip-in event, the company is involved in a business combination or substantial asset sale with any person, all stockholders (except the raider) become entitled to purchase, at a 50 per cent discount to market price, the most senior voting securities of the ultimate corporate parent resulting from the transaction (this is the discriminatory '*flip-over*').

The flip-over feature of the current pill is largely an anachronistic carryover from the earlier form of pill considered in *Household*. Today, it is the flip-in which accounts for the pill's effectiveness. Because the level of dilution it would inflict on both the voting power and the economic value of the stock of a raider who unilaterally crossed the ownership trigger level has proven universally unacceptable, the flip-in has proven an effective deterrent to several tactics. Thus while the pill has not eliminated takeover vulnerability or stopped hostile takeovers, it has significantly ameliorated the susceptibility of targets to transactions that do not offer full value to all stockholders and, equally significantly, has given boards far more time to explore value-maximizing alternatives to hostile tender offers than is afforded by the SEC's tender offer rules.[25]

Second Generation State Takeover Laws

Following the Supreme Court's rejection of state takeover regulation in 1982 and the absence of federal initiatives in the wake of that decision, the states themselves developed a number of second-generation takeover statutes. Each approach was premissed on the traditional role of the states in defining the framework for corporate governance. By framing statutes in terms of corporate governance, states successfully avoided the Williams Act pre-emption and Commerce Clause concerns that prompted the Supreme Court to overturn the first generation statutes.

CONTROL-SHARE STATUTES

In 1982 Ohio enacted the first control-share acquisition statute,[26] which was copied by a number of other states, including Indiana. Although Ohio acted first, Indiana's statute became the subject of a Supreme Court decision

---

[25] Arthur Fleischer, Jr. Alexander R. Sussman, and Henry Lesser, *TAKEOVER DEFENSE* (1990), 209–12.

[26] Ohio Gen. Corp. Law, s. 1701.831 (A). The Ohio statute was declared unconstitutional in *Fleet Aerospace Corp.* v. *Holderman*, 796 F.2d 135 (6th Cir. 1986), but the Sixth Circuit decision was vacated by the Supreme Court (*Ohio* v. *Fleet Aerospace Corp.*, 481 US 1003, 107 S. Ct. 1623, 95 L. Ed. 2d 197 (1987)) in light of its decision in *CTS Corp.* v. *Dynamics Corp. of America*, 481 US 69, 107 S. Ct. 1637, 95 L. Ed. 2d 67 (1987) ('CTS').

validating this approach to state regulation of takeovers.[27] The Indiana Act denies voting rights to a purchaser who brings its voting power to or above the threshold of 20 per cent of the stock of the target, unless such purchaser first obtained permission of the target's shareholders at a special meeting. Thus, the Indiana Act requires a vote of the target's shareholders before a tender offer for control may be consummated.

FAIR-PRICE PROVISIONS

With greater freedom to protect shareholders, several states also amended their corporation laws to include a 'super-majority/fair-price' provision similar to those found in many corporate charters. These provisions operate by imposing super-majority voting requirements for mergers, sales of assets, liquidations, and recapitalizations (but not tender offers) between a corporation and an 'interested shareholder' (generally, a holder with at least a 10 per cent stake), unless the transaction meets statutory fair-price requirements. The fair-price requirement assures that shareholders receive in the second stage of an acquisition a price at least as high as the highest price paid by the interested shareholder for any shares within the past two years. If the fair-price standards are not met, the statutes generally require an 80 per cent vote of the outstanding shares and a $66\frac{2}{3}$ per cent vote of the shares held by disinterested shareholders.

BUSINESS COMBINATION STATUTE

States also adopted statutes that delay the ability of a hostile acquiror from squeezing out majority shareholders, and thereby deter bootstrap financing. These laws also block a transaction between the acquiror and the target after the delay period unless the shareholders are provided with a 'fair' price for their shares. The New York statute, for example, prohibits New York corporations from entering into a 'business combination' with a 20 per cent stockholder for five years after the 20 per cent threshold is crossed, unless the board of directors approved the combination in advance of the 20 per cent acquisition.[28] Any business combination after the five-year period must be approved by a majority of the disinterested stockholders or must satisfy a fair-price test. No business combination is permitted if the 20 per cent shareholder acquires additional stock after crossing the 20 per cent threshold, unless the additional shares are purchased at the fair price or in a fashion, prescribed by the statute, designed to allow all shareholders to share proportionately.

More recently, the Wisconsin Business Combination Act, after being challenged in court, led to a broad endorsement of the power of the states to regulate takeover transactions. In essence, the court construed the Williams

---

[27] Ind. Bus. Corp. Law, s. 23–1–42–1, *et seq*. The Indiana statute was upheld in *CTS*.
[28] NY Bus. Corp. Law, s. 912.

Act as nothing more than a procedural statute; it did not provide any particular entitlements to shareholders. The court held that because '[i]nvestors have no right to receive tender offers' and the Williams Act 'does not create a right to profit from the business of marking tender offers', the Wisconsin law is not pre-empted.[29]

CORPORATE CONSTITUENCY STATUTES

In response to the perceived societal injustices of takeovers and the enormous dislocation inherent in bust-up takeovers, states developed laws that allowed directors to consider a variety of constituency interests in addition to shareholder interests. A number of the state statutes are broad enough to allow a board to consider all types of interests in evaluating a takeover bid. For example, the Ohio statute[30] and the Missouri statute[31] provide that for the purpose of performing his duties to the corporation, a director could consider the interests of employees, creditors, the community, and even the economy of the state and the nation.

While all the constituency statutes do not reach as far as the Ohio and Missouri statutes (the New York statute, for example, authorizes directors to consider both the long- and short-term interests of the corporation and its shareholders) the statutes none the less lessen the pressure on a board to accede to the demands of arbitrageurs and institutional investors in connection with a hostile bid. In particular, constituency statutes may provide support for a 'just say no'[32] defence and are often supported by legislative history indicating that the legislature rejects the heightened *Unocal* standard, the standard adopted by Delaware for evaluating director conduct in response to a takeover bid.[33] In addition, constituency statutes are often accompanied by statutes validating rights plans.

MASSACHUSETTS STAGGERED BOARD STATUTE

Most recently states have begun to legislatively codify what had previously been the subject of individual corporate action. This move reflected the broad political consensus that hostile takeovers had come to threaten communities and lead to unjust enrichment for the few. A Massachusetts statute[34] legislatively mandates that every publicly held Massachusetts corporation, unless its board of directors opts out of the statute, will have a staggered board of directors, with one-third of the directors being elected each year. This statute was adopted after BTR PLC announced an

---

[29] *Amanda Acquisition Corp.* v. *Universal Foods Corp.*, 877 F.2d 496, 504 (7th Cir. 1989), cert. denied, 493 US 954, 110 S. Ct. 367, 107 L. Ed. 2d 353 (1989).

[30] Ohio Rev. Code Ann., s. 1701.59.

[31] Mo. Rev. Stat., s. 351.347.

[32] See text at n. 9.

[33] See e.g. Indiana Code, s. 23–1–35–1 (1989). See text at n. 42.

[34] s. 50A of Ch. 156B of Massachusetts General Laws.

unsolicited tender offer and a proxy fight for Norton Company, a Massachusetts corporation. The Massachusetts statute also contains tin parachute and labour-contract provisions similar to those enacted in Pennsylvania.

Pennsylvania Statute

In April 1990 Pennsylvania adopted what can be seen as the culmination of the evolution of state takeover regulation. The statute applies to takeovers and proxy contests and effectively combines a variety of state statutes and corporate charter provisions. The statute has several distinct aspects:

- Profit-disgorgement provisions:[35] to discourage raiders from acquiring a stake and then putting the target in play, this section provides that any short-term profit realized by an acquiror in connection with a bid for 20 per cent or more of the voting power of a publicly traded Pennsylvania corporation is forfeited to the corporation.

- Control-share provisions: the statute incorporates 'control-share' provisions along the lines of control-share statutes adopted by other states. A person who acquires 'control-shares' will not have any voting rights with respect to such shares until such rights are granted by shareholder referendum. The referendum is particularly restrictive in that both the raider and any short-term holders, such as arbitrageurs, are excluded from the vote.

- Directors' duties provisions: this provision incorporates the concept of the constituency statutes adopted by other states. Directors can consider the long-term interests of the corporation, the identity and history of a bidder, and 'all other pertinent factors'. It is also made clear that the board need not regard the interests of any given constituency as 'dominant or controlling'. The directors' duties provisions explicitly provide that the duties of the board are owed 'solely to the corporation'. Such duties 'may not be enforced directly by a shareholder, member or by any other person or group'. They also make clear that these statutory provisions do not 'create any right or cause of action' against the board. These provisions also provide that the 'fiduciary duty of directors shall not be deemed to require them to act ... solely because of the effect such action might have on an acquisition ... of control of the corporation or the consideration that might be offered or paid to shareholders in such an

---

[35] Ohio recently adopted a statutory provision similar to Pennsylvania's profit-disgorgement statute. In addition, the Ohio statute, among other things, creates a moratorium on Ohio companies acquired by 10 per cent shareholders using the company's assets to retire debt and restricts the sale of assets to the acquiror at below-market prices. The Ohio company's board of directors is able, however, to opt out of these provisions prior to a 10 per cent shareholder becoming such.

acquisition'. The provision legislatively overrules the application by Pennsylvania courts of *Unocal*'s 'enhanced business judgement rule'.

- Tin parachutes and labour-contracts provisions: finally, the statute explicitly protects the interests of workers in the takeover context.

  (a) Any employee who was employed for at least two years by a Pennsylvania corporation that was subject to a control-share approval, who was employed within ninety days prior to or on the day of the control-share approval, and was terminated within ninety days prior to the control-share approval pursuant to an agreement or within twenty-four months following the control-share approval, is entitled to receive a severance payment from the company. The payment is equal to the employee's weekly compensation multiplied by the employee's number of completed years of service, to a maximum of twenty-six, less other severance payments paid to the employee by the company.[36]

  (b) No labour contract covering employees engaged in employment in Pennsylvania that was negotiated by a labour organization or a collective-bargaining agent and that is in effect and relates to the business of a Pennsylvania corporation at the time of a control-share approval may be cancelled as the result of a business-combination transaction occurring within five years of a control-share approval. The statute includes a provision for successor liability under such contracts.

Under the statute, Pennsylvania corporations, through action by the Board of Directors, could opt out of the new law until 26 July 1990. Unlike some other state takeover statutes, Pennsylvania does not allow corporations to opt out by shareholder action. Out of approximately 300 Pennsylvania public companies, at least ninety-one companies opted out of at least some portion of the new law: thirty-two opted out totally; forty-nine opted out of the control-share and disgorgement provisions; eight opted out of the control-share provisions only; and two opted out of the disgorgement provisions only. Eleven of the sixteen Pennysylvania Fortune 500 companies opted out of at least some portion of the statute.[37]

The Courts

The judicial response to the takeover wave has been varied and complex. On the one hand, the judiciary often found itself as the arbiter of complex and

---

[36] 'Tin parachutes' provide for severance payments for certain salaried employees who are terminated during an interim period (typically two years) following a 'change in control'. They are a variation of 'golden parachutes' which provide protection—either through employment or severance agreements—to the executives of a company that has been taken over. See Lipton and Steinberger (n. 1 above), at s. 6.02[4][a][i], 6.02[4][a][iv].

[37] See also Margaret M. Blair, 'Who's in Charge Here? How Changes in Corporate Finance are Shaping Corporate Governance', *The Brookings Review* (Fall 1991), at 9.

high-stakes contests. On the other, the courts have expressly eschewed taking sides in the public debate over whether takeovers are good or bad in terms of national policy. In *Norlin Corp.* v. *Rooney, Pace Inc.*,[38] the Second Circuit took care to note that, while it had ruled against director action to give themselves effective voting control in response to an undesired stock-purchase programme, its holding should not be read as reflective of any general views on the takeover debate: 'Although we are cognizant that takeover fights, potentially involving billions of dollars, profoundly affect our society and economy, it is not for us [the courts] to make the policy choices that will determine whether this style of corporate warfare will escalate or diminish. Our holding here is not intended to reflect a more general view of the contests being played out on this and other corporate battlefields.'[39] Similarly, in the *CTS* opinion,[40] the US Supreme Court, upholding the constitutionality of the Indiana Control Share Acquisitions Act, declined to second-guess the judgement of the Indiana Legislature regarding the utility of the Indiana Act, noting that 'the Constitution does not require the States to subscribe to any particular economic theory'.

THE BUSINESS JUDGEMENT RULE

The starting-point for a judicial evaluation of director conduct in a takeover context is the 'business judgement rule'.[41] This rule creates a presumption that directors act in good faith, on an informed basis, and in the best interest of the company when making corporate decisions.[42] The doctrine acknowledges that an informed board of directors is in the best position to make the complex decisions necessary to administer a modern corporation.[43] In short, courts ordinarily will not second-guess board decisions.

The pressures and conflicts inherent in a contested takeover challenged the judicial assumptions underlying the business-judgement rule. In response, the courts developed a doctrine which places an enhanced duty on directors, subject to judicial examination, before the directors will be entitled to rely on the presumptions of the business-judgement rule.[44] The

---

[38] 744 F.2d 255 (2d Cir. 1984).

[39] Ibid., at 269.

[40] *CTS Corp.* v. *Dynamics Corp. of America*, 481 US 69, 92, 107 S. Ct. 1637, 1651, 95 L. Ed. 2d 67 (1987).

[41] The Delaware judiciary is one of the most important fora for judicial pronouncements on corporate governance. Reflecting the highly developed state of its corporate law, half of the Fortune 500 companies are incorporated in Delaware. The courts of other states frequently look to the Delaware courts for guidance.

[42] See *Unocal, Inc.* v. *Mesa Petroleum Co.*, 493 A.2d 946, 954 (Del. 1985).

[43] Ibid.

[44] Note that once the sale of the company becomes 'inevitable', the *Unocal* test is not applicable. Then the board must shift its efforts to obtaining the highest price for the sale of the company. *Revlon, Inc.* v. *MacAndrews & Forbes Holdings, Inc.*, 506 A.2d 173, 182 (Del. 1986) (when sale of the company is inevitable, the board is no longer faced with 'threats to corporate policy and effectiveness, or to the stockholder's interests, from a grossly inadequate bid'). For a discussion of the transactions or events which may put the company into a sale mode, see

test, developed in *Unocal* v. *Mesa Petroleum*, requires the directors to show: (1) 'reasonable grounds for believing that a danger to corporate policy and effectiveness existed', and (2) that the defensive measure chosen was 'reasonable in relation to the threat posed'. In essence, directors would be entitled to the protection of the business judgement if (1) they acted in good faith and upon reasonable investigation to satisfy the first prong of the *Unocal* test, and (2) if they acted in the interests of the corporation rather than to maintain their own positions.

The court, however, made clear that the second prong of the *Unocal* test is to be interpreted broadly. A board could consider:

inadequacy of the price offered, nature and timing of the offer, questions of illegality, the impact on 'constituencies' other than shareholders (i.e., creditors, customers, employees, and perhaps even the community generally), the risk of nonconsummation, and the quality of securities being offered in the exchange. See Lipton and Brownstein, Takeover Responses and Directors' Responsibilities: An Update, p. 7, ABA National Institute on the Dynamics of Corporate Control (8 December 1983).[45]

The extent to which the board could look to other constituencies under the second prong of the *Unocal* test, however, remained unclear. The *Unocal* case arose out of a challenge to a defensive self-tender by Unocal Corp. that excluded the shareholder-raider. *Unocal* sought to effect the tender in response to a two-tiered bid by Mesa Petroleum that was to be followed by a 'squeeze-out' merger of the remaining shareholders with consideration made up of junk bonds with a lower value than the cash consideration offered. Later court decisions suggested that the nature of the offer was the critical element in the *Unocal* decision. With the advent of junk-bond financing and the ability of raiders to provide an all-cash offer to shareholders, courts suggested that the other constituencies' language of *Unocal* lost its force when the board considered an all-cash, premium offer for all of the target's shares.[46]

JUST SAY NO

The Delaware Supreme Court's recent decision in *Paramount Communications, Inc.* v. *Time Inc.*[47] however, rejected the efforts to undermine *Unocal* and constitutes a broad affirmation of a board of directors' ability to consider the interest of other constituencies in evaluating a takeover offer. In short, a board of directors can 'just say no' to a hostile bid where the corporation is pursuing its long-term, strategic interests.

Ronald T. Gilson and Reinier Kraakman, 'What Triggers Revlon' (1990) 25 *Wake Forest L. Rev.* 37.

[45] 493 A.2d at 955 (footnotes omitted).
[46] See *Grand Metropolitan PLC* v. *Pillsbury Co.*, [1989 Transfer Binder] Fed. Sec. L. Rep. (CCH) [•] 94,104 (Del. Ch. 16 Dec. 1988); *City Capital Assocs. Ltd. Partnership* v. *Intercom, Inc.*, 551 A.2d 787 (Del. Ch. 1988).
[47] 571 A.2d 1140 (Del. 1989).

The *Time* decision arose out of an effort by Paramount Communications to break up a friendly merger between Time Inc. and Warner Communications. Approximately two weeks before the scheduled shareholder votes on the merger, Paramount announced an all-cash, any-and-all tender offer for the shares of Time. The Time board rejected the offer, persuaded that the Warner merger was in the best long-term interests of the company. Ultimately, Time restructured the transaction with Warner so that no shareholder vote was required. A subsequent higher bid by Paramount was again rejected, even though the board acknowledged that the offer by Paramount would be likely to exceed the market price for the Time-Warner stock immediately after the merger. Time shareholders and Paramount sued. The Court refused to enjoin Time's defensive actions.

The Court made clear that there is no obligation to sacrifice long-term plans for short-term gain. Because the 'authority to set a corporate course of action, including time frame, designed to enhance corporate profitability' rests with the board, and the board is *'obliged to charter a course for a corporation which is in its best interests without regard to a fixed investment horizon'*, except in limited circumstances, the board 'is not under any per se duty to maximize shareholder value in the short term, even in the context of a takeover'.[48] In this respect, the Court's decision corresponds to the broad constituency statutes adopted by a number of states.

Shift to Institutional Investor Power

Institutions own more than 50 per cent of shares of most of the major companies in the US and have demonstrated that they will use their proxy power to force a target to dismantle its takeover defences and enter into a transaction that maximizes shareholder value. The decade's largest hostile transactions—ATT's bid for NCR, Georgia Pacific's bid for Great Northern Nekoosa, BTR PLC's bid for Norton Company, and Schneider's bid for Square D—were tender offers combined with a proxy contest. The combination of a fully financed bid combined with a proxy contest effectively overcame all of the defences that had been put in place by the respective target companies.

Institutions have led the way in seeking a new focus on improving corporate performance through enhanced monitoring of corporate activity and strategy by the board of directors. The role of independent directors is critical in this conception of corporate governance. For example, Chancellor William Allen of the Delaware Court of Chancery, one of the leading judicial scholars of corporate law, has set forth his views on the role of corporate directors:

---

[48] *Paramount Communications, Inc.* v. *Time, Inc.*, 571 A.2d 1140, 1150 (Del. 1989).

The conventional perception is that boards should select senior management, create incentive compensation schemes and then step back and watch the organization prosper. In addition, board members should be available to act as advisors to the CEO when called upon and they should be prepared to act during a crisis: an emergency succession problem, threatened insolvency or an MBO proposal, for example.

This view of the responsibilities of membership on the board of directors of a public company is, in my opinion, badly deficient. It ignores a most basic responsibility: the duty to monitor the performance of senior management in an informed way. Outside directors should function as active monitors of corporate management, not just in crisis, but continually; they should have an active role in the formulation of the long-term strategic, financial, and organizational goals of the corporation and should approve plans to achieve those goals; they should as well engage in the periodic review of short- and long-term performance according to plan and be prepared to press for correction when in their judgement there is need. . . .

Effective long-term monitoring requires more of outside directors than an appreciation of the scope of their responsibility. It requires a sympathetic and productive relationship between the outside board members and the CEO and the acknowledgement by the CEO of the legitimacy of the monitoring role and its requisites. More than this, effective sympathetic monitoring requires a commitment of time and resources, especially information, and sometimes independent advice. A few hours a quarter may satisfy the role of passive advisor in good times; it is not sufficient to meet the obligation to act as a monitor. The demands of the position, if properly understood, are inconsistent in my opinion, with service on an impressively long list of boards. . . .

When I consider the role of corporate director in the context of global economic competition, I begin to see the role of outside director as a private office imbued with a public responsibility. In most contexts, the director's responsibility runs in the first instance to the corporation as a wealth producing organization. Promotion of the long-term, wealth producing capacity of the enterprise insures ultimately to the benefit of the shareholders as the residual risk bearers of the firm, but it also benefits creditors, employees as a class, and the community generally.[49]

1992 Corporate Governance Initiatives

As the 1992 annual meeting season ended, we summed up the events as follows:

SHAREHOLDER ADVISORY COMMITTEES

In 1992, the SEC Staff required Exxon to include in its annual meeting proxy materials a shareholder proposal to adopt a by-law establishing a shareholder advisory committee, funded by the company, to review and evaluate the performance of Exxon's board of directors. This action indicated a shift by the SEC

---

[49] Chancellor William T. Allen, Address at the Ray Garnet Jr. Corporate and Securities Law Institute, Northwestern University (30 Apr. 1992).

towards allowing shareholders to vote on substantive corporate governance proposals. Nevertheless, despite considerable interest by institutional investors in the 'shadow board' concept, the proposal received the support of only 8 per cent of the shares voted. This lower-than-anticipated vote may indicate that institutional shareholders have some concern over the competitive impact of this type of proposal on day-to-day operations.

SEARS'S ANNUAL MEETING

Sears faced five shareholder proposals at its annual meeting. Two proposals—one mandating confidential voting in all events, the other requesting declassification of the board and the annual election of all directors—received favourable votes from more than 40 per cent of the shares voted. Increasingly, it appears that shareholders, particularly institutions, are likely to vote in favor of these 'ideological' shareholder proposals. Less-ideological shareholder proposals, such as a proposed by-law amendment to require separate chairman of the board and chief executive officer positions, and another proposal to study the divestiture of certain businesses, received significantly less support from Sears's shareholders. Finally, a shareholder proposal requiring minimum stock ownership by directors received support from less than 20 per cent of the shares voting. Despite widespread publicity and a high-profile campaign in support of the Sears shareholder proposals by shareholder activist Robert Monks, fewer than 6 per cent of the shares withheld support from the Sears board's nominees in the election of directors.

EXECUTIVE COMPENSATION

The most significant issue raised during this year's proxy season involved executive compensation and its relationship to corporate performance. For the first time, the SEC Staff required several companies to include precatory shareholder proposals dealing with executive compensation in their proxy statements. Despite the scrutiny that this issue has received from Congress and the general public, these executive-compensation proposals have to date on average received the favourable vote of less than 25 per cent of the votes cast at annual meetings. Responding to pressure from shareholder activists and the current environment, companies such as Gannett and UAL have revised their proxy statements to improve the presentation of compensation information—in the case of Gannett, by showing all elements of compensation on a person-by-person basis rather than the traditional format that makes it difficult to determine what each individual is receiving; and in the case of UAL, by providing more detailed information. In addition, at the Westinghouse and IBM annual meetings, several significant institutional shareholders withheld their votes from the board's own nominees for director in order to protest chief-executive compensation in light of perceived poor performance. Executive compensation is expected to receive additional attention next year.

GENERAL MOTORS

The outside directors at GM sent a very strong message to management by removing the chairman of the board from his position as chairman of the board's executive committee and replacing him with an outside director, by demoting GM's president, and by shuffling other members of management. Although the independent directors affirmed their support for the chairman of the board and vowed not to be involved in the day-to-day business of GM, they clearly expressed their displeasure with what they perceived to be the company's poor financial performance and management's slow response to a changing business environment. The actions taken by the independent directors drew substantial praise from institutional investors and, if GM's financial results improve, it is expected that institutional investors will increase pressure on other boards to take similar actions.

CALPERS

Although in 1992 CalPERS did not use shareholder proposals as means to force management changes, it remained an active participant in the debate on corporate governance. In addition to urging a number of companies to adopt formal shareholder advisory committees, it actively campaigned for changes at GM, publicly announced its positions on a number of significant shareholder proposals, and voted against (or withheld its votes from) board nominees for directors at several companies. In addition to publicly targeting twelve companies for corporate governance changes, CalPERS indicated that during the 1993 proxy season it may again use shareholder proposals as one option for dealing with unresponsive management.

SUBCOUNCIL ON CORPORATE GOVERNANCE

As part of the Competitiveness Policy Council legislated by the omnibus Trade and Competitiveness Act of 1988, the Subcouncil on Corporate Governance and Financial Markets has been formed to study whether the US system of corporate governance constrains the ability of American corporations to realize their strategic goals and to compete successfully in the global market-place. The Subcouncil, which is chaired by Edward Regan, Comptroller of the State of New York, includes the SEC chairman, the chairman of the New York Stock Exchange, and a number of other recognized leaders in the business, labour, government, financial, legal, and academic fields. The Subcouncil is expected to hold a series of meetings in order to fashion policy recommendations to be forwarded to the Council by November and eventually to Congress and the President.

Securities and Exchange Commission Proposals

The debate over corporate governance continues at the administrative agency level. Recently the SEC proposed for public comment a series of changes to current shareholder proxy rules as well as substantial revisions of its rules governing the disclosure of executive compensation. Both sets of proposals reflect the ongoing trend in corporate governance toward increasing the involvement of shareholders in the corporate governance process. The SEC aims to implement the revised rules prior to the 1993 proxy season.

PROXY RULE PROPOSALS

The SEC is easing shareholder communication and lightening the filing requirements in connection with proxy solicitations.[50] The new proposals:

- Remove barriers for shareholders not seeking proxy authority: currently, if a shareholder communicates with ten or more shareholders of the same company, that shareholder must file and distribute a proxy statement (containing detailed disclosure) to the shareholders receiving the communication. Under the revised rules, if a person is not seeking proxy authority, the filing and proxy-statement distribution requirements would no longer apply. Written materials would be required to be mailed to the SEC after use. There would be no filing requirement for press releases or advertisements.

- No prior review of additional soliciting material: proxy statements and proxy cards would continue to be pre-cleared with the SEC, but additional soliciting material would not be required to be pre-cleared.

- Preliminary proxy material would no longer be deemed confidential and not subject to public access prior to clearance by the SEC: there would be an exception for undisclosed mergers and acquisitions.

- No requirement to provide shareholder lists: rather than supply a shareholder list to someone soliciting proxies, companies would be able to mail for the soliciting person.

- Proxy solicitation, but not distribution of actual proxy card, would be permitted prior to filing proxy statement.

- Partial opposition slates would be permitted: shareholders who seek board representation, but who do not seek control of the company's board, would be able to list their own nominees as directors for election to the board together with other management nominees. This would avoid shareholders who might want to vote for one or two alternative directors from being unable to vote for the remainder of the management slate.

- Bundling of related but separable proposals would not be permitted: proxy cards would provide for separate votes to be taken on shareholder resolutions, rather than 'bundling' related, but separable, matters.

- Shareholder statement on management performance: the SEC is also seeking comment on a proposal by Edward Regan, Comptroller of the State of New York, to provide proxy-statement access to shareholders who have held half of 1 per cent of the shares for three or more years and who wish to include up to 700 words as to their views of management performance.

[50] See SEC, Revisions of Proposed Rules: Regulation of Communications Among Securityholders, Release Number 34–30849; IC-18803 [File No. 57–15–92], 24 June 1992.

DISCLOSURE OF EXECUTIVE COMPENSATION

The SEC also proposed a major overhaul of its disclosure rules governing executive compensation. The proposed rules would significantly increase the quantitative information required to be disclosed about pay packages. Moreover, the SEC proposals would require for the first time a discussion of the qualitative, judgemental factors implicated in compensation decisions in the form of a report signed by compensation committee members. The SEC's proposals respond to a growing debate about the manner in which executives are compensated and how these decisions are made.[51]

The proposed rules would replace narrative-plan descriptions with a summary table that would provide a detailed overview of the compensation packages of each of the CEO and the four other most highly compensated executives, and for the executive group as a whole, for each of the preceding three years. There would also be a series of back-up tables providing extensive information about, among other things, executive stock ownership and awards under long-term incentive plans. It is noteworthy that the proposed rules would not require companies to value stock-option grants. Rather, there would be a table illustrating the 'spread' inherent in stock options granted in the last fiscal year assuming various levels of stock-price appreciation. The valuation of stock options and their accounting treatment remain controversial points.

The SEC's release describes the proposed compensation committee report as '*intended to bring shareholders into the compensation committee or board meeting room and permit them to see and understand the specific decisions made through the eyes of directors*'. Complementing the compensation committee report would be a graph comparing cumulative shareholder returns over the preceding five years with the S&P 500 Stock Index and with a nationally recognized or company-constructed peer-group index. Finally, in cases where the compensation committee does not meet certain criteria of independence or where the company has re-priced options within the last fiscal year, additional disclosure regarding the members of the compensation committee would be required.

---

[51] See SEC, Proposed Rules, Executive Compensation Disclosure, Release Number 33–6940, 34–3085 [File No. 57–16–92], 23 June 1992. See also Andrew R. Brownstein and Morris J. Panner, 'Who Should Set CEO Pay? The Press? Congress? Shareholders?', *Harv. Bus. Rev.* (May/June 1992).

9

CORPORATE GOVERNANCE IN THE CONTEXT OF TAKEOVERS OF UK PUBLIC COMPANIES

Alan Paul

Introduction

The significance of the distinction between the corporate entity and its shareholders, fundamental in English law and regulation of companies, reaches a crescendo in the context of a takeover. Coupling that distinction with the free market in a company's shares, ownership and management control can change, over the heads of an incumbent board. The critical major issue of corporate governance is a public-policy one as to whether the balance of power between an unwelcome bidder, the directors of a target company, the interests of employees and creditors and customers, and the ability of shareholders to deliver control is correctly weighted. What the answer is depends on objectives.

Five propositions may be worth considering:

- A UK public company should not be capable of being taken over unless its board agrees, and then only if the approval of an appropriate governmental authority is obtained.

- The target board should not resist a takeover or expend the company's resources on defence but should passively give shareholders information to decide whether the price is right.

- UK takeover regulation is biased in favour of bidders and therefore unjustifiably interferes with normal corporate governance.

- Executive directors of a company that is bid for have such a conflict of interest that the conduct of the process should be directed or substantially directed by non-executive directors.

- Given that the everyday position on corporate governance is regulated by statute or common law, is it right in the takeover context to add to the basis through a non-statutory takeover code?

This paper seeks not to answer these questions but to put them in the context of current applicable law and regulation which especially affect the target company, under the following main headings: the regulatory framework; special duties of target directors; how can a target company defend itself?; conflicts of interest; and possible changes to the system.

The Regulatory Framework

There are two distinct areas of principal relevance: (a) regulation of the conduct of a takeover; and (b) the permissions needed for takeover to occur.

The first area is not covered by legislation of specific application to takeovers, but by the non-statutory takeover code ('Code'), published and enforced by the Panel on Takeovers and Mergers ('Panel'). The second area is, generally, the range of governmental consents that may be necessary, in the UK principally involving the decision of the Secretary of State for Trade and Industry on whether or not to refer the takeover to the Monopolies and Mergers Commission following recommendation by the Office of Fair Trading. However, for a multinational group, with material businesses in other countries, various consents under foreign jurisdictions may also be relevant.

The Code is designed principally to ensure fair and equal treatment of target shareholders in relation to a takeover and to provide an orderly framework within which takeovers are conducted. It is notably not concerned with the financial, commercial, social, or political merits of takeovers, or their economic effect. While the remit of the Office of Fair Trading and the Secretary of State for Trade and Industry includes the general public interest, it focuses on the effect on competition, rather than on wider commercial and social interests. Therefore, in general there is no UK body which considers the merits of a takeover from a wider perspective, such as the interests of UK industry as a whole.

Special Duties of Target Directors

The fundamental duties of target directors in a takeover situation are the same as at other times: that is to act bona fide in the best interests of the company as a whole, with a duty to consider, as well as the interests of shareholders, those of employees and in some circumstances creditors. Whilst there is general acceptance by directors that they should comply with the Code, which therefore has at least market-practice authority, it is not inconceivable that such compliance could conflict with what directors regard in good faith to be in the best interests of the company concerned at any particular time. Given the purposes of the Code, it has the effect of placing the decision of the company's fate in the hands of the shareholders; subject to certain timing restrictions, and provided a bidder treats shareholders equally in compliance with specific requirements of the Code, a bidder can, through market purchasing of shares, take control of any UK company over the head of the board.

In addition, the Code imposes onerous positive duties on target directors which are additional to the responsibilities they normally have. For example:

THE DIRECTOR AS ADVISER

Directors must advise shareholders. In the normal course there is not in the UK any duty on directors to advise their shareholders when to buy or sell a company's shares. Rather, their duty is to act in the best interests of the company as they may decide, acting in good faith. Nor is there any duty on them to do their best to ensure that the best price is offered by a purchaser for shares in the company. However, the Code's requirement is that target-company directors give shareholders their view on whether or not to sell their shares to the bidder or, failing that, to set out in detail their views on the pros and cons of the relevant offer.[1] Since directors must take express responsibility for this advice in the document which contains it, stating that the view has been arrived at carefully, the directors assume a direct personal liability to each shareholder who relies on that advice. However, there are no recently reported instances of directors having actions brought against them for views expressed on an offer.[2]

USE OF RESOURCES

In addition, the directors have to instruct, effectively at the expense of the target company, an adviser qualified to give financial advice who in turn has to express a view on the takeover.[3] This forces the board into committing the company's resources to the defence of the bid.

With a hostile takeover the directors have to make significant decisions as to the deployment generally of the company's resources in its best interests in circumstances where they have no duty to procure the best price. Bid statistics show that substantial sums can be used in defence employing financial, accounting, legal, PR, and other specialist advisers. This has been the source of considerable complaint on the part of both target companies and shareholders, particularly in circumstances where it seems arguable that the bid, or threat of takeover, was not realistic (for example, where a bid is

---

[1] Rule 25.1 of the Code.
[2] Cf. *Morgan Crucible Co. PLC* v. *Hill Samuel Bank* [1991] BCLC 178.
[3] Rule 3.1 of the Code.

threatened publicly but is not actually made):[4] there is no obligation on a bidder to make a realistic opening shot bid.

DIRECTOR AS INFORMER

The Code[5] expressly requires that shareholders are given sufficient information and advice to enable them to reach a properly informed decision and must have sufficient time to do so. No relevant information should be withheld from them. Target directors, therefore, not only have to advise shareholders on the value of an offer, but must also take responsibility for giving them all necessary information and for its accuracy, and so again assuming a direct personal liability to shareholders which is not normally there. On the other hand, arguably, this is not a substantially greater responsibility than directors of a listed company normally have, since at all times, under London Stock Exchange rules, 'any information necessary to enable holders of the company's listed securities and the public to appraise the position of the company and to avoid the establishment of a false market must be published'.[6]

AN ILLUSTRATIVE PROBLEM

In theory, the legal duties of directors and their Code duties can come into conflict. This is exemplified by the Code's requirement[7] that, if information relating to the target is given to a favoured actual or potential bidder, the same information must be given to any other bona-fide bidder or potential bidder even if less favoured. Given the Code's assumption that it is in shareholders' interests to get the best price, this is an inevitable provision.

Conflict arises most obviously where the less-favoured person is a competitor of the target company. The passing to him of confidential information on the target's business is potentially damaging and the board may consider that it is not in the best interests of the company. This argument will have been propounded in the bid in 1992 for Midland Bank, when Lloyds Bank, the potential bidder less favoured by the Midland board, sought the same information as had been received by Hong Kong & Shanghai Bank, the favoured bidder. Nevertheless, it had to be handed over, even in circumstances where it was not clear that Lloyds would clear a reference to the Monopolies and Mergers Commission: the argument runs that at the time of deciding to provide Hong Kong & Shanghai information,

---

[4] In 1990, for many months, Mr Edelman threatened to make a bid for Storehouse PLC. The Panel eventually ruled that he must actually bid, or he would be prohibited from doing so for twelve months (applying Rule 35 of the Code which imposes such a twelve-month restriction on a bidder who has made a takeover which failed): Panel statement 1989/9.

[5] General Principle 4 of the Code.

[6] Para. 1 of ch. 2 of s. 5 of 'Admission of Securities to Listing', published by the London Stock Exchange.

[7] Rule 20.2 of the Code.

the Midland board will have taken into account the consequences of the relevant rule.[8]

How Can a Target Defend Itself Against Takeover?

SOME RESTRICTIONS

The methods of defence against hostile takeover available to UK companies are considerable: in theory a target board is able to take any action necessary provided they act bona fide in the best interests of the company itself and do not use their powers for a purpose for which they were not intended. Normal legal restrictions apply in a takeover as with any other activity (for example, it is established that a board may not use its powers for a collateral purpose: issues of shares to raise money may be proper, but to do so in order to dilute a shareholder may not be).[9] However, again due to the Code, the target's board's behaviour and normal management responsibility become restrained as, once a takeover attempt is imminent or taking place, actions which could frustrate it (that is, deprive shareholders of their ability to decide the outcome) may only be carried out with majority shareholder approval.[10]

The specific restrictions prevent material acquisitions and disposals; issues of shares and options; the buying-in of own shares; payment of unusual dividends; and generally transactions outside the ordinary course of business which could have the effect of depriving shareholders of the bid. Nevertheless, all these transactions can be undertaken with majority shareholder approval—thus, the decision-making is taken out of the hands of management and, for the takeover exercise, the balance of power is placed into the hands of shareholders.

By way of example, the use of UK court proceedings to prevent a bid going through is not common as a defensive measure. This may be because the well-developed Code forum takes the place of what would otherwise be a potential court action, in that the non-statutory Panel can resolve issues which could otherwise lead to legal proceedings. Whether or not a company's resources should be used in litigation is normally a matter for the board: it is clear, however, that the Panel will interfere and require such proceedings to be the subject of shareholder approval where it is perceived that the proceedings could thwart the wishes of shareholders. This was the case in Minorco's bid for ConsGold in 1989: once Minorco had achieved over 50 per cent acceptances of its offer (together with shares it owned), litigation in the US against Minorco which ConsGold was actively

---

[8] Panel statement 1992/15.
[9] *Smith (Howard) Ltd.* v. *Ampol Petroleum Ltd.* [1974] AC 821; cf. *Cayne* v. *Global Resources PLC* (unreported, 12 Aug. 1982).
[10] General Principle 7 and Rule 21 of the Code.

pursuing was required by the Panel to be abandoned, unless ConsGold obtained shareholder's approval to continue it; otherwise the board of ConsGold, in the Panel's view, might have thwarted the wishes of majority shareholders that the takeover should proceed. As it happened, an associated company of ConsGold, Newmont, found to be independent of ConsGold, could continue the action and so the bid failed.[11] There are (thankfully, most UK practitioners would say) few cases in UK takeover practice where the bid outcome is dependent on legal proceedings, and none where an action has been successful in the UK courts to prevent a takeover.[12] This is in marked contrast to, say, the US.

POISON PILLS

In theory, it is available to any UK company to structure itself constitutionally and/or by contract with third parties to ensure that a hostile takeover is unattractive to the predator, or that a change of control has such severe consequences for an unwanted controller that only an agreed takeover is possible. Variations of US techniques, such as 'crown jewel lock-ups', effectively flip-in share rights, shark repellants, and poison pills which operate when a bid is made could legally be put in place outside an actual takeover, when the Code does not apply. However, statutory and Stock Exchange controls on the terms of issues of shares means that their introduction would require shareholder approval in advance, and shareholders in UK companies have shown no enthusiasm generally to encourage such arrangements.

Today it is rare for listed companies to have two-tier voting structures (although there are a few left), which leaves the voting power in friendly hands while spreading the equity amongst the public, thus making a hostile takeover in voting-control terms difficult (Trust House Forte's designs on the Savoy Hotel represent a well-publicized case of frustration with the two-tier voting structure). Paradoxically, the 'golden share' has most recently arisen in respect of companies privatized by the government.[13] In theory, however, it would be open to any company to adopt a constitution which prohibited acquisitions of substantial shareholdings without permission of the board; but this has not occurred, presumably either because boards do not wish to propound them or because shareholders would not support such proposals. It may reasonably be concluded that shareholders generally do not perceive it to be in their interests to inhibit a takeover or the possibility of a takeover. It seems reasonable to conclude, too, that this attitude is

---

[11] Panel Statement 1989/7.

[12] The courts have attempted to prevent legal proceedings from being used to stymie bids: *R* v. *Panel on Takeovers and Mergers, ex p Datafin and Prudential-Bache Securities Inc.* [1987] QB 815.

[13] Gower, *Principles of Modern Company Law* (5th edn. 1992, London, Sweet & Maxwell), 77.

motivated largely by an interest in maximizing investment value. The writer at least is sceptical of any theory that the threat of takeover is the investment community's principal means of enhancing management performance; while there are cases where a takeover threat has prompted management of a target to take measures to increase shareholder value, research has not proved that such theories have general validity.[14]

One deterrent to bids that can be put in place by management, often without shareholder approval, is contractual standstill arrangements with a significant shareholder under which the shareholder agrees not to acquire shares above a limited percentage for a fixed period; the typical standstill not only prevents the affected shareholder from bidding but also from accepting any hostile offer without target-company board approval, and so it operates to remove the shares from the market-place, making a controlling interest considerably harder for any third party to acquire. Opportunities to seek standstills are taken with increasing frequency (such as on issues of shares to vendors on acquisition of private companies).

THE ARMOURY

Despite the lack of structural defences such as those mentioned above, the regimented but flexible framework for takeovers seems to allow defences to succeed with reasonable regularity—on average, between 40 and 50 per cent of hostile takeovers fail, with a higher failure-rate where cash is not offered. (The Panel's annual report for 1991/2 records that seventeen out of the thirty-four bids in the period, which were unrecommended at their close, failed.)[15] The types of defence can be categorized as follows:

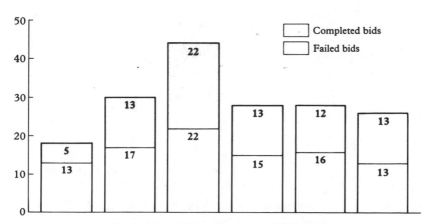

FIGURE 9.1   Bid success-rate, 1984–1989

[14] See Morgan and Morgan, *The Stock Market and Mergers in the United Kingdom*, Hume Occasional Paper No. 24 (David Hume Institute, Edinburgh,).

[15] See figs. 9.1–2 where statistics on defences and bid success-rates are set out.

- the financial or credibility argument, including profit forecasting, dividend uplift, and asset revaluation;
- white knights;
- regulatory intervention (for example, reference to the Monopolies and Mergers Commission or the interference of an equivalent foreign authority); and
- restructuring (proposing demerger/divestment of businesses, as in the case of the bid for Racal by Williams Holdings, and BAT Industries' response to the Hoylake consortium's offer in 1989).[16]

Of these basic tools, the first, winning the argument with shareholders, is statistically the most common and most successful.

Since a bid runs in general terms a maximum of eighty-eight days from announcement, the time factor is critical and the use of this time to best advantage is the defence's aim. It is accordingly the combination of that time with other regulatory features that enables many companies to fend off bidders. Since the Code requires a bid to be conditional on achieving control of shares representing over 50 per cent of voting rights, the composition of the shareholder register can make that target difficult to achieve. In practice this is not a real 50 per cent: rather, a number of shareholders will, as a matter of policy, not accept a hostile offer; some shareholders always follow their board's recommendation; some are activated by computer, for example, index funds; some are 'dead'; and perhaps a block of shares rests

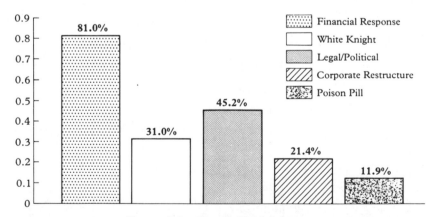

FIGURE 9.2   Usage of bid defences

[16] The offer by Hoylake Investments Ltd. for BAT Industries in 1989 lapsed due to the inability of the bidder, within the Code timetable for the offer, to obtain certain necessary US regulatory approvals in respect of the indirect change of control of Farmers Group Inc., a subsidiary of BAT, which would result from the bid, if successful.

in target directors' hands. Therefore, in many cases a reasonable proportion of the share capital is in fact unavailable to the hostile bidder.

In a regulatory system where the balance of power in a takeover rests with shareholders, in a market where in general there is pressure on bidders not to overpay and an investor demand for premium prices for change of control, targets seem agile at surviving. This is to ignore, however, the cost and uncertainties for employees and others, as well as the management stress which defending a takeover brings.

Conflicts in Takeovers

The market inevitably perceives that the target's directors have a conflict of interest in the takeover.[17] Oddly, these conflicts can be of opposite types.

THE EXECUTIVE DIRECTOR AS EMPLOYEE

The first is the concern that a director, who may lose his position in consequence of a bid, will for that reason do everything he can to prevent it going through: and therefore his advice not to recommend could be tainted. There is no particular evidence that directors are generally unable to resolve this perceived conflict. On the contrary, it could be argued that, with a secure written service contract, it may be in a director's interest to be taken over.

This concern is really an extension of the controls that are perceived to be necessary on directors to decide their own terms of service. Statutory restriction on service contracts of over five years duration is well known.[18] Directors' service terms have to be fully disclosed to their shareholders, who can disapprove of them if they so wish.[19] The roles of non-executives on remuneration committees to help ensure conflicts are resolved independently is a general subject of corporate governance dealt with elsewhere. However, in the takeover context the Code imposes a further restriction on the ability of directors to change their service contracts without shareholders' approval:[20] would this really be necessary if independent directors dealt with such matters as an internal housekeeping matter? Where the conflict is so resolved in a takeover situation, it is arguably unreasonable that shareholders should have to approve a contract simply because of a takeover.

THE DIRECTOR AS SHAREHOLDER

The opposite conflict can arise where a director is a significant shareholder in a company—that is, for personal reasons he may wish to

[17] As Morgan and Morgan point out (n. 14 above, at 62–5), there can be at least six different, conflicting interests in a bid situation.

[18] Companies Act 1985, s. 319, requires such contracts to be approved by shareholders. See also Cadbury Report (London, 1 Dec. 1992), para. 4.41 (service contracts should not exceed three years).

[19] Companies Act 1985, s. 318.

[20] Rule 21 of the Code.

realize his shareholding at a value less than the real value of the company as a whole and so sell out, and advise other shareholders to sell out, to suit his own circumstances. The Code says that: 'It is the shareholders' interests taken as a whole, together with those employees and creditors, which should be considered when directors are giving advice to shareholders.'[21] It is important that the system allows an individual who is a director and a shareholder (whether through trusts or otherwise) to differentiate between his capacities and act accordingly. There has to be an element of faith in his ability to differentiate his role. This is particularly so where directors are encouraged to take shares in the companies which they run. In these cases, the role of independent directors, perhaps non-executive,[22] can acquire special importance in formulating and publishing their advice on the value of a bid.

The Management Buy-Out

The management buy-out gives rise to an area of conflict where the resolution of the problem rests entirely with independent directors, usually non-executive, who are not participating in the buy-out. Reflecting common-sense rules of conflicts of interests, the Code requirements are such that the management effecting the buy-out cannot participate in advising shareholders whether or not the price is right.[23] However, this imposes on non-executive directors a significant responsibility, and I suspect that in this circumstance they have a special sensitivity to get the best price reasonably obtainable: but this arises not from a legal requirement but from the obligation on them under the Code to advise shareholders whether the particular offer is appropriate. In the normal course, the non-executive director may not have the detailed knowledge of the business available to management on whom he normally relies for information. He continues so to rely in the management buy-out context. Since such buy-outs of UK public companies are now of relatively rare frequency, probably for economic reasons, this has not been a particular issue since 1990. In 1988/9 scepticism of underpaying by management (that is, conflict concerns) was at its height (for example, the management buy-out of Magnet PLC) and, as a matter of corporate governance, investors then expressed a significant cynicism with regard to management buy-outs of listed public companies, which probably still exists. More recently in November 1992 the 'offer' by Mr A. Sugar to shareholders of Amstrad stirred the debate.[24]

---

[21] General Principle 9 of the Code.

[22] To ensure independence of non-executive directors, Cadbury recommends, *inter alia*, that non-executive directors should not participate in share option schemes: Cadbury Report, n. 18 above, para. 4.13.

[23] Note 4 on Rule 25.1 of the Code.

[24] This case involved an attempt by the chairman and major shareholder to take a public company private by way of a management buy-out effected under s. 425 of the Companies Act

In recognition of these problems, in the management buy-out situation, the Code imposes specific requirements, for example, that independent directors (not being members of the management team) and their advisers receive all the information they need from management, on whom is imposed a considerable onus of good faith to resolve the evident conflict.[25]

GENERAL RESOLUTION OF CONFLICTS FOR DIRECTORS

If directors, particularly executive directors, are perceived to have a conflict in the takeover situation, such a conflict can be and is generally resolved. Just as disclosure resolves conflicts in a number of other circumstances, so too in the takeover: specific directors' interests in the takeover or its outcome are required to be publicly disclosed; their approach and views are then assessed in the light of such disclosure. At the most extreme, for example, if a director is also a director of the bidder, that director stands aside from the decision-making process in relation to the takeover.

It is also recognized in takeovers that day-to-day management of the bid can properly be conducted through a committee: but proper arrangements have to be put in place to keep all directors informed of significant issues.[26] The Panel introduced specific rules on this following one or two takeovers in the late 1980s (including Guinness's takeover of Distillers), when there was concern that powerful executives might sideline the other directors, who, the Panel considers, should take active responsibility. It is notable that in the normal course (outside a takeover), a director in good faith can often discharge his legal obligations by responsible delegation to a committee or in reliance upon a responsible executive. The Code requirements of involvement of the full board in the conduct of a takeover may reflect common good practice but impose positive and equal duties on both executive and non-executive directors. This is with a view to minimizing the risk of regulatory abuse.

The involvement of non-executive directors on 'bid' committees is not required, but often occurs, and may be perceived to allay fears that the enthusiasm of the 'war cabinet' may otherwise be untempered.

Also, the public role of the independent financial adviser,[27] highly public and visible in the takeover situation, is designed to operate, among other things, to bring objectivity to issues where directors' conflicts of interest can arise.

1985. There were no non-executives on the board and there was criticism of the quality of the disclosure made to the shareholders. Because of considerable institutional pressure, the proposal failed and the company has agreed to appoint non-executive directors: see *Financial Times*, 6 December 1992, pp. 1 and 22; 1 December 1992, p. 91.

[25] Rule 20.3 of the Code.
[26] App. 3 of the Code.
[27] Rule 3 of the Code requires a target to have a financial adviser who must express publicly his view of the takeover terms.

Bids—Recent Recommendations for Change

Nobody would be so unwise as to suggest that the current system of UK takeover regulation is perfect. However, as is so often the case in any area, suggestions for change are motivated perhaps by self-interest groups with their own particular gospels. Many of the suggestions made from time to time could lead to more regulation, not improvement, providing more scope for problems. It may sometimes be perceived that the law of self interest would be for lawyers to encourage more regulation—it is fairly clearly the case that most UK lawyers who are takeover practitioners would not regard major changes to the system involving greater regulatory involvement to be worthwhile, since in fact their interest is the client's interest: that things should be done as efficiently and economically as possible.

Having said that, there have been, year after year, a number of suggestions for change which have excited a measure of interest. All changes of regulation in this area affect the method by which corporations are run.

FEES

To focus on recommendations of the Trade and Industry Committee's First Special Report on Takeovers and Mergers 1992, three of their recommendations on fees illustrate a point:[28]

[*Recommendation 13*]: We recommend that an unsuccessful bidder should pay 50 per cent of the easily identifiable professional fees and charges incurred by a target company.

[*Recommendation 14*]: We recommend that a bidder for a company listed on the [London] Stock Exchange should be required to lodge with the Takeover Panel at the time of the bid the sum of the value equal to the Takeover Panel's estimate of the likely recoverable costs of the bid as a security for the eventual costs of the bid for the company in the event of the bid proving unsuccessful.

[*Recommendation 15*]: We recommend that the government should press for the inclusion in the draft EEC Takeover Directive of provisions for an unsuccessful bidder to pay half the easily quantifiable professional fees and charges incurred by a target company of a bid below £100,000,000 and for a security deposit to be lodged with the National Takeover Authority of the country in which the target company is domiciled at the time of the bid as security for the payment of such cost.

What a target company does, and how much it spends, by way of defence against the takeover bid is a matter for it. It is very difficult to understand the rationale behind recommendations such as these. They are possible to understand if one has the view that companies that are bid for are unfairly suffering. The contrary view, of course, is that the only debate in a bid for a UK company is between its shareholders and the bidder. Thereafter,

---

[28] See also Manser, *The U.K. Panel On Takeovers and Mergers*, Hume Occasional Paper No. 21 (David Hume Institute, Edinburgh).

applying normal corporate governance rules, it is up to the board of the target company acting in good faith in the interests of the company to decide what it does by way of defence. There is no need to defend; equally, there may be every justification for vigorous defence. This does not seem to put the takeover in a different category to that of any other corporate activity. The logic for such recommendations is, therefore, quite difficult to sustain. If, however, it is thought that the takeover of UK companies should not be resolved through the existing methods, and if the government believes that it should judge whether a takeover is or is not in the best interests of the public, that would actually avoid the need for this fees debate.

Perhaps such suggestions are artificial ways to make companies less liable to takeover. That may be a proper aspiration; if that is the objective, why do it indirectly? In addition, if these recommendations were taken up, the bid-price would no doubt have to reflect the requirements. As things stand, if a bid is successful such costs are effectively 'eaten' by the bidder.

In a similar area there seems to exist a theory that bids could be fee-driven by advisers, which would erode normal principles of corporate decision-making. This sounds like the stuff that sensationalizes takeovers: one would expect directors to be somewhat offended by suggestions that the board of a company is so influenced by advisers as to be persuaded to enter into a transaction which that board did not believe was appropriate. There is quite a separate debate as to whether or not any particular fees are appropriate. Experience, however, shows that in general boards of companies are more than able to negotiate fees which they believe represent value for money for their corporate entity in the activity for which the relevant advisers are employed. Takeovers in this sense represent a situation no different to any other corporate activity in which advisers are necessary.

BID THRESHOLDS AND DEALINGS

From the same report (which contained a number recommendations), two others are highlighted. First, the recommendation that the mandatory bid threshold[29] be reduced from 30 to 20 per cent. The rationale for any mandatory bid threshold in the UK has always rested on the principle that, if there is an effective change of control, minority shareholders should have the opportunity to 'get out' and, if applicable, share the premium for control. No magic percentage at less than 50 + per cent can be shown to represent effective control in all cases: but it must be in few cases that 20 per cent represents *de facto* control. If, however, the purpose of a reduction to 20 per cent is to protect companies from the influence of material shareholders, other mechanisms to achieve it may be more appropriate (for example,

---

[29] Rule 9 of the Code requires that a person who acquires shares representing 30 per cent or more of the voting rights must take an offer to all shareholders holding voting shares at the highest price paid by that person in the preceding twelve months.

through constitutional provisions requiring a shareholder who reaches this level to make a bid for all the shares. This would give shareholders of individual companies, who control the constitution, case by case, a choice as to whether to adopt such provisions.)

The second recommendation was that, (a) in a takeover, no share transactions should take place during the twenty-one days following the publication of an offer document; and (b) that management of a target should be able to extend a bid timetable to give more time to respond. The first proposal would seem to be a restraint on shareholders' freedom to deal in shares that is hard to justify. If the proposal is designed to slow down the pace at which bidders can buy shares, the Code already contains restrictions[30] with a 29.9 per cent limit for the same period. The second proposal exists in the system already, as the Panel can agree extensions for good reason. In any event, having regard to the normal sixty-day bid timetable,[31] it is largely not the first twenty-one days that are critical, but the last. On the other hand, since a bidder has the advantage of surprise and can time the making of a bid to suit himself, there may be an argument of fairness to allow a target board the latitude this recommendation suggests.

Regulation of Takeovers by Law

The proposed EC directive,[32] which could push takeover regulation into (or at least much closer to) a statutory regime, still appears to be 'on hold'. The Trade and Industry Committee's overall impression was that the current non-statutory Panel system is 'viewed positively and is beneficial to British industry'. There is also a large body of opinion, among practitioners at least, which does not favour a move to a statutory system. The present regulatory structure seems to work, with (inevitably) some rough edges at times, as with any system. The move to a statutory system, where strict legal interpretation of the application of rules, rather than a purposive one, prevails, must lead to a risk of a greater involvement of UK courts in dispute resolution between bidders and targets, and perhaps shareholders.[33] That must lead to greater delay and uncertainty for all participants, as well as increased costs. Perhaps recent 'trials', well publicized in the UK (the Blue Arrow and Guinness-related cases), point to a worse case: civil dispute can last even longer than criminal prosecution. The greatest risk with a move to a statutory system would be a leap into the unknown. It is evident that a thorough and reasoned

---

[30] Rule 5 of the Code restricts the speed with which any person can acquire shares or rights over shares (e.g. options) representing 30 per cent or more of voting rights.

[31] Rule 31.6 of the Code requires a takeover to lapse if within no later than sixty days after posting of the offer document shareholders representing over 50 per cent have not accepted.

[32] The EC harmonization programme includes a possible directive on takeover regulations: see proposal for Thirteenth Directive COM (88) 823, (OJ C64/8 14 Mar. 1989).

[33] On the role of litigation in corporate governance see G. P. Stapledon, Ch. 11 below, p. 187.

debate, not an emotive political one, would be needed before the known advantages of the current system (with whatever faults it may have) are replaced by an entirely unknown quantity, with potentially unquantifiable disadvantages.

The first task would be to resolve the objectives of regulation of takeovers—is it to allow shareholders to decide the outcome in an open market, or should other public-interest factors, not related to regulation of securities markets, prevail?

10

TAKEOVERS VERSUS INSTITUTIONS IN CORPORATE GOVERNANCE IN GERMANY

Theodor Baums*

I. Introduction

The corporate governance systems in the UK and in Germany differ markedly. German large firms have a two-board structure, they are subject to employee co-determination, their managements are not confronted with public hostile takeover bids, and banks play a major role in corporate governance, through equity stakes, proxies given to them by small investors, and bankers' positions on the supervisory boards of these firms. One of the main issues of corporate governance in large firms, the problem of shareholders' passivity in monitoring management in Berle–Means-type corporations, is thus addressed by an institutional provision, the role of the banks, rather than by a market-oriented solution as we find it in the UK, with its 'market for corporate control' through the threat of hostile takeovers. These two different approaches to corporate governance have been compared several times recently, and it was argued that a bank-based or institutional solution has clear advantages and should be preferred. Cosh, Hughes and Singh,[1] for example, argue at the conclusion of their discussion of takeovers and short-termism in the UK that:

'the institutional shareholder [in the UK] should take a much more active and vigorous part in the internal governance of corporations . . . In order for such a proposal to be effective both in disciplining inefficient managements and promoting long-term investments, far reaching changes in the internal workings and behaviour of the financial institutions would be required. The financial institutions would need to pool their resources together, set up specialized departments for promoting investment and innovation—in other words behave like German banks.'

The following remarks seek to continue this discussion from the German

* Helpful comments have been given by Jonathan S. Berck, Jeremy S. Edwards, Philipp v. Randow, Roberta Romano, Dieter Schmidtchen, and Mark Wingerson.

[1] Cosh, Hughes, and Singh, 'Analytical and Policy Issues in the UK Economy', in A. Cosh *et al.* (eds.), *Takeovers and Short-Termism in the UK* (Institute for Public Policy Research, 1990), 19, 20.

perspective. The article will first attempt to evaluate the monitoring potential of our domestic bank or institution-oriented corporate governance system, and then, in a further part, compare it with that of a market-oriented solution. It will be argued that both systems focus on different problems and have specific advantages and drawbacks, and that there are still quite a few puzzles to be solved until all pros and cons of each of these monitoring devices can be assessed. The perception that both systems focus on different problems suggests combining institutional monitoring with a 'market for corporate control' rather than considering them to be contrasting and incompatible approaches.

The article is organized as follows. Section II will describe the legal structure of the large corporation in Germany in more detail. Section III explains why a 'market for corporate control' by the threat of public hostile takeover bids does not exist in Germany. Section IV then shows how corporate governance in publicly held corporations with small investors is organized instead, and deals with the role of banks in corporate governance in these firms. Section V will then try to compare the monitoring potential of a market-oriented and our bank- or institution-oriented corporate-governance system. Concluding remarks follow.

II. The Structure of the Large Corporation

1. Legal Forms of Firms and Distribution of Ownership

In Germany firms can be organized and run either by a sole proprietor, a partnership,[2] or by a corporation. The most important forms of corporations are the private company with limited liability[3] and the stock corporation.[4] The following remarks will only deal with the publicly held stock corporations, the stock of which is either owned by scattered individuals or by institutions. While only focusing on these publicly owned corporations we have to keep in mind that, although we are speaking of a small number of firms, they are also Germany's largest firms: In 1990 there were about 2 million firms in Germany; of these about 430,000 were private companies with limited liability, and less than 2,700 were stock corporations.[5] Of the latter, only 551 are quoted on a stock exchange[6] and of

---

[2] Unlimited partnership (*offene Handelsgesellschaft*); limited partnership (*Kommanditgesellschaft*).

[3] *Gesellschaft mit beschränkter Haftung* or *GmbH*.

[4] *Aktiengesellschaft*.

[5] Numbers as of 31 Dec 1990: Gesellschaften mit beschränkter Haftung 433,731; Aktiengesellschaften and Kommanditgesellschaften auf Aktien 2,682. *Source*: Statistisches Bundesamt, oral information, and *Statistisches Jahrbuch 1991*, 141.

[6] *Source*: Arbeitsgemeinschaft der Deutschen Wertpapierbörsen, *Jahresbericht 1990*, 157 (numbers for 1990); over-the-counter traded stock excluded.

these 551 about eighty are widely held and traded.[7] However, most of these corporations with widely distributed ownership are among the 100 largest firms in Germany.[8]

2. THE THREE 'ORGANS' OF THE STOCK CORPORATION

To understand corporate governance in these large stock corporations, the impediments to hostile takeovers (see Section III), as well as the role of the banks in this respect (see Section IV), it is necessary to mention some special features of German corporate law.

First, the two-tier or *dual boards* system, which was established in 1870. It consists of a management board and a separate supervisory board. Management is appointed, mostly for five-year terms, and is dismissed by the supervisory board.[9] The management runs the day-to-day business of the firm independently and can only be dismissed for cause. Complete power rests with neither the management nor the supervisory board. A more detailed picture would show a complex structure of balance of powers between these two organs. The powers of the shareholders' meetings are restrained to basic decisions such as changes of the statutes, approval of the annual statements of accounts, distribution of (half of) the annual balance-sheet profits, election of (half the) members of the supervisory board, and consent to such specific structural changes as mergers, issuance of new stock, and the like.

Secondly, the *co-determination system*[10] involves members of the super-visory board who are neither elected nor appointed by the shareholders. In firms with more than 2,000 employees, half of the members of the supervisory board are elected by the shareholders and the other half by the employees (blue and white collar as well as lower-ranking management) and labour unions. Hence, the members of the supervisory board and the

---

[7] More than 50 per cent of stock widely held: about 80 companies; more than 75 per cent of stock widely held: 38 companies (*Source*: Saling, *Aktienführer* (84th edn., 1991) (numbers as of Sept. 1990); Commerzbank ed., *Wer gehört zu wem?*, *A Guide to Capital links in German Companies*, (17th edn., 1991).

[8] Cf. the list of the largest 100 firms (measured by their value-creating potential—*Wertschöpfung* = surplus or loss of the firm corrected by additional factors) in: *Bundestag-Drucksache* 11/7582, pp. 176 ff., and the list of German firms and the structure of their ownership in: Commerzbank (n. 7 above).

[9] Cf. the detailed description by A. F. Conard 'Comparative Law: The Supervision of Corporate Managements: A Supervision of Developments in European Community and United States Law' (1984) 82 *Mich. L. Rev.* 1459 ff. and C. Meier-Schatz, 'Corporate Governance and Legal Rules: A Transnational Look at Concepts of International Management Control' (1980) 13 *Journal of Corporation Law* 431–80.

[10] Cf. thereto H. Wiedemann, 'Codetermination by Workers in German Enterprises' (1980) 28 *Am. J. Comp. L.* 79–82. Although the present co-determination laws came into force after the end of the Second World War, there is an older tradition of obligatory representation of employees on the supervisory boards.

management board are considered to be agents of all stakeholders in the firm, rather than of the shareholders only.[11]

Thirdly, the *voting process*. There is no proxy system with proxies for the management. In the shareholder meetings shares are either voted by the shareholders themselves or—in the case of smaller shareholdings—by institutions, mainly banks, which act as custodians for the shares. This voting power of a few banks, sometimes not more than three or four, each with a large block of votes, gets their representatives on the supervisory boards (alongside the representatives of the employees and trade unions). This will be described in more detail in Section IV.

III. Impediments to Hostile Takeovers

1. Specific Structural Features of German Corporate Law

To date, no public hostile takeover bid has been successful in Germany. One actual case is still pending—although a bid in its technical sense has not yet been launched—the struggle between the two tyre-makers Continental AG and Pirelli of Italy. The attempt of the French company AGF to take over the insurer AMB has recently been settled by an agreement. What are the reasons for this pattern, which obviously is so different from the Anglo-American corporate world?

To start with, these recent cases may indicate an ongoing change which will probably be reinforced by the further internationalization of markets and changes of the economic and regulatory environment in the EC. Apart from that, the fact that public hostile takeovers did not occur until now does not mean that there are no hostile takeovers at all. The management of Hoesch AG, the shares of which were recently taken over by Krupp, would probably have liked to hinder this shift of control if there had been a chance to do so. Resistance to a hostile takeover is not always possible, as will be shown later, and will become particularly difficult for an incumbent management if it loses the support of one or even several depository banks. That means that in such cases these institutions will still play an important, if not a decisive, role, and that means in turn that these cases cannot—in terms of our differentiation between inside monitoring by institutions versus outside control by a takeover market—be attributed clearly to the latter. Hence it is justified to exclude such 'private' hostile takeover activities which are accompanied or supported by the depository institutions and focus on public hostile takeover bids only.

---

[11] In the German system employees are stakeholders in a firm not only in the regular and usual sense as partners of long-term (labour) contracts and relationships with the corporation but also because their pension capital is—unlike the practice in the Anglo-American countries—to a large extent kept within the employing firm and serves as an important source of capital of the firm. 'Co-determination' finds its legitimation also in this specific structure.

We need not speculate about different corporate cultures here to explain why this technique to gain control even against the will of the incumbent management is not used in corporate Germany so far. There are quite a few more tangible and concrete arguments which explain this pattern as a result of specific structural features of German company law, as well as of the conditions of corporate finance and other peculiarities. The following remarks will try to describe some of these impediments to hostile takeovers in more detail.

First, remember the comparably small number of potential targets: there are less than 100 listed stock corporations with widely distributed shares.[12] The continued concentration of equity holdings in families or small groups of shareholders can to a large extent be explained by the relative importance of internal as well as of debt (bank) rather than equity financing.[13]

As to the large corporations with widely distributed stock, the shares in these firms are normally not voted by the shareholders themselves but by depository banks as *proxy-holders*. Hence these few large banks play a key role in this respect. Until recently the majority of these banks firmly opposed public hostile takeovers ('blunders of American capitalism') and supported managements in protecting firms and themselves against possible attempts by amending the statutes through anti-takeover provisions. Is this attitude likely to change if the banks' competitors from abroad finance hostile takeover bids in the future? Only if the benefits from supporting a hostile takeover bid outweigh the disadvantages that our large banks still fear from their corporate clientele if they were to support such an attack. In this context, it should be mentioned that the *Großbanken* (large banks) themselves are also (or were at least until recently, before the cross-holding alliance between Dresdner and Allianz) large corporations with widely dispersed shareholders; hence, their managements have no interest in being exposed to a hostile takeover either. On the other hand, the banks as depository institutions have been increasingly criticized in the literature as well as in the media. Not least because of this criticism, two of the three *Großbanken* recently abstained from voting in the Conti case where the issue was whether they, as the proxy-holders of their clients, were to abolish an anti-takeover provision in the company's statute.

A second structural impediment to hostile takeovers is the *two-boards structure*. The representatives of the shareholders on the supervisory boards (half the members of this board) can be removed before the expiration of their office term (usually five years) only with a super-majority of 75 percent of the votes cast. The members of the management boards can, by resolution

---

[12] Cf. IV. 1.(*a*), below.

[13] Cf. H. Hax, 'Debt and Investment Policy in German Firms—The Issue of Capital Shortage' (1990) 146 *Jour. Institutional and Theoretical Economics* 106–23; *Monatsberichte der Deutschen Bundesbank* (Oct. 1991), 22 ff. and n. 50 below.

of the supervisory board, be removed prematurely only for cause, although removal without cause is valid until nullified by a court.

A further impediment for takeovers financed by means of the assets of the target (LBOs) are the *strict capital protection rules* of German corporate law which prohibit these finance techniques. By the same token, repurchases of shares as an anti-takeover device are also prohibited.

Anti-trust law, the *law of groups of companies*, and *labour law* specialities can render takeovers difficult. If a bidder is a 'group of companies' or is going to be such a group by virtue of its acquisition, it will be subject to the rules of the law of groups of companies which provide for the protection of minority shareholders and creditors of subsidiaries. Shutting down plants or laying off employees can be a cumbersome and costly undertaking.

2. STATUTORY ANTI-TAKEOVER PROVISIONS; PREVENTIVE ACTIONS

Apart from these and other structural impediments, some specific statutory anti-takeover provisions and preventive actions are possible and can be observed. For the purpose of this article it should suffice to mention the most common or sweeping ones rather than to display the whole palette.

In 1990 the statutes of twenty-three of the large stock corporations with widely distributed shares provided for *caps on voting rights*.[14] In such a case a shareholder cannot vote more than (usually) 5 per cent of the stock irrespective of the number of voting shares held by him. Since 1990 several firms have eliminated this provision. In the long run a firm with a controlling shareholder will have to come to terms with a major shareholder despite a voting limit if the latter is not to block everything, since the voting cap affects only the voting right and not the other rights of a shareholder.[15] Apart from that, this provision can be overcome by help of 'friends' who vote together with the shareholder who seeks the control. That is the main issue in the Conti–Pirelli case.

A much more effective means of preventing takeovers is *registered shares*. It is contended in the literature that about one third of the German stock corporations, among them forty-seven companies listed on stock exchanges, are equipped with this device.[16] In such a case the management board has broad discretion whether or not to register an acquirer.[17] The acquirer's rights as a shareholder depend on registration.

---

[14] *Höchststimmrechte*; cf. T. Baums, *Höchststimmrechte* (1990) Die Aktiengesellschaft 221–42.

[15] In particular, changes of the statutes mostly can be effected only if three-quarters of the shares represented in the shareholder meeting agree irrespective of whether the present shares may not be voted because of a statutory cap on voting rights.

[16] R. Lüttmann, *Kontrollwechsel in Kapitalgesellschaften* (1992), 158, 159.

[17] Most recently thereto Landgericht Aachen in the ABM–AGF case; the action of the French AGF to get its shares registered was dismissed (19 May 1992, *Der Betrieb* 1992, 564).

Cross-ownerships between two firms up to a stake of 25 per cent of the other firm's stock can be organized by the managements of these firms. The shareholders' consent is not necessary. A famous example which was recently reported by the financial press is the interlock between Dresdner Bank and Allianz, the largest European insurer. This example shows, however, that such an alliance cannot be entered into by management without an underlying business rationale other than to provide a defence against takeovers, and the acquisition of a stake of, say, 15 per cent of the stock of another large firm has to make sense in other respects, and has to be approved by the supervisory board and explained to the shareholders and the public.

Another model which avoids these drawbacks which can be found in practice consists of several large firms setting up a *joint subsidiary* which acquires small blocks of shares of the participating firms and acts as a 'white knight' in the event of a hostile takeover bid.[18]

There are other devices, such as staggered boards, the issuance of preference shares without voting rights, and so forth which need not be explained here fully to show that hostile takeovers face cultural and structural impediments as well as obstacles set up for the purpose of obstructing the acquisition of a controlling block of shares.

This takes us back to our question of how, if not by the threat of takeovers, management in these firms is monitored. Theoretically there are several instruments and devices which could serve to align the interests of the management with those of the stockholders, employees, and creditors of the firm:

- monitoring of the management by the supervisory board;
- pressure from the various factor markets (product, capital, labour) as far as these are competitive;
- competition in the market for managers;
- incentives in contracts, with the compensation of managers tied to their performance;
- monitoring by creditors;
- the threat of bankruptcy and the resultant loss of prestige and reputation; and
- legal rules under which managers must act with loyalty and care with respect to the firm and its various stakeholders.

To be sure, not all of these devices are thought of as aiming at the same goal; the liability rules, for example, are more concerned with misbehaviour

---

[18] Cf. Herdt, 'Strategie der kleinen Schachteln,' *Börsen-Zeitung* 58 (23 Mar. 1991); E. Sünner 'Zur Abwehr feindlicher Unternehmensübernahmen in Deutschland', in *Festschrift für Karlheinz Quack* (1991), 469–75.

such as self-interested conduct by management, rather than with monitoring managerial efficiency.

Our focus here is not on all of these devices but only on the attempt of the German system to overcome the problems of shareholders' passivity in monitoring management in Berle–Means-type corporations by an institutional arrangement rather than a market-oriented solution (that is, through the 'market for corporate control' or the threat of hostile takeovers). This institutional solution consists of financial intermediaries (universal banks) which act as proxy-holders for small investors. The banks are better informed than small investors and have the advantage of economies of scale when monitoring the management. Hence, the 'agency costs' due to asymmetric information and collective action problems of small shareholders in Berle–Means-type corporations can perhaps be reduced by inserting these institutions. But new questions arise: What incentives do these institutions have to monitor corporate activities? Do they really act on behalf of the shareholders? And how well do they perform? Does 'internal monitoring' by institutions have limitations which a market solution does not have? Are there other interests which distract or deter them from pursuing their clients'—the small shareholders'—interests? Are the 'controllers' themselves 'controlled'? Before these questions can be addressed, the system and practice of the depository banks should first be described for the benefit of the foreign reader.[19]

IV. Banks as Institutional Monitors

1. THE INSTRUMENTS

(A) PROXY HELD BY BANKS

The typical large German firm with dispersed shareholders finds its shares in voting blocks which are voted by a few banks and which, if aggregated, comprise up to 30 per cent or more of all votes.[20] This voting power, which helps place representatives of the banks on the supervisory board,[21] comes from different sources: from directly owned stock,[22] from investment companies controlled by banks,[23] or from voting the shares held by banks as custodians for their clients.

Since the separation of commercial banks and securities firms is unknown in German banking law, banks are allowed to trade stock. They may also

---

[19] The following description is a slightly changed version of my article, 'Corporate Governance in Germany: The Role of the Banks' (1992) 40 *Am. J. Comp. L.* 503–26.
[20] Cf. Table 10.1 (p. 160 below).
[21] See (C) below.
[22] See (B) below.
[23] German banks may own investment companies and do so to a large extent. Data in A. Gottschalk, 'Der Stimmrechtseinfluß der Banken in der Aktionärsversammlungen von Großunternehmen' (1988) *WSI-Mitteilungen* 295–6; data on the engagement of investment funds in corporate stock most recently in F. W. Mühlbradt, (1992) 'Kennziffer Fondsengagement', *Die Bank* 72–7. Other than for banks (cf. n. 37, 38 below), there is a 10 per cent ceiling

offer their customers custodial or depository services for those shares, administer them (for example, collect dividends), and vote them at shareholder meetings. Shares of German publicly held corporations are predominantly bearer shares; smaller shares are mostly part of a single global document. A shareholder who wants to hold actual stock certificates will have to pay additionally for them. This drives stock into institutions.

Banks need a special written power of authority to vote the deposited shares. There is no ceiling or cap limiting the exercise of the voting rights by banks to a certain percentage of the firm's stock capital. The power of authority for the bank, or proxy, cannot be given for more than fifteen months, and it is revocable at any time. Before a shareholder meeting banks have to recommend to their customers how to vote, and must ask for special instructions. As a practical matter, special instructions are extremely rare.[24] If the shareholder does not give the bank special instructions, the bank is to vote according to its recommendations. Generally, banks can vote their customers' stock on any matter. In its own shareholder meeting,[25] however, a bank may only vote stock if it receives explicit instructions from its shareholders.[26]

Banks do not charge extra fees for voting their clients' stock. There is only a basic fee for their depository (custodial) service.

There are several older empirical studies on banks as proxy holders.[27] The most recent ones were published by Gottschalk[28] and Böhm.[29] Gottschalk selected those companies from the list of the 100 largest firms in 1984 where more than 50 per cent of their stock was either widely held or owned by banks. These thirty-two companies, with a (nominal) equity capital of DM 29.5 billion, represented about a quarter of the nominal capital of all German stock corporations. Among them were seven of the ten largest[30]

on shares of a portfolio firm for investment companies (Gesetz über Kapitalanlagegesellschaften, s. 8 a). Investment companies have to vote the shares in their portfolio personally and may not give a general proxy to another person or institution (Gesetz über Kapitalanlagegesellschaften, s. 10). This provision does not exclude, however, that an investment company and its parent company bank agree to vote in the same sense.

[24] Only in 2–3 per cent of all cases; U. Immenga, *Beteiligungen von Banken in anderen Wirtschaftszweigen*, Stüdien zum Bank-ünd Börsenrecht (1978), 103; Gottschalk (n. 23 above), 296.

[25] Esp. the large banks which act as proxy-holders are (or until recently were) corporations with widely held shares themselves.

[26] Cf. s. 128, 135 Aktiengesetz (Stock Corporation Act).

[27] Monopolkommission, *Zweites Hauptgutachten 1976/7, Fortschreitende Konzentration bei Großunternehmen* 1978), 283 ff.; Bericht der Studienkommission *Grundsatzfragen der Kreditwirtschaft* (1979), 111 ff. This commission concluded that in 1974/5 in seventy four stock-exchange listed companies (with a nominal capital of at least DM 50 millions) 52.5 per cent of the present shares were voted by banks or investment companies as proxy-holders and another 10.2 per cent as owners (*Report*, 290–1).

[28] Gottschalk (n. 23 above).

[29] J. Böhm *Der Einfluß der Banken auf Grossünternehmen* (1992).

[30] Measured by their *Wertschöpfung* (= surplus or loss of the firm corrected by additional factors). The contribution of the largest ten to the *Wertschöpfung* of all firms in the national economy was about 8% in 1986.

TABLE 10.1. *Voting blocks of banks at shareholder meetings of the 100 largest firms, 1986**

Rank of company in 1984	% of shares present at the meeting	% of shares voted by				
		Deutsche Bank	Dresdner-Bank	Commerz bank	All three big banks	All banks
1 Siemens	60.64	17.84	10.74	4.14	32.52	79.83
2 Daimler Benz	81.02	41.80	18.78	1.07	61.66	69.34
Mercedes-Holding	67.20	11.85	13.66	12.24	37.75	57.35
3 Volkswagen	50.13	2.94	3.70	1.33	7.98	19.53
5 Bayer	53.18	30.82	16.91	6.77	54.50	95.78
6 BASF	55.40	28.07	17.43	6.18	51.68	96.64
7 Hoechst	57.73	14.97	16.92	31.60	63.48	98.34
9 VEBA	50.24	19.99	23.08	5.85	47.92	98.18
11 Thyssen	68.48	9.24	11.45	11.93	32.62	53.11
12 Deutsche Bank	55.10	47.17	9.15	4.04	60.36	97.23
13 Mannesmann	50.63	20.49	20.33	9.71	50.53	95.40
18 MAN (GHH)	64.10	6.97	9.48	13.72	30.17	52.85
21 Dresdner Bank	56.79	13.39	47.08	3.57	64.04	98.16
27 Allianz-Holding	66.20	9.91	11.14	2.35	23.41	60.08
28 Karstadt	77.60	37.03	8.81	33.02	78.86	87.27
29 Hoesch	45.39	15.31	15.63	16.73	47.67	92.39
34 Commerzbank	50.50	16.30	9.92	34.58	60.81	96.77
35 Kaufhof	66.70	6.29	13.33	37.18	56.80	98.45
36 Klöckner-Werke	69.13	17.30	3.78	3.55	24.63	53.00
37 KHD	72.40	44.22	3.82	1.50	49.54	85.29
41 Metallg'schaft	90.55	16.42	48.85	0.35	65.62	75.95
44 Preussag	69.58	11.15	5.60	2.59	19.34	99.68
51 Degussa	70.94	6.86	33.03	1.89	41.79	67.09
52 Bayr. Vereinsbank	62.40	11.42	2.71	3.59	17.72	68.69
56 Continental	35.29	22.77	9.99	6.04	38.81	95.55
57 Bayr. Hypobank	67.90	5.86	7.05	1.20	14.11	92.09
59 Deutsche Babcock	67.13	7.58	9.67	5.29	22.54	97.01
67 Schering	46.60	23.86	17.46	10.17	51.50	99.08
68 Linde	52.99	22.76	15.73	21.36	59.87	90.37
73 Ph. Holzmann	82.18	55.42	0.91	6.49	62.82	74.81
94 Strabag	83.02	6.80	19.15	1.37	27.32	95.24
96 Bergmann	99.12	36.89	—	—	36.89	62.15
98 Hapag-Lloyd	84.50	48.15	47.82	0.39	96.36	99.50
On average	64.49	21.09	15.30	9.05	45.44	82.67

*Source: Gottschalk, 'Der Stimmrechtseinfluß der Banken in den Aktionärsversammlungen von Großunternehmen', *WSI-Mitteilungen* (1988), 298. The numbers for Siemens, Veba, and Continental refer to the 1987 meeting. The list adds up the shares of banks held by them on own account, their proxy holdings, and the shares held by investment companies which are subsidiaries of the respective banks.

firms of the Federal Republic. Böhm extends this study on a smaller sample of firms.[31]

Unlike Böhm, Gottschalk's study adds up the voting power of the banks' own shares, their depository shares, and shares held by investment companies, which are bank subsidiaries. His study shows the following results: on average, banks represented more than four-fifths (82.67 per cent) of all votes present in the meetings. With one exception, they represented at least a majority (more than 50 per cent) of those votes present. Consequently, they were able to elect the members of the supervisory board elected by the shareholders (as opposed to those elected by the employees). Changes of the statutes of the corporation could not be effected against their votes. In twenty-two or two-thirds of the firms, the banks voted more than three-fourths of the stock present and thereby could change the statutes. No other shareholder could block these decisions. Note that most of these corporations (by the votes of these very banks) have adopted provisions in their statutes to the effect that no one shareholder may vote more than (typically) 5 per cent of all shares of the company.[32] This rule, however, does not apply to banks in their capacity as proxy-holders voting for different clients.

The breakdown in Gottschalk's study shows that the voting rights are highly concentrated in the three largest private banks (Deutsche Bank, Dresdner Bank, and Commerzbank). Together, these three banks voted on average approximately 45 per cent of the stock that was represented at the general meetings of the thirty-two companies.[33] In almost half of these cases (fifteen firms), they together held the majority; in a further one-third (ten firms) they had a blocking minority. In individual cases, one or another of the big banks dominates; in most cases the votes are distributed roughly equally among them, or the other two banks together have about the same number of votes as their competitor.[34]

The extent of co-ordinated behaviour of these banks in the voting process[35] has not yet been empirically determined. A government commission in its report of 1978, noted that 'the banks mostly vote in the same sense'.[36]

(B) BANKS AS SHAREHOLDERS

A second source of influence of banks in corporate affairs is their position as stockholders for their own account. According to German banking law,

---

[31] Böhm (n. 29 above), 242.
[32] Cf. n. 14 above.
[33] This corresponds with the data of the Bundesbank according to which by the end of 1988 the three Großbanken held 43% of all depository shares in their custody; Die Aktiengesellschaft, *AG-Report* (1989), 412.
[34] See Table 10.1.
[35] Cf., e.g., Immenga (n. 24 above), 103–4; Gottschalk (n. 23 above), 300.
[36] Bericht der Studienkommission (n. 27 above), 171.

credit institutions may acquire and hold stock in non-bank firms for their own account; there are no rules which forbid or limit such holdings to a certain percentage of the firm's capital. There are only caps or limits with respect to the bank's capital to protect the depositors and creditors of the bank: a single participation in one firm may not exceed 50 per cent of the capital of the bank.[37] Further, investments of a bank in stockholdings and other illiquid assets may not exceed its own capital.[38]

The Second EC Banking Directive lowers these limits: in the future no single holding may exceed 15 per cent, nor all holdings together 60 per cent of the capital of the bank.[39] Additionally, the recent draft of an EC directive concerning large credits limits each single 'credit' (including participations on own account) to 25 per cent of the capital of the bank.[40] Practically, however, these new rules will not mean significant changes for German banks and their equity holdings.

By the end of 1989 German credit institutions, directly and through subsidiaries, held 4.69 per cent of all shares of domestic stock corporations[41] (this number includes subsidiaries of banks, such as corporations that own bank premises, and so on). For the issue of 'banks and corporate control' this number alone is not very informative. It does not tell us whether or in which banks these holdings are concentrated; in how many cases these holdings are mere portfolio investments rather than controlling blocks of shares; whether they are acquired only for the short term (for placement or trading purposes), or as a long-term investment; or what the structure of the remaining shares is (that is, whether they are widely dispersed or concentrated).

In his recent study, Böhm analysed the shareholdings of banks in the 100 largest industrial firms (measured by turnover). In 1986 twelve credit institutions held participations in twenty-two of these firms.[42] The list shows that the holdings on own account have little relation to the blocks of shares voted by banks in the name of their clients. Secondly, the size of the holdings is not distributed equally; they rank from about 5 per cent (holdings of all banks in one firm) up to more than 50 per cent (holding of a single bank in one firm). Thirdly, the holdings are rather stable over time. This impression is confirmed when we compare recent with older data.[43]

(C) INTERLOCKING DIRECTORATES

Influence on management, its decisions, its appointment, and dismissal is

[37] s. 13 (4), 19 (1), No. 6 Kreditwesengesetz (Banking Act).
[38] s. 12 Kreditwesengesetz.
[39] Amtsblatt der EG Nr. L 386 (30 Dec. 1989), Art. 12.
[40] Kom. (91) 68 endg. (23/4/1991).
[41] Source: Deutsche Bundesbank, written testimony for the hearing before the Committee for Economy of the Federal Parliament (*Bundestagsausschuß für Wirtschaft*. Anhörung vom 16. Mai 1990) of 16 Apr. 1990, p. 9.
[42] Cf. Table 10.2.
[43] Böhm (n. 29 above), 231–8.

TABLE 10.2. *Stockholdings of banks in the 100 largest industrial firms, 1986* (% of nominal capital)

No	Rank (size of turn-over)	Company	Nominal capital (million DM)	Deutsche Bank	Dresdner Bank	Commerz-bank	Other banks	All banks
1	1	Daimler Benz AG	2,116.0	28.50	1.6	1.6	3.20	34.90
2	8	Thyssen AG	1,565.0			>5.00		>5.00
3	12	Klöckner Werke AG	469.03	7.20	3.1	3.2	16.40	30.00
4	14	BMW AG	750.0		5–10.00			5–10.00
5	19	Metallges. AG	280.0	11.25	16.5		0.56	28.30
6	21	MAN AG	674.5			>8.25		>8.25
7	26	AEG AG	931.2	16.00	0.9	0.90	1.80	19.60
8	27	Degussa AG	284.0		>10.0			>10.00
9	32	Preussag AG	401.6				43.00	43.00
10	37	Ph. Holz-mann AG	90.0	35.00		7.55		42.55
11	41	VEW AG	1,000.0	6.30			10.46	16.76
12	42	MBB GmbH	600.0		5–10.0	>0.30	5.00	10–15.00
13	46	Hochtief AG	200.0			>16.25	>25.00	>41.25
14	47	Dt. Babcock	250.0				>5.00	>5.00
15	49	Continental AG	312.1	>10.00				>10.00
16	54	AGIV	80.0				44.00	44.00
17	58	Linde AG	237.7			>10.00		>10.00
18	80	Strabag AG	55.1				>50.00	>50.00
19	81	PWA AG	200.0				44.00	44.00
20	83	Bilf. u. Berger AG	70.0		>25.0			>25.00
21	91	Fichtel u. Sachs	128.0			35.00		35.00
22	99	Dyckerhoff u. Widmann AG	57.0	6.72		1.45	13.00	21.17

Source: Böhm, *Der Einfluß der Banken auf Grossunternehmen* (1992), 225–60.

not exercised directly by the shareholders but by the supervisory board. Therefore, seats on the supervisory board are crucial for every shareholder or institution that wants to have a say in corporate governance, obtain relevant information, and so on. Banks influence or strengthen their influence on firms by appointing members to the supervisory board of the companies. One can find bank managers and other professionals on these boards who are appointed to multiple boards with the votes of the same institution, but such 'informal' relationships between a bank and these professional supervisory-board members are difficult to identify; however, interlocks with firms by board members of the bank must be disclosed.[44]

Members of the managing board or the supervisory board of a bank can be members of the supervisory board of a firm, be it as a consequence of the equity participation of the bank, its position as a holder of proxies, or as a consequence of its business relationship with the firm, especially a long-term credit relationship. That does not mean that management does not also try to influence the selection of its supervisors to a certain extent. As mentioned earlier, the members of the supervisory board are—except those elected by the employees—elected by the shareholders. A single person may not be a member of more than ten boards at the same time. This rule, however, does not restrain the institution which he or she represents. There is no rule in German law that prohibits service on boards of competing firms. Direct cross-interlocks (the member of the supervisory board of company A sitting on the management board of company B, and vice versa) are forbidden.

As mentioned above, the supervisory board appoints the members of the managing board and may dismiss them, though only for cause. It is reponsible for monitoring the management, although practically it acts as an advisory committee rather than as a monitoring panel[45] except in times of financial distress of the firm. To accomplish its duties the board has the right to receive comprehensive information. The management must report to it periodically on all important questions, and the supervisory board may always ask the management for reports. The supervisory board reviews the annual reports and balance sheets of the firm. The board may require management to obtain its prior approval before entering into certain important transactions, such as obtaining (or granting) loans above a specific amount. Board members must treat company information confidentially.

The chair of the supervisory board has a particularly influential position.[46] He prepares the meetings of the board—which are less frequent than, for example, board meetings in the US[47]—proposes the agenda, and stays in steady contact with the management. The management has to brief the chair immediately on all important developments. If there is a stalemate in a vote on a board under a co-determination regime (a rare event), the chairman breaks the tie.

---

[44] s. 128 (2) (5) Aktiengesetz (Stock Corporation Act).

[45] Cf. in more detail 2 below.

[46] That corresponds with the self-assessment of their position; K. Bleicher, *Der Aufsichtsrat im Wandel*, (1987), 58.

[47] Three to four times per year; cf. K. Bleicher and H. Paul, 'Das amerikanische Board-Modell im Vergleich zur deutschen Vorstands-Aufsichtsratsverfassung-Stand und Entwicklüngstendenzen' (1986) 46 *DBW* 273; Bleicher (n. 46 above), 41.

Comprehensive data on personal links between firms and banks in Germany do not exist. Various studies have been done at different times in different sectors.[48] Let us have another look at the list of the 100 largest firms which has been provided by Böhm.[49] Ninety-two of these firms had a supervisory board (numbers as of 1986); banks were represented on seventy-five (= 81 per cent) of these boards. They held more than 10 per cent of all seats and more than 20 per cent of the seats of the shareholders' side of the board. On average they had more than two representatives on each board. The three *Großbanken* held more than 61 per cent of all banks' seats; the Deutsche Bank alone held fifty-four seats in forty-four of these largest firms. The key position as president of the supervisory board was held by banks' representatives in 1986 in twenty of the ninety-two firms.

Although these numbers, which refer only to direct personal links between a bank and the large firms, do not give us the whole picture of the potential influence which can be exerted by banks through the supervisory boards, it is safe to say that there is a significant potential for banks to get information, give advice, and monitor management in most of these large firms. But do banks really exert their influence and, if so, to what extent and with what results? If these questions cannot be answered satisfactorily, can we at least say something about the incentives and disincentives to monitor or behave in a way which might be advantageous for the bank, but disadvantageous for the other shareholders, among them the bank's clients?

2. CONTROL, INCENTIVES, AND DISINCENTIVES TO MONITOR

(A) CONTROL

Control can mean various grades on a scale that starts with the right of a shareholder or a bank to information, which in turn causes management to refrain from certain actions, and ends with the power to remove the incumbent management. In the following we consider (first) control by means of better access to information; (secondly), influence by giving advice to management on an ongoing basis; (thirdly), influence by appointing the members of the management board; and (fourthly), interim and *ex-post* monitoring. There are certainly other ways for a bank to exert control, especially if it is also a lender to the firm (scrutinizing of the borrower before granting or extending a credit; monitoring during the credit relationship; pressure of the claim to fixed payments irrespective of the unsteady flow of returns to the borrowing firm; threat of bankruptcy), and these means are perhaps even more important for monitoring management than the

---

[48] Cf. Bericht der Studienkommission (n. 27 above), 122–6 and the tables on pp. 440–5 and 585–98; Immenga (n. 24 above), 109 ff.; Informationen des Bundesverbandes deutscher Banken, *Zur Diskussion um die 'Macht der Banken'* (1989), 20; Gottschalk (n. 23 above), 299 ff.; survey in K. Fischer 'Haüsbankbeziehungen als Instrument der Bindüng zwischen Banken und Unternehmen: Eine theoretische und empirische Analyse', Diss. (Bonn, 1990), 148–9 with further references.

[49] Böhm (n. 29 above), 194–6 and 257–63.

instruments described here if one looks at the extent and importance of credit finance for German firms[50]. Although the means and devices available to a bank as a creditor do not stand at the centre of our interest here, we also have to consider in the following the extent to which the banks' role as custodians is either reinforced or hampered by their other role as (major) creditors of the firm.

First, *information* about somebody may influence that person's behaviour if the person is aware of it. As mentioned above, the management board must report to the supervisory board on a continuing basis. Hence, information about the firm and its management, so far as it is given to the superisory board at all, is almost always immediately available to at least one bank on the supervisory board. Thus, information about the plans and the quality of the firm's management can be disclosed to these institutions without the need to make this information public—information which the banks, perhaps, would not get otherwise.

However, it is doubtful whether this argument is valid. Remember the rather infrequent meetings of the supervisory board. A poll of banks done by Fischer shows that a bank does not expect to get any better or more thorough information from its representatives on the board than it already has as the firm's creditor.[51] In addition, members of the supervisory board must keep confidential the information they get in that capacity.[52] Board members are normally well aware of this, because the breach of this duty is a criminal offence.[53].

In all, it does not seem very likely that the information which a bank gets from its position on the supervisory board puts a tighter rein on management than would be the case without board membership.

Secondly, bank representatives on supervisory boards have specialized knowledge, particularly in the field of finance. Very often they have an office back in their bank with special facilities, such as the help of an assistant, to support them in their work as a board member. The large banks have departments specialized in corporate finance, analysing the financial markets as well as the financial needs of their client firms. This information, too, is available to the representatives of these banks. Thus, these representatives can provide the respective firms with *specialized advice, financial knowledge* and *information*.

Banks may not be able to run industrial firms themselves, but from the activities of their representatives on supervisory boards they know the

---

[50] Cf. the comparison in G. Mayer/Alexander, 'Banks and Securities Markets: Corporate Financing in Germany and the U.K.' (1990), 4 *Jour. of the Japanese and Int'l. Economics* 456–63.

[51] Fischer (n. 48 above), 80–1, 149; cf. also O. H. Poensgen 'Between Market and Hierarchy—The Role of Interlooking Directorates' (1980) 136 *Jour. Institutional and Theoretical Economics* 208–25.

[52] s. 116, 93 (1) Aktiengesetz (Stock Corporation Act).

[53] s. 404 Aktiengesetz.

manager market quite well. They should at least be able, by the exercise of their stock voting rights, to appoint the right people to the supervisory board, which in turn can provide management with information and experience in other fields.[54] A poll done by Bleicher shows that nine out of ten board members in his sample believe that the actual influence of their advice on management is 'strong'.[55] This belief, of course, does not mean that this is, in fact, the case, especially given the rather infrequent sessions of the supervisory board, although there is some evidence that there are informal contacts between board members and management between the sessions.[56] Certainly one must make a distinction between the chairman of the supervisory board and the members of certain subcommittees on the one hand, and the 'regular' members on the other.

Thirdly, where advice cannot be given because of institutional impediments (infrequent sessions, for instance), and where the supervisory board cannot monitor the management (see below), all the more important is the question of whether the supervisory board is capable of *selecting managers from the beginning* who appear capable of doing a good job—because of the pattern of their behaviour in the past, their career, and previous success—even if their efforts cannot be observed on an ongoing basis. This seems, indeed, to be the most important task of the supervisory board, and banks seem to play some role in this respect.

It has already been mentioned that the members of the management board are appointed by the supervisory board and that—in large German corporations—half the members of the supervisory board are elected by the shareholders. That means that, in our sample,[57] all banks together determine who sits on the shareholders' side of the supervisory board, even if there are no personal interlocks. Furthermore, if there is an open conflict between shareholders' and employees' representatives on the board, the shareholders' could push their management candidate through, because of the tie-breaking vote of the chairperson.[58] That means that banks have a decisive influence on who gets into the management boardroom, even though the members of the supervisory board are legally independent and may—should a conflict arise—act independently. To the extent that one bank dominates the shareholders' meeting, is represented on the nominating committee of the supervisory board, or holds the position of chairperson, its influence will be greater accordingly.[59]

---

[54] For empirical data on the composition of the supervisory board, see e.g., the study of Gerum, Steinmann and Fees, *Der mitbestimmte Aufsichtsrat: Eine empirische Untersuchung* (1987).

[55] Bleicher (n. 46 above), 57.

[56] Ibid. 54 ff.

[57] Cf. Table 10.1 (p. 160 above).

[58] Cf. s. 32 Mitbestimmungsgesetz (Codetermination Act).

[59] On the role of the nominating committee (Vorstandsausschuss) and the nominating process, see e.g. Brinkmann-Herz *Entscheidungsprozesse in den Aufsichtsräten der Montanindustrie* (1972).

In their roles as creditors, shareholders, proxy-holders, and their representation on many supervisory boards, banks should know the market for managers quite well. Nevertheless, bankers' influence on the appointment of managers could be detrimental if only one institution, with perhaps doubtful knowledge about the firm's particular sector, had to decide. But that seems not to be the case. If we keep in mind that the three big banks often have similar voting holdings, or that two of them can outvote the other, that the members of the supervisory board are not bound to follow the instructions of the shareholders, and that the shareholders' representatives would think long and hard before they pushed a candidate through against the vote of the employees, then it becomes clear that a candidate for the management board has to pass several tests of qualification and approval, and is not simply appointed by one dominating institution.

Fourthly, with regard to *monitoring management*, it is useful to differentiate between interim and ex-post monitoring. *Interim monitoring* can occur especially in cases where the management must ask the supervisory board for its consent; when, for instance, the management plans to shut down a plant, enter into a loan agreement, and so forth. Another case where the supervisory board is likely to interfere is when the firm is in financial distress. Apart from these cases, 'interim monitoring' activities seem to be limited.[60]

But the supervisory board may be able to measure the performance of the management by its results at the end of certain periods. If so, there may be an incentive for management to perform well even if it is not monitored continuously, if management can be recalled in the case of disappointing results. At first sight, *ex-post monitoring* in this sense does not seem to be directly related to the role that banks in particular have in corporate governance, and could theoretically occur without them. There is, however, a link between the *ex-post* monitoring role of the supervisory board and the existence of depository institutions. It becomes evident when one considers the difference between a board system with outside directors on the board who are there because of the influence of the managing director, the chairman, or the Chief Executive Officer, on one side, and a two-tier system on the other, where you have 'outside' supervisory-board members who are appointed by large, influential institutions in the shareholder meetings rather than by the incumbent management. The readiness of the supervisory-board members to act and, if necessary, even to dismiss or not to prolong the contracts of the members of the management board should be stronger because of the independence guaranteed through the existence and role of influential institutions in the shareholder meetings.

How does the supervisory board measure the performance of the incumbent management? According to German law, management must

[60] Cf. ibid. 81, 82.

prepare and publish the firm's balance sheet and profit-and-loss statement annually. Both are reviewed by independent public accountants who are responsible to the supervisory board and report to it. There are additional obligatory interim reports that are provided to the supervisory board only. The supervisory board can then put further questions to the management, compare the results of the firm with past results as well as with those of the firm's competitors (to the extent that such information can be obtained), and thus get at least a partial picture of the performance or mistakes of the incumbent management as a whole, and perhaps also of individual members of the management board.

The observation that this internal monitoring system relies very much on comparisons with previous results, plans, and the results of the industry competitors hints at a limitation of such an internal monitoring system which will be examined later, in the context of and in comparison with, takeovers. A potential outside bidder may have information about, say, a new technology which the board of a specific firm does not have. Is 'outside' governance by (hostile) takeovers which forces a firm to react to technological changes before the competitive process on the product markets will do so a necessary supplement to an internal monitoring system which fails in such cases?[61]

Can boards react, and do they really react, if they observe bad performance? If so, this can be anticipated by management and can give it an incentive to try harder. A member of the management board can be removed only for cause before the expiry date of his or her term.[62] For this reason, as well as because of the attendant bad publicity, such removals occur only in cases of criminal offences, and the like.

Practically, there is the more subtle threat of not renewing the contract after its expiry (a manager's term may not last longer than five years; at that point the supervisory board must explicitly decide whether or not to renew it).[63] Poensgen and Lukas have published an interesting empirical study in which they show that there is significant involuntary 'fluctuation' of management-board members, not only in cases of very serious problems or the financial distress of the firm,[64] but also in 'lighter' cases in which the supervisory board was not content with the performance of individual managers or with the management board as a whole.[65] To be sure, the fact that there is significant involuntary fluctuation does not by itself say anything about the monitoring 'performance' of the supervisory boards. Did they react too late, did they dismiss the right people, on what signals did

[61] Cf. Ch. 5. below.
[62] s. 84 (3) Aktiengesetz (Stock Corporation Act).
[63] s. 84 (1) Aktiengesetz.
[64] Poensgen and Lukas 'Fluktuation, Amtszeit und weitere Karriere von Vorstandsmitgliedern' (1982) 42 *Die Betriebswirtschaft* 187, 188.
[65] Cf. ibid. 183, 184, 188, 190.

they react, and are there certain directions in which their incentives might drive management? This issue certainly deserves further research, and until such studies are made it seems difficult to maintain that one corporate governance system or the other shows better results and should be preferred.

To get closer to an answer to this question we also need to take into consideration the incentives and disincentives for institutions like banks for corporate control. The following sections try to address this.

(B)   INCENTIVES FOR CONTROL

Why do banks get involved in corporate governance, act as proxy-holders, and hold positions on supervisory boards?

Banks are compensated through *fees for their custodial services*. But that alone does not explain why banks vote their own and their clients' stock, appoint their managers to the supervisory boards of other firms, and spend money to support their monitoring work. Banks could (as owners of stock) free-ride, and their customers could re-deposit their stock with institutions that promised no monitoring, but also no expenses.

As to the latter, such services are not offered in the market. Banks could easily drive such competing institutions out of the market by cross-subsidizing their depository business. Further, investment companies that are subsidiaries of banks will not try to dilute the position of their parent banks.

There may be other incentives or advantages that accrue to banks from their governance activities. First, they can try to *protect their own equity investment*. As our overview has shown, banks hold, besides their position as proxy-holders of their clients, equity stakes that rank from stakes as small as 1 per cent of a firm's stock up to more than 50 per cent.[66] The right to vote their clients' stock (at low additional costs) gives banks leverage to protect or strengthen their own investment without making a capital infusion. For instance, if a bank holds an equity position of 12 per cent of a firm's stock and commands another 15 per cent through its clients' deposited shares, it has a blocking position against the issuance of new stock and the elimination of shareholders' pre-emptive rights[67] that it would not have as a 12 per cent owner alone. This explanation has to be ruled out, however, in all cases in which banks have proxy voting power without own equity holdings.

Furthermore, banks could try to *protect their other (credit) investment in the firm*. Creditors face the problem of 'asymmetric information', both before the conclusion of a loan contract and thereafter. It is often argued that an equity stake of a bank in the borrowing firm will improve the information

---

[66] Table 10.2 (p. 163 above)
[67] Cf. s. 186 (3) Aktiengesetz (Stock Corporation Act).

for the bank, and reduce the problem of asymmetric information.[68] That is doubtful. Typically, a shareholder will not receive earlier or better information than would a creditor bank (although, to be sure, a small creditor and a majority shareholder with immediate access to the management should not be compared). Even if the bank is represented on the firm's board, this will normally not provide the bank with better or earlier information than it already has as creditor.[69]

If these positions do not provide the bank with better information, they may nonetheless help to exclude or minimize risks for the bank during the course of a credit relationship, and thus lower the agency costs associated with debt.

There is no doubt that a bank can improve its position as creditor in certain aspects if it is an equity owner or votes stock of the firm for its clients at the same time. A creditor commanding 51 per cent of the votes in the shareholders' meeting of this borrower can choose who manages the firm. Perhaps the creditor is not capable of electing the best managers, but at least he will choose people who implicitly promise not to harm the interests of the creditor by engaging in risky projects, distribution of assets to shareholders, and so on, without the bank's approval. As the threshold at which the bank's own equity investment is able to command a majority will be normally too high, the addition of the depository shares of the bank's clients seems to be a perfect arrangement to achieve the necessary leverage on the management to protect the bank's own (equity as well as) credit investment. Certainly, this power usually has to be shared with other banks, but as creditors of the firm they have, at least to a large extent, parallel interests with regard to the management.

If this is so, we can expect that credit finance for these firms plays a more important role (in terms of availability and costs of credit finance as well as higher leverage) than it does for firms in an environment in which banks do not have a comparable position. Astonishingly, however, large firms in Germany seem to raise less bank finance than do comparable large U.K. public limited companies where banks have neither proxy voting power nor board seats.[70]

Another incentive for a bank to acquire and vote stock could be to capture

---

[68] J. Cable 'Capital Market Information and Institutional Performance: The Role of West German Banks' (1985) 95 *Econ. Jour.* 118–32; R. J. Pozdena 'Commerce and Banking: The German Case', *Fed. Reserve Bank of San Francisco Weekly Letter*, 18 Dec. 1987; id., 'Banking and Venture Capital', ibid. 1 June 1990; id., *Why Banks Need Securities Powers* (Fed. Reserve Bank of San Francisco Working Paper, 1990); McCauley and Zimmer, *Explaining International Differences in the Cost of Capital: The US and UK versus Japan and Germany* (Fed. Reserve Bank of NY, Research Paper No. 8913) (1989); E. Berglöf, 'Capital Structure as a Mechanism of Corporate Control: Comparison of Financial Systems', in Aoki *et al.* (eds.), *The Firm as Nexus of Treaties* (1990), 237–62.

[69] Cf. no. 51 above and accompanying text.

[70] Cf. G. Mayer and Alexander, n. 50 above.

all or at least a part of the firm's financial business. In his study on 'house-bank relationships,' however, Fischer concludes that exclusive relationships between banks and firms are rather the exception today. They still can be found between small firms and banks. But publicly held corporations with widely distributed stock (which to a large extent is, as shown, voted by the banks) may have five to ten 'primary' banking relationships and a number of additional connections with other banks.[71] Regrettably, the study does not analyse the question whether there are syndicates rather than exclusive business relationships with a single bank, as has always been contended in the literature, especially for the fee-based business like underwriting,[72] and whether these syndicates reflect the shares of their members in the shareholders' meeting. Certainly, a management board will think long and hard before it chooses to give a considerable part of its financial business, such as raising capital through issuance of bonds or shares, to the competitors of those banks represented in its shareholders' meeting if the latter offer the same services on roughly the same conditions.

To conclude, although there may be—apart from reputational reasons— no clear incentives discernible for banks to act in their clients' interests as their proxy holders, it is, on the other hand, not obvious that these banks follow their incentives to protect or promote their other finance business by means of their position as depot institutions.

(C) DISINCENTIVES

Are there also disincentives to banks in engaging in corporate control activities?

A bank which is an institutional shareholder and offers other (financial) services at the same time could be eager *to get into or keep up a business relationship,* and might therefore refrain from being a nuisance to management at least as long as things run comparably well.[73] This depends on questions that differ in each individual case: what position do the offering banks and other banks have regarding management, and can management independently decide to prefer a competitor or an 'outside' bank?

Another disincentive could come from *implicit management coalitions.* The large banks themselves are generally corporations with widely distributed ownership.[74] That could lead to the same 'sympathetic' understanding of how corporate governance should function, or even to certain 'arrangements'. The most simple way would be to have cross-interlocks (manager A sits on the supervisory board of company B, and vice

---

[71] Fischer (n. 48 above), 21–2; 102–3. Fischer looked at the credit relationships between banks and firms only. Whether the same is true for other services, especially underwriting and floating new shares, is not clear.

[72] See e.g. Böhm (n. 29 above), 154–5, with further references.

[73] Ibid. 138–41.

[74] Cf. Commerzbank (ed.), *Wer gehört zu wem? A Guide to Capital Links in German Companies* (17th. edn., 1991).

versa). That, however, is forbidden.[75] In the past, banks have helped managements of other large firms, whose stock they vote, to protect their own and the other managers' interests against takeovers, by changing the statutes of the respective corporations.[76] This may have been done to protect the banks' position as proxy-holders and thereby the banks' own equity investments, or to protect or promote such banks' business relationships rather than to do the management of these firms a favour. But for whatever reasons, protection against hostile takeovers as a means of management control does not mean protection against control altogether if there are other 'institutional' devices of control.

A last remark on disincentives to monitor should be made with respect to the banks themselves. As our statistics prove, managements of these banks can punish each other to a certain extent because they hold and vote roughly similar amounts of proxies for voting shares in the other banks.[77] Hence there seems to be a strong disincentive at work in monitoring and controlling the other banks' managements. Instead of a control through this method and through the other monitoring devices mentioned earlier,[78] monitoring of bank management may occur through state supervision (that is, the central bank and the banking supervisory authority) and the media.

3. DRAWBACKS

As we analyse institutions which represent small investors in shareholder meetings and on boards and act as corporate monitors in the shareholders' place, we should ask three questions. What are their incentives? Are there conflicts of interests or other drawbacks? And how, in turn, are these institutions monitored themselves? So far I have only tried to describe the role of banks in corporate governance, their instruments, incentives, and disincentives. This may be accepted as a substitute for the more precise measurements of their performance which our economists still owe us. The following part will deal briefly with the question of whether there are drawbacks connected with this governance system (other than those already mentioned as possible disincentives). 'Drawbacks' means disadvantages for the shareholders as well as for the respective firms. They may result from conflicts of interests on the part of the depository banks. Or there may be disadvantages for the shareholders who are clients of the depository banks if these institutions, which are thought to control management on behalf of their clients, remain uncontrolled themselves.

The following remarks on drawbacks will, however, not deal with the political debate. The role and 'power' of German banks, especially the

---

[75] s. 100 (2)(3). Aktiengesetz (Stock Corporation Act).
[76] See n. 14 above, and accompanying text.
[77] Table 10.1 (p. 160 above).
[78] Cf. p. 157 above.

Großbanken, have been discussed for decades. This section also does not deal with the possible risks for the banks and their depositors (which is not presently an issue, and for which prudent regulation should be sufficient),[79] the impacts on the German stock market, the question of the 'equity capital shortage' of German firms,[80] the abuse of confidential information, the role of the banks in the concentration process,[81] or other anti-trust questions— issues which normally dominate the discussion about bank–firm relationships.[82]

Large voting-right holdings of a bank and its representation on the supervisory board may drive management into an *exclusive business relationship* with this bank. This can be advantageous to the firm (through the commitment of the bank as a source of finance and lowered risks because of better possibilities to monitor and control management and the resulting easier and cheaper access to credit finance).[83] On the other hand, such a situation may be exploited by a controlling bank to the detriment of 'its' firm. When we look at the distribution of votes among several institutions,[84] however, such an 'exploitation' by one offeror does not seem very likely. Even if this were proved empirically, it would be difficult to weigh up the advantages and drawbacks of such 'stable' business relationships.[85] As there are several large banks represented in the general meetings, the question rather is whether these banks share at least a part of the respective firm's business. Such oligopolistic behaviour is often contended in the literature for the fee-based underwriting and flotation business.[86] As to the lending business, 'exploitation' through the imposition of interest rates above the market price seems unlikely.

Another charge in this context is that institutional proxy-holders who are also creditors *might not support* a profitable, innovative (and—perhaps— more risky) policy aimed at *maximizing shareholder value*. Or, to put it differently, banks may influence investment decisions of the firm to protect an already existing credit relationship, and they may prefer projects which need (higher) external (credit) finance to those with a comparatively higher net present value for the firm (rather than the banks), and which are of greater benefit for the shareholders.[87] Banks may indeed have this

---

[79] Overview and discussion in T. Baums 'Should Banks own Industrial Firms? Remarks from the German Perspective' (1992) 56 *Rev. de la Banque/Bank-en Financiewezen* 249–55, and *Verbindungen Zwischen Banken und Unternehmen im amerikanischen Wirtschaftsrecht* (1992).

[80] Cf. Hax (n. 13 above).

[81] Cf. W. Eckstein 'The Role of Banks in Corporate Concentration in West Germany' (1980) 136 *Jour. of Institutional and Theoretrical Economics* 465–82.

[82] See most recently Böhm (n. 29 above).

[83] Cf. the interesting study of Fischer (n. 48 above).

[84] See Table 10.1 (p. 160 above).

[85] Cf. for the credit relationship Hellwig 'Banking, Financial Intermediation and Corporate Finance', in Giovannini and Meyer (eds.), *European Financial Integration* (1991), 55 ff.

[86] Cf. n. 72 above.

[87] Böhm (n. 29 above), 142, 144.

preference if they are not themselves shareholders. And if the assertions of the managerialists are correct, that corporate managers do not pursue profit-maximization, but rather size- or growth-maximization,[88] then there seems to be an implicit agreement between managers and depository banks on a mutually favourable pattern at the expense of the shareholders.[89] On the other hand, debt is always looked at as a device to discipline management.[90] So why should management yield to its alleged incentives for growth-maximization with the help of credit finance? Here we simply need a more systematic analysis of the relation between the financing patterns of large firms and the underlying interests.

A related issue concerns the *dividend policy* of firms. Management may prefer to retain earnings rather than distribute them as they accrue since this provides a way to conceal fluctuations in future earnings and thereby to reduce management's accountability for losses. And retained earnings give management the means to achieve growth-maximization without being monitored by outside financiers, even at the expense of the shareholders (that is through 'free cash flow').[91] It is contended in the literature that banks support this restrictive dividend policy of managements either because they want to get at least a share of the firm's financial business,[92] or—and this seems to be the main argument—in order to protect their credit investments.[93] On the other hand, retaining dividends means that managements become increasingly independent and 'emancipated' from external finance the larger the internal funds grow. But perhaps banks tend to neglect this long-term development in order to protect their present interests. Furthermore, there are limits to the 'emancipation' of managements because of the role which banks play in their function as proxies in shareholder meetings and on supervisory boards. Here again one would like to see more theoretical and empirical studies on this point, with reference to the tax and other cost issues which affect a firm's dividend policy.

Even if there is no abuse there is, as our summary has shown, certainly a potential for it because of conflicts of interests. There is a long-standing discussion about how abuse can effectively be avoided without destroying the advantage of having an institutional arrangement which overcomes shareholders' passivity and serves as a professional monitor. It is not necessary to go into this discussion here in detail; suffice it to say that the existing rules and provisions against potential abuse seem not to be

---

[88] Cf. Klein and Coffee *Business Organization and Finance. Legal and Economic Principles* (4th edn. 1990), 161, 162, with further references.

[89] Cf. Böhm (n. 29 above), 142, 144.

[90] See e.g. M. C. Jensen, 'Agency costs of free Cash Flow, Corporate Finance, and Takeovers', in C. W. Smith, Fr (ed.), *The Modern Theory of Corporate Finance* (2nd edn., 1989), 660.

[91] Ibid. 659.

[92] Böhm (n. 29 above), 139, 140.

[93] Immenga (n. 24 above), 121; Böhm (n. 29 above), 143, 144, 149, with further references.

sufficient and could and should be amended.[94] Another problem which can only be mentioned here is how the efforts and the performance of these institutions which monitor managements on behalf of small investors can themselves be measured and controlled. By installing an institution to solve the 'principal-agent' problem on the level of the corporation, we get a new 'principal-agent' problem on the level of the intermediary. Do we have similar problems (that is asymmetric information, collective action problems, and so on) on this second stage too, and how can these be solved?[95]

Although these questions concerning the monitoring performance of the depot institutions as agents of the shareholders remain unanswered, in the following section a first attempt is made to compare this institutional solution with a market solution: more specifically, with the threat of hostile takeovers. This threat has often been claimed in the literature to align adequately the interests of shareholders and managers, and to address the problem of managerial inefficiency. Would such a solution avoid the problems which are connected with the institutional solution, such as conflicts of interests, lack of control, and so on? Would it even show better results, or are there other imperfections and drawbacks connected with this solution? The following section will try to address these questions.

V.   Market and Institutional Monitoring—A Comparison

A comparison between market and institutional monitoring systems has to start with several caveats.

First, such a comparison is necessarily narrowly focused in that it picks out only one instrument from among several which are meant to cope with managerial inefficiency, self-dealing, and related problems, and which are meant to supplement each other within a given legal system. If, for instance, the takeover market cannot deal with individual instances of management self-dealing but the institutional control of managers perhaps can, there may be, in a system which relies on market rather than on institutional control of managers, supplementary instruments available which may be even more capable of dealing with this specific problem.

Secondly, such a comparison is of limited value because the possible policy consequences seem to be very limited. Even if such a comparison could provide us with reliable results at this time and show us the advantages and disadvantages of both systems, that would not necessarily mean that the other system could be adopted and implanted into a completely different

---

[94] Cf. the overviews in U. Körber, *Die Stimmrechtsvertretung durch Kreditinstitute* (1989); Böhm (n. 29 above), 157–67 and 211–21; J. Köndgen Duties of Banks in Voting their Clients' Shares', in Baums *et al.* (eds.), *Institutional Investors and Corporate Governance* (1993).

[95] For references on the theoretical discussion about agents watching other agents and how to solve the control of controllers problem, see B. S. Black, 'Agents, Watching Agents', The Promise of Institutional Investor Voice (1992) 39 *UCLA Law Rev.* 811–93.

environment. For example, since there are specific structural impediments to takeovers in German corporate law, as was shown earlier,[96] the threat of takeovers would presumably show different results than in a system which is more responsive to this incentive. On the other hand, it does not seem very likely that public policy and regulators in the Anglo-American countries would permit banks to play a role similar to that in Germany, even if banks had more and better incentives to monitor management on behalf of small shareholders than other institutions (such as pension funds).

Thirdly, the following comparison cannot deal with all aspects, all the pros and cons of (hostile) takeovers on the one hand[97] and the influence of banks on firms on the other.[98] The focus has to be, and will be, limited to the potential of these monitoring systems for monitoring management efficiently.

1. DIVERGENCE OF INTERESTS OF SHAREHOLDERS AND MANAGERS

A good starting-point for a comparison is Professor Eisenberg's list of cases in which the interests of shareholders and managers diverge.[99] Eisenberg differentiates between 'shirking', 'traditional conflicts of interests', and 'positional conflicts'. If the efforts of an agent cannot be observed, and his performance not be controlled, he has no disincentive to work at a slack pace and to avoid the effort and discomfort involved in adapting to changed circumstances ('shirking'). 'Traditional conflicts of interest' means the potential interest of agents in diverting the principal's assets to their own use through unfair self-dealing. The third potential divergence of interests are 'positional conflicts': the interest of top corporate managers in maintaining and enhancing their position even at the shareholders' expense. Positional conflicts may occur in a great variety of ways: among other measures, managers can make it particularly difficult to monitor their performance, impose high barriers to their own removal, seek to increase corporate size or 'free cash flow' in order to maximize their power, prestige, and salary rather than to maximize the firm's value. How do both hostile takeovers and institutional monitoring through banks cope with these problems?

To start with, neither device is aimed at prohibiting or lessening problems like shirking and self-dealings if these are problems at all. Most top managements will certainly refrain from *shirking* because their self-esteem is tied to work and accomplishment, and the selection process on the

---

[96] See III.1. above.

[97] A thorough overview has been given recently by R. Romano, 'A Guide to Takeovers: Theory, Evidence, and Regulation' (1992) 9 *Yale Journal on Regulation* 199–80.

[98] Most recently thereto Böhm (n. 29 above).

[99] M. A. Eisenberg, 'The Structure of Corporation Law' (1989) *Columbia Law Review* 1471–4.

management market, as well as the mutual control among agents,[100] tends to exclude this pattern.

Also, most top managers will probably refrain from *unfair self-dealing* because they have internalized the rules of social morality.[101] The takeover market likely has very little impact on such traditional conflicts of interest. A hostile takeover bid does not succeed unless it includes a premium that is significantly above the market price.[102] A hostile bidder must also pay large fees to advisers such as lawyers, investment bankers, and others. Hence, a takeover bid would not be economically justified if the bidder's only aim is to end unfair self-dealing by managers.[103] That means that other legal provisions must deal with this particular conflict of interest, and the same is true for a system which relies on institutions like banks rather than on takeovers as a monitoring device. If a supervisory board finds out about unfair self-dealing of management, that does not happen just because banks have representatives on the board.

Much more interesting are the effects of takeovers and institutional control on *positional conflicts*. It seems clear that takeover activity is, among several other factors, like synergy gains, and so on, also motivated by the inefficiency of the target's management.[104] Here the first question is whether the 'outside' bidder has information about the inefficiency of incumbent management, such as whether the stock price of a firm is lower than that of industry peers because of inefficient management. An 'inside' monitor like a bank may have an informational advantage in this respect. The next question, then, is whether and under which circumstances an outside bidder and an inside institutional monitor will react when they observe inefficiency. Putting to one side for the moment other factors such as synergy gains, and so on, the bidder will only act if a takeover and replacement of incumbent management will produce sufficient gains to justify the huge premium and out-of-pocket transaction costs required—something that does not seem very likely if management is not excessively inefficient.[105] An 'inside' monitor who is represented on the supervisory board can act without incurring these costs. The problem here, however, is that an institutional monitor with personal business interests in the firm has an incentive not to act in cases in which 'inefficiency' of the management, such as seeking to increase corporate size or maximize cash and other resources at the expense of the firm and its shareholders, is favourable to the monitor.[106]

---

[100] Cf. H. R. Varian, 'Monitoring Agents with other Agents' (1990) 146 *Jour. Institutional and Theoretical Economics* 153–74.

[101] See also Eisenberg (n. 99 above), 1473.

[102] M. C. Jensen, 'Takeovers: Their Causes and Consequences' (Winter 1988) 2 *Jour. Ec. Perspectives* 22, 28.

[103] Eisenberg (n. 99 above), 1498.

[104] Jensen (n. 102 above), 28; a recent thorough overview is given by Romano (n. 97 above).

[105] Eisenberg (n. 99), 1497; evidence on management turnovers after takeovers in Romano, (n. 97 above) 129, 130.

[106] Cf. the discussion under IV. 3. above.

Hence, it is not very likely that initiatives for restructuring, disposing of under-performing subsidiaries, or splitting up a conglomerate will come from banks' representatives as long as the firm is not in financial distress.[107]

2. EX-ANTE, INTERIM, AND EX-POST MONITORING

A further difference is remarkable. Institutional and market control by threat of hostile takeover differ also in that control by management replacement by way of a takeover is merely *ex-post control*, whereas institutional control is not. To be sure, the idea of control by the threat of replacement is thought to give management an incentive in advance to try harder. But it works differently from the *ex-ante*, *interim*, and *ex-post monitoring* by an inside institutional monitor. As Eisenberg has pointed out, the threat of takeover will not affect the behaviour of managers who do not realize that they are inefficient, and who do their best as they see it: they are already doing all they can.[108] Especially for such cases a system should be preferred which does not react only after the firm has incurred considerable losses. Identifying competent managers from the beginning, gathering information continuously, and familiarity with the qualifications of management could avoid this.

3. TURNOVER VERSUS 'RELATIONAL' MONITORING

The notion that the governance system which we are examining is based on a long-term relationship between a few depository institutions and the respective firms reveals another contrast to a system in which no 'intermediaries' stand between management and institutional or private shareholders, shareholders who themselves are not active in corporate governance except by 'voting with their feet', especially in the case of a takeover. Private shareholders, like institutional shareholders, may have short 'shareholding horizons'. That may be because they have to sell their shares, in the case of an individual, for purposes of private needs for liquidity or, in the case of, say, a pension fund, because it has to make disbursements to pensioners. Or shares may be sold because the investor or fund manager believes he has identified a mis-priced share, or because the shareholder is offered a higher price than the actual market price by a bidder. Short shareholding horizons and a high turnover in a firm's shares make it difficult for the company to establish meaningful relationships and two-way communications with its shareholders. Short-term investments in a firm's stock not only make it difficult for shareholders to influence a company's affairs, leaving the takeover mechanism as the major corrective device to align the interests of management with those of constantly changing shareholders. It may even lead to the question of the extent to which

---

[107] Cf. also 5 below.
[108] Eisenberg (n. 99 above), 1498.

shareholders who own stock only for a comparably short period of time should be given influence and a say in corporate affairs at all by those who formulate the charter, by-laws, and applicable regulations of the corporation. In a system where proxies are given to 'professional' institutions which remain the same over time irrespective of the turnover in the underlying shares, long-term relationships and two-way communications between management and such interested and responsive proxy-holders can be established, and there may be a greater willingness to give more information and to concede more rights and influence to shareholders represented by such institutions. Of course, the question arises again of whether and to what extent such stable relationships between management and professional proxy-holders with own business or equity interests in the firm are favourable or detrimental to the small investors because of the conflicts of interests or the lack of control in the relationship between these intermediaries and the shareholders, as mentioned above.

4. LONG-TERM VERSUS SHORT-TERM

How do managers behave in a system without stable long-term relationships with their shareholders and the threat of a hostile takeover above their heads? Do they, in order to satisfy the greediness of the investors and to keep the stock prices high, slash expenditures which pay off only in the long term? That has frequently been contended in the literature as well as in the political debate, and Anglo-American scientists and policy-makers are apparently becoming increasingly concerned about the short-term issue.[109]

Research-and-development expenditures of firms in various nations are compared, and specific institutional features like quarterly reports, interim dividends, or the investment policy of pension funds and other institutional investors are blamed for forcing managements to take short-term views. Hostile takeovers are said to contribute to this, too. The plans of the EC Commission to abolish caps on shareholder voting rights and dual class voting (*Höchststimmrechte* and *Mehrfachstimmrechte*) under the Fifth EC Directive has been strongly opposed by German industry, especially on the grounds that (hostile) takeover activity would lead to short-termism and have negative impacts on resource allocation and the German economy as a whole. Is a bank-oriented corporate governance system (without hostile takeovers) advantageous in this respect?

As to hostile takeovers, the debate among economists seems to date to be unsettled. In one version investors are short-sighted and behave myopically to sacrifice long-term benefits for immediate profits. As a consequence, firms that engage in long-term planning and make substantial investments in research and development (R&D) are supposedly undervalued by the

---

[109] See the report in *The Economist*, 27 June 1992, pp. 77–8.

market and become takeover targets.[110] Shleifer and Vishny have argued that the short time-horizon of arbitrage investors, who focus on short-term assets because they are relatively less expensive to arbitrage, may result in market underpricing of a corporation's equity. This phenomenon in turn is said to impose a short time-horizon on managers, who thus avoid long-term investments that depress share prices over the short term and make the corporation vulnerable to a hostile takeover.[111] Stein has developed a formal model in which the threat of takeovers encourages myopic behaviour on the part of managers. A central prediction of this model is that firms which construct barriers to takeovers are able to increase profitable long-term investments such as research and development.[112] There is, however, empirical evidence that firms actually decrease R&D intensity after the introduction of shark repellents, thus failing to support this prediction. These findings suggest that takeover impediments may even reduce incentives to engage in long-term investments.[113] Furthermore, there is evidence that the market responds positively to announcements of increases in R&D and other capital-investment expenditures[114] which, on the other hand, does not mean that informational asymmetries between the markets and firms with respect to such expenditures may not still remain, such as instances where management does not want to communicate commercially sensitive information to the market. And it may well be that managers, in order to avoid undervalued stock which might lure hostile bidders, shift from profitable long-term investment to short-term projects—although this hardly seems to be a good defence against unwanted bids.[115]

As this debate cannot be continued from the outside, would it be possible at least to establish that the corporate governance structure in German large firms supports long-term views of management? Although to my knowledge there are no empirical data available with respect to these large firms, my guess certainly is that management in these firms is encouraged to maintain a focus on the long term: first, managers in these firms are usually elected for five years, and can be removed prior to the expiration of their term only for

---

[110] Cf. Lipton and Rosenblum 'A New System of Corporate Governance: The Quinquennial Election of Directors' (1991) 58 *U. Chicago L. Rev* 208–9 and 213–14 with further references.

[111] Shleifer and Vishny, 'Equilibrium Short Horizons of Investors and Firms' (1990) 80 *Am. Econ. Rev.* 148–53.

[112] J. C. Stein, 'Takeover Threats and Management Myopia' (1988) 96 *Jour. Pol. Economy* 61–79.

[113] L. K. Meulbroek *et al.*, 'Short Repellents and Managerial Myopia: An Empirical Test' (1990) 98 *Jour. Pol. Economy* 1108–17; see also Gordon and Pound, *Governance Matters: An Empirical Study of the Relationship Between Corporate Governance and Corporate Performance* (The Corporate Research Project, JFK School of Govt., Harvard, June 1991); Romano (n. 97 above), 145, with further references.

[114] Han Chan, Martin, and Kensinger, Corporate Research and Development Expenditures and Share Value' (1990) 6 *Jour.Fin. Economics* 255–76; see also Jensen (n. 102 above), 26–7, and P. Marsh, Short-Termism on Trial (1990), with further references.

[115] Cf. Marsh (previous note), 46.

cause.[116] Secondly, the equity holdings of banks, as well as the amount of proxies which are given to them, remain rather stable over time irrespective of the fact that the underlying stock is traded. That means that the monitoring institutions remain the same over time. Thus, long-term projects can be discussed and explained to them, and this discussion is a dialogue rather than merely giving a 'signal' to an anonymous market which will 'mirror' it by pricing the firm's value. On the other side, we must also take into account the incentives of banks as creditors. Banks might, as creditors, prefer projects which are comparatively less profitable.[117]

In short, there is no clear-cut answer to our question as to whether the elements of the governance systems discussed here favour rather than discourage long-term investments with higher net present values.

5. ADAPTABILITY TO CHANGE

It has already been mentioned that, in order to assess the efforts and results of the management, an internal monitoring system must rely on a comparison of actual results with the results of the firm for former periods, the firm's plans, and the results of the firm's competitors within the same industry. This hints at a limitation of such an internal monitoring system where 'outside governance' may have an advantage: a potential outside bidder may have information about, say, a new technology which management and the supervisory board of a firm do not have and which is not yet in use within the industry. Is outside governance by (hostile) takeovers which forces a firm to adapt and react to technological changes a necessary supplement to an internal monitoring system which fails in such cases?

In this respect one should differentiate between the mere dissemination of information on one side and the failure of the incumbent management and supervisory board to exploit it on the other. Hostile takeovers are not necessary to disseminate new information about, for example, new value-increasing technologies. Information can be sold to the firm or shared with it in other ways.

Management and the members of the supervisory board may, however, be reluctant to make changes that raise the market value of the firm, even if the steps that have to be taken to raise the value are known. This may be because the required changes in a declining industry, such as lay-offs, wage reductions, investment cut-backs, or divestitures would harm the employees who are considered more important to the organization than shareholders, or because members of the supervisory board fear the negative publicity or problems with local authorities that would result from such unpopular decisions. In such cases, a hostile bidder could buy the firm and

[116] See n. 62 above.
[117] See IV.3. above.

implement profit-increasing changes against the wishes of both the board and the top management of the target. More generally, takeovers could play a role in bringing about a necessary shift in a firm's policy and in replacing managers whom the supervisory board is unable or unwilling to force to take the necessary steps.

There is interesting empirical evidence especially for this role of hostile takeovers during the merger wave of the eighties in the US. Morck, Shleifer and Vishny examined the circumstances under which a company's poor performance leads to an internal governance response—the incumbent board replacing management—as opposed to the external governance response of a hostile takeover. Tracking a sample of 454 of Fortune 500 companies over the period 1981–5, the authors concluded that an internal governance response is more likely when a company performs poorly compared with industry competitors, but that hostile takeovers are predictable based on poor performance of the entire industry. In cases in which whole industries (for example, airlines, steel, or oil) were performing poorly, corporate boards apparently were reluctant to take the necessary steps to increase the value of the firms by removing irresponsive managers. Instead, this function has been accomplished by hostile takeovers. Apparently takeover organizers have taken advantage of opportunities raised by the ineffectiveness of internal control devices.[118]

VI. Concluding Remarks

This overview and the thoughts expressed above may have shown that the German experience with its corporate governance system in large firms is both ambivalent enough and empirically unexplored to suggest great care in using it as a point of comparison for discussion of these issues or for making policy recommendations in other national contexts. It nevertheless seems safe to say that an institution-based or 'relational' governance system and a market for corporate control focus on different problems for which the other system is less able to offer solutions. Hence they should be considered as supplementary, rather than as mutually exclusive, systems.[119] But this approach, which has also been adopted by the EC Commission in its proposals for the Fifth and Thirteenth Directives on company law leads to new questions: can these two governance systems really be combined, or will the development of a takeover market destroy the existing 'relational' governance system or change it, and if so, with what results? The proposals of the EC Commission for the Fifth and Thirteenth Directives must be further discussed in this light.

[118] Morck, Shleifer, and Vishny, 'Alternative Mechanisms for Corporate Control' (1989) 79 *Amer. Ec. Rev.* 842–52.

[119] Cf. also R. J. Gilson, 'The Political Ecology of Takeovers: Thoughts on Harmonizing the European Corporate Governance Environment', in Hopt and Wymeersch (eds.), *European Takeovers* (1992), 49–75.

Part V
The Role of Litigation

Part V
The Role of Litigation

In this essay Geoff Stapledon analyses the recent important case of *AWA Ltd.* v. *Daniels*,[1] a decision of the Supreme Court of New South Wales. This case examines the application of the duty of care and skill to a board composed of executive and non-executive directors in which the chairman was also the chief executive. It also examines the monitoring role of the board and the important question as to whether auditors sued by a company for negligence can invoke the defence of contributory negligence. Unlike in the US, litigation has had a limited role to play in the UK in dealing with corporate governance issues, partly because here there has been greater reliance on non-statutory codes of conduct, the derivative action is less easily available, and the cost rules are different.[2] However, *AWA Ltd.* v. *Daniels* indicates that nevertheless, in certain circumstances, common-law duties could still have some significance. There remains, however, the important issue of the extent to which these duties can be enforced by persons other than the company itself, an issue which *AWA Ltd.* v. *Daniels* did not have to address.

---

[1] (1992) 7 ACSR 759.

[2] In the USA the normal rule is that each party bears its own legal costs, whereas in the UK costs are borne by the losing party.

11

THE AWA CASE: NON-EXECUTIVE DIRECTORS, AUDITORS, AND CORPORATE GOVERNANCE ISSUES IN COURT

G. P. Stapledon

I. Introduction

The decision of Rogers C.J. in the Commercial Division of the Supreme Court of New South Wales in *AWA Ltd.* v. *Daniels*[1] could hardly have been more timely. In the midst of the lively corporate governance debate in the UK and the US (which incidentally also has been taking place in Australia[2]), we have a case dealing with issues such as the role of auditors and non-executive directors, and indeed at last recognising that the governance structures of large public companies are not as simplistic as the structure envisaged in the companies legislation and statutory model articles of association. This chapter comprises an analysis of those aspects of *AWA* which concern corporate governance. Amongst other things, the analysis questions—and attempts to answer—whether the approach of Rogers C.J. on the relevant issues would and/or should be followed by courts in the UK.

The background facts of *AWA* are quite straightforward. The plaintiff company, AWA, was engaged in the manufacture, import, and export of electronic and electrical products. To minimize the risk associated with foreign-currency fluctuations, it purchased foreign-currency contracts against actual or anticipated import requirements. In late 1985 the plaintiff appointed a young man, K, as its foreign-exchange manager. Shortly thereafter, the plaintiff's foreign exchange (FX) dealings ceased to involve simply risk management. The plaintiff, through the activities of K, engaged in what is known as managed hedging; this activity grew so rapidly that, for the 1986/7 financial year, 25 per cent of the company's budgeted profit was

---

[1] (1992) 7 ACSR 759. The judgment has been appealed to the NSW Court of Appeal.

[2] See e.g. Australian Senate Standing Committee on Legal and Constitutional Affairs, *Report on the Social and Fiduciary Duties and Obligations of Company Directors* (Canberra, 1989); Australian House of Representatives Standing Committee on Legal and Constitutional Affairs, *Report on Corporate Practices and the Rights of Shareholders* (Canberra, 1991).

to come from it. K was so apparently successful that, for the eight months to February 1987, the reported profit from FX dealings (A\$35.5 million) exceeded budget by some 400 per cent. In fact, it later became apparent that K's activities had led the plaintiff to a loss of A\$49.8 million from its FX transactions (which amounted to almost 10 per cent of the company's annual turnover). K had been disclosing principally those contracts showing a profit, whilst not disclosing loss-making contracts and concealing the losses.

The plaintiff company, under the direction of a new board and management, sued its former auditors for damages for *breach of contract*[3], claiming negligence in respect of two audits carried out at the peak of K's activities. The auditors denied any breach of duty, asserted that the plaintiff was guilty of contributory negligence, and issued third-party proceedings seeking contribution against, *inter alia*, the non-executive directors and chief executive/chairman of the plaintiff holding office at the relevant time. The judgment deals only with questions of liability, and covers six broad areas: (i) negligence of the auditors; (ii) causation; (iii) contributory negligence of the plaintiff company; (iv) the possibility of the auditors being relieved, under the equivalent of Section 727 of Companies Act 1985, from liability for negligence; (v) third-party proceedings by the auditors against two banks; (vi) third-party proceedings by the auditors against the plaintiff's non-executive directors and chairman/chief executive. All except issue (v) are of relevance to the corporate governance debate. The five pertinent issues are addressed in Section 2 of this chapter.

Aside from those legal issues, Rogers C.J. also made a number of comments that are of great interest and relevance to the current debate on corporate governance. His Honour recognized the realities of corporate governance within very large public companies, and the associated difficulties for legal concepts developed more than a century ago. This would appear to be the first such acknowledgement by a judge in an English-speaking jurisdiction outside the USA. The matters raised by Rogers C.J., together with three corporate governance issues related to the case but not mentioned by his Honour, are discussed in Section 3.

II. Legal Issues of Relevance to Corporate Governance

2.1. NEGLIGENCE OF THE AUDITORS

The plaintiff's main complaints against the auditors were that they failed to detect and/or report important matters arising from the two audits. The plaintiff alleged that when the auditors *did* uncover deficiencies in the company's recording and supervisory systems relating to FX, they: first, left it too late in informing senior management; and second, failed to inform the

---

[3] The fact that the plaintiff brought its action in contract and not in tort was significant, and potentially costly for the plaintiff, on issues (iii), (iv), (v), and (vi), listed below. See discussion under Subsections 2.3–5.

board, even when directly questioned about FX, either about the inadequate systems of recording and supervision or that senior management had not responded to directions to improve the systems. The plaintiff's case, therefore, rested heavily on it being proven that the recording and control systems of its former management were severely deficient. Rogers C.J. found this to be quite ironic[4] in the light of the plaintiff's strongly argued case that the auditors could not rely on a defence of contributory negligence. For reasons formulated in detail in Subsection 2.3.3, below, it is submitted that there is not, in fact, any irony in the plaintiff's approach.

Rogers C.J. found that the auditors had been *continuously* negligent mainly through omissions during the period from, roughly, June 1986 to March 1987.[5] There were six main 'events' that led to the findings of negligence against the auditors.

(i) During the first audit, in respect of the year ended 30 June 1986, the auditors uncovered weaknesses in internal controls and accounting procedures relating to FX. They were negligent here in not immediately *and formally* taking the matter up with senior management (the audit partner, 'by custom', chose to leave the matter until the 'exit meeting' at the end of October).[6] However, the audit partner did during June and July informally raise the matters with the plaintiff's general manager (who was not a member of the board).

(ii) The audit partner attended a board meeting of AWA on 22 September 1986. The board invited him to the meeting to discuss the FX results in the draft accounts. He negligently failed to tell the directors about the inadequacy of internal controls and reporting systems and about the lack of action in this regard by the general manager. Further, he positively misled the board in his explanation of some of the FX transactions into which K had entered. The audit had discovered 'hedges upon hedges', and this was not revealed to the directors. A major finding of his Honour, which also impacted heavily upon his findings on the cross-claims against the non-executive directors, was that one of the non-executive directors had asked the audit partner whether the board should be aware of anything arising from the audit, and had been given a negative answer. This was negligence.[7]

(iii) The auditors took no further action on the deficiencies until the exit meeting of 28 October. At this meeting of the auditors with AWA's finance manager, internal auditor, and corporate accountant (none of whom were board members), more 'modest suggestions' for improvements were made by the auditors.

(iv) The second audit was not a statutory audit, but rather an investigating

---

[4] See AWA (n. 1 above) (hereafter the page references are to this report) at 768, 833–4.
[5] See AWA (n. 1 above) at 838.
[6] See at 835: 'it was unreasonable and contrary to the defendants' own audit manual . . . to leave the problem in abeyance until the audit exit meeting.'
[7] See AWA (n. 1 above) at 814, 837.

accountant's report in anticipation of a hostile takeover bid for AWA. The improvements suggested by the auditors at the October audit exit meeting still had not been implemented at this time. The audit partner became aware of this during the second audit, but 'did nothing'.[8] As Rogers C.J. noted, 'these defects had been in existence now to the knowledge of the auditors for over eight months', and 'the remedies for them were glaringly obvious'.[9] However, the aspect of the second audit most damaging to the auditors' case was that the audit partner signed a profit statement, which proved to be 'grossly erroneous', before all relevant FX information had been obtained by the auditors. This, too, was negligence.[10]

(v) The auditors met with the general manager, finance manager, and another senior executive of AWA on 13 March 1987. The auditors revealed that the audit had identified what Rogers C.J. described as 'an appalling state of affairs' in the FX area.[11] At the conclusion of the meeting AWA's general manager told the audit partner that they should go to see AWA's chief executive/chairman, which they did the same day. At the meeting with the chief executive, all the matters covered in the earlier meeting between management and the auditors were discussed. Therefore, the chief executive was fully aware of the serious deficiencies in the FX operation as at 13 March 1987, at the latest. It would appear that, as a result of the meetings of 13 March, some piecemeal steps were taken to try to improve the reporting and supervision of the FX operation.

(vi) There was a meeting of the board of AWA on 30 March 1987. The audit partner was asked to attend *specifically to discuss the FX operation*. The employee of the defendant auditors who had carried out the day-to-day audit work of AWA's FX department (for the second audit) prepared a situation summary for the audit partner. It detailed the inadequacy of internal controls and records (of which the audit partner was already fully aware, and about which he had told the chief executive on 13 March). Significantly, it also revealed a 'terrifying exposure to loss', the risk of concealment of large losses, and the opinion that K was speculating beyond the requirement of hedges (seemingly matters new to the audit partner).[12] Regrettably, the audit partner did not raise these matters with the board. He did not even inform the directors of the concerns expressed by him to the chief executive on 13 March. The audit partner's explanation was that he expected that the chief executive would himself have told the other directors.

Rogers C.J. held that in 'normal circumstances' it would be justifiable for an auditor, having drawn the attention of the chief executive/chairman to

[8] At 818.
[9] At 819.
[10] At 838.
[11] At 826.
[12] See at 828.

deficiencies, to assume that the chief executive would in turn bring the matter to the attention of the board.[13] However, there were two vital factors in this case which led his Honour to find that the audit partner was *not* justified in so assuming: the audit partner knew that he had been invited to attend the meeting because the board was 'deeply troubled by the extraordinary profit figures which had been revealed',[14] and 'the attitude and questions from the board suggested that they had not been advised by [the chief executive] of his meeting with the auditors'.[15] In addition, the audit partner was not justified in failing to tell the board about the further matters revealed in the situation summary prepared by his employee. His Honour's basis for this finding seems to be that the additional revelations involved such serious potential losses for the company that the audit partner had no choice but to tell the board himself (again, reinforced by the fact that he was at the board meeting specifically to discuss FX).[16]

2.2. Causation

Rogers C.J. was satisfied that there existed a causative link between the auditors' negligence and the plaintiff's loss. The negligence of the auditors was *a* cause of AWA's loss.[17] The decisive finding in this regard was Rogers C.J.'s acceptance of the evidence of each non-executive director that, 'had he been made aware of the inadequacy of the internal controls and accounting records and that [K] was trading hedges upon hedges he would have sought expert advice, commenced an investigation, dismissed [K], and ensured the installation of proper internal controls'.[18]

Rogers C.J. recalled that the audit partner had failed, when in attendance at the board meeting on 22 September 1986, to draw to the attention of the board the defects in the plaintiff's FX operation. Had the defects been disclosed to the board, and an inquiry been made, it would have been discovered that the approximate value of 'open contracts' was A$750 million. His Honour remarked: 'The FX market would not have moved

---

[13] At 828, 838.

[14] At 828–9.

[15] At 838. One of the non-executive directors 'opened the discussion with [the audit partner] by saying that the directors were really concerned about the whole FX operation. He went on to say that the directors found it hard to believe that AWA could be making profits [from the FX area] of the order which were emerging in the monthly results . . . He went on: "the directors want to be reassured by you that you really have dug into the whole area and that we are not kidding ourselves in accepting these figures . . ." [The audit partner] responded by acknowledging an awareness of the board's concerns and went on: "We have done so (looked very hard at the area of FX operations) and we are satisfied that there is nothing funny about the figures" ' (at 829).

[16] See at 828, 838.

[17] See *Simonius Vischer & Co.* v. *Holt* [1979] 2 NSWLR 322, 346 *per* Samuels J. A. (Moffitt P. & Reynolds J. A. concurring on this matter); *Smith Hogg & Co. Ltd.* v. *Black Sea & Baltic General Insurance Co. Ltd.* [1940] AC 997, 1,007 *per* Lord Wright.

[18] At 839.

with greater rapidity than the directors would have done once they learnt that fact!'[19]

2.3. CONTRIBUTORY NEGLIGENCE

The approach of Rogers C.J. on the matter of contributory negligence is perhaps the most important aspect of the *AWA* case. It is submitted, with respect, that his Honour was incorrect in allowing the auditors' defence of contributory negligence. His Honour chose not to follow a (short) line of Australian authorities. More importantly, though, Rogers C.J. seems to have either overlooked or found outweighed the important policy rationale for not allowing auditors' claims of contributory negligence where the client company is plaintiff. This point is developed in Subsection 2.3.3.

Initially, it is important to appreciate a factor which seems to have strongly influenced the overall approach of his Honour to the matter of contributory negligence. The defendant auditors argued that the plaintiff company's directors and senior management had breached their duties of care and skill (owed to the company) in their implementation and supervision of the FX operation. The auditors submitted that the directors' (alleged) negligence was: (i) negligence of the plaintiff company grounding the auditors' defence of contributory negligence; and (ii) a joint cause of the plaintiff company's loss such that the auditors were entitled to recover contribution (by way of third-party proceedings) from the directors in respect of their share of the damage. It is clear that Rogers C.J. was dissatisfied with the remedy of the auditors in the form of third-party proceedings seeking contribution from the allegedly negligent directors.[20] Indeed, in cases involving large companies and large claims, defendant auditors may decide, in view of the relatively insignificant resources of the directors, to forgo contribution proceedings. Even if third-party proceedings seeking contribution *are* issued against the directors, any orders granting contribution[21] may prove to be of little worth if the directors have insufficient resources to meet the amount ordered recoverable from them. The net result, if no claim for contributory negligence against *the company itself* is possible, is that the 'deep pocket' defendant—the auditor[22]—pays for

---

[19] At 841.

[20] '[T]he solution suggested . . . that relief be sought by the auditors by way of contribution from other persons who may have been negligent is not always appropriate to yield the desired result' (at 856). 'The defendant may indeed seek contribution from other persons responsible for the major damage [but] Why should the whole of the burden of possibly insolvent wrongdoers fall entirely on a well insured, or deep pocket, defendant?' (at 877). See also at 852.

[21] The statute—the UK provision is identical to the NSW provision in this respect—sets the amount of contribution recoverable as: 'such as may be found by the court to be just and equitable having regard to the extent of that person's responsibility for the damage'. See Civil Liability (Contribution) Act 1978, s. 2(1); Law Reform (Married Women and Tortfeasors Act) 1935, s. 6(2) (the 1935 Act applies where relevant damage occurred before 1 Jan. 1979; the 1978 Act where it occurred on or after that date).

[22] Or, more likely, the auditor's professional indemnity insurer.

virtually the entirety of the damage suffered by the company, despite being only one of a number of concurrent wrongdoers responsible for the company's loss. The rule of joint and several liability is of great concern to, *inter alia*, those in the accounting profession.[23] However, for reasons developed later, it is inappropriate to seek, as Rogers C.J. did, to overcome its unsatisfactory effects by allowing auditors a defence of contributory negligence against the claims of client companies.

The auditors' defence of contributory negligence was attacked by the plaintiff on three alternate grounds: (i) as a matter of law, a defence of contributory negligence is not available where the action is one in contract rather than in tort; (ii) whether the action be in contract or tort, a defence of contributory negligence is unavailable to an auditor as against the client company, 'by reason of the nature of an auditor's duties'; (iii) only the negligence of the directors and perhaps the chief executive/chairman could be considered as negligence of AWA; the negligence of senior management could not be imputed to the company. For convenience, argument (ii) is discussed last.

2.3.1. AVAILABILITY OF DEFENCE OF CONTRIBUTORY NEGLIGENCE WHERE ACTION BROUGHT IN CONTRACT

This is not an issue new to the UK. In fact, it has been the subject of judicial pronouncements, a working paper and a report of the Law Commissions,[24] and numerous journal articles.[25] It is, therefore, not proposed to treat it in any detail here. The sections of the New South Wales statute interpreted by Rogers C.J. are in material respects the same as the relevant sections of the UK's Law Reform (Contributory Negligence) Act 1945.[26] Rogers C.J. found, in the face of conflicting Australian authorities, that the NSW provision did not preclude the auditors' defence. As a result of (*a*) recent Court of Appeal authorities on the UK provision,[27] and (*b*) the coincidence

---

[23] See Section 3.5, below.

[24] *Report on Civil Liability—Contribution* (Scot. Law Com. No. 115 (HMSO, Edinburgh, 1988)); *Contributory Negligence as a Defence in Contract* (Law Com. Working Paper, No. 114 (HMSO, London, 1990)).

[25] See e.g. P. S. Marshall and A. J. Beltrami, 'Contributory Negligence: A Viable Defence for Auditors?' [1990] *LMCLQ* 416, 417–20; J. Swanton, 'Contributory Negligence as a Defence to Actions for Breach of Contract' (1981) 55 *Aust. LJ* 278. The topic is, of course, also treated in most of the standard texts.

[26] These provisions were introduced to overcome the common-law rule whereby a finding of contributory negligence wholly defeated the plaintiff's claim. Section 1(1) of the UK Act states: 'Where any person suffers damage as the result partly of his own fault and partly of the fault of any other person or persons, a claim in respect of that damage shall not be defeated by reason of the fault of the person suffering the damage, but the damages recoverable in respect thereof shall be reduced to such extent as the court thinks just and equitable having regard to the claimant's share in the responsibility for the damage . . .' The important term is 'fault', which is defined in s. 4 as 'negligence, breach of statutory duty or other act or omission which gives rise to a liability in tort . . .'

[27] *Forsikringsaktieselskapet Vesta* v. *Butcher* [1989] AC 852; *Tennant Radiant Heat Ltd.* v. *Warrington Development Corp.* [1988] 1 EGLR 41, 43. In *Vesta*, the Court of Appeal followed

of auditors' liability in contract and tort, where there has been a breach of an implied term to exercise reasonable care and skill,[28] it is submitted that the same result would—and should[29]—be reached in the UK.

2.3.2. NEGLIGENCE OF SENIOR MANAGEMENT AS NEGLIGENCE OF THE COMPANY

The auditors, of course, argued that AWA's directors and chief executive/chairman were negligent and that their acts were the acts of the company. The plaintiff did not dispute that any negligence on the part of the directors and chief executive would be negligence of AWA[30] and that, should the plaintiff's two other arguments[31] fail, AWA would by this means be guilty of contributory negligence. However, the auditors also argued that AWA's senior management, below board level, had been negligent and that this could found a defence of contributory negligence on the grounds, either (*a*) that the negligent acts and omissions of senior management were to be taken as the acts of the company, or (*b*) that the acts and omissions of senior management, in the course of their employment, could be imputed to AWA such that AWA would be responsible vicariously. The plaintiff did not deny that senior management had been negligent,[32] but took issue with both grounds (*a*) and (*b*).

Rogers C.J. preferred the auditors' arguments to those of the plaintiff in respect of both grounds (*a*) and (*b*). On (*a*), his Honour said:

As a general rule, members of the board are the directing mind and will of a corporation and their negligence will be taken to be that of the company. If, because they delegated their powers, except for the general guidelines provided, to senior management and as a consequence they were not the directing mind and will of the company then those charged with the conduct of FX operations must have been. [Here] the board had left the entirety of the FX operation to be structured and implemented by management. In the circumstances, the actions and omissions of

---

Hobhouse J.'s first instance holding that the Act applies to claims brought in contract if 'the defendant's liability in contract is the same as his liability in the tort of negligence independently of the existence of any contract': [1986] 2 Lloyd's Rep. 179, 196.

[28] *Caparo Industries plc* v. *Dickman* [1989] QB 653, 682 *per* Bingham L. J. (not disputed in the House of Lords); *Employers Corporate Investments Pty. Ltd.* v. *Cameron* (1977) 3 ACLR 120, 125–6; *Arthur Young & Co.* v. *WA Chip & Pulp Co. Pty. Ltd.* [1989] WAR 100, 102–3 *per* Burt C. J.; 114–15 *per* Brinsden J.; *Esso Petroleum Co. Ltd.* v. *Mardon* [1976] 1 QB 801, 819–20 *per* Lord Denning M.R.

[29] As Rogers C.J. stated, at 877: 'There is absolutely no reason, in principle, why, now that it is recognised that, in many cases, there is concurrent liability in contract and tort a defendant, if sued in tort, should be entitled to claim contributory negligence on the part of the plaintiff but not when the plaintiff sues in contract.'

[30] In the sense of 'primary' as opposed to 'vicarious' negligence.

[31] i.e. the arguments discussed in Subsections 2.3.1 and 2.3.3.

[32] In fact, as noted by Rogers C.J. at 768 and 834, the plaintiff went to great lengths, in order to develop its case against the auditors, to show how inefficient and incompetent its former management had been in relation to the FX operation.

management are properly to be taken as acts of the plaintiff itself and, *if otherwise they qualify*, to be taken into account as acts of contributory negligence.[33]

It is submitted that Rogers C.J. was correct in finding that the acts and omissions of AWA's senior management were in law the acts of the company itself.[34]

His Honour found, alternatively, that neither precedent nor principle stood in the way of a finding that it is possible to impute the negligence of senior management to a company so as to found a defence on contributory negligence.[35] In so doing, his Honour rejected the plaintiff's argument that 'the principles of vicarious liability, which are engaged in relation to acts and omissions of employees of a company when the company is sought to be made liable, are not applicable when, as against the company plaintiff, it is alleged that the company has been guilty of contributory negligence'.[36] This argument is, as found by Rogers C.J., lacking in support both in terms of authority and principle. Atiyah points out that, although the point appears never to have been argued in an English case, it has long been assumed in many cases that 'a master is vicariously responsible for the contributory negligence of his servants acting in the course of their employment'.[37] And, although some commentators find the concept of 'imputed contributory negligence' to be lacking in policy support even in the case of master and servant (it used to apply more broadly),[38] the better view is that, in light of today's apportionment legislation,[39] the doctrine is 'not seriously objectionable'.[40]

To summarize, therefore, it is submitted that senior management's negligent acts and omissions in *AWA* were properly construed as acts of the company itself. However, if this view be wrong because management was not the directing mind and will of the company in this instance, authority

---

[33] At 850–1, (emphasis added).

[34] *Lennard's Carrying Co. Ltd.* v. *Asiatic Petroleum Co. Ltd.*. [1915] AC 705, 713 *per* Viscount Haldane L. C.; *Arthur Guinness, Son & Co. (Dublin) Ltd.* v. *The Freshfield (The Lady Gwendolen)* [1965] P 294, 355–6 *per* Winn L. J.; *Tesco Supermarkets Ltd.* v. *Nattrass* [1972] AC 153, esp. at 170–1 *per* Lord Reid.

[35] At 851–3.

[36] At 833.

[37] P. S. Atiyah, *Vicarious Liability in the Law of Torts* (London, 1967), 409. As noted by Atiyah, ibid., dicta of the House of Lords in *Mills* v. *Armstrong (The Bernina)* (1888) 13 App. Cas. 1 removed any uncertainty.

[38] See e.g. C. D. Baker, *Tort* (5th edn., London, 1991), 193: 'the basis of policy underlying the doctrine of vicarious liability is that the servant's liability is transferred to a financially solvent defendant [i.e. the employer], whereas imputed negligence affects the case where the employer is the injured party, and there is no reason of policy requiring financially solvent plaintiffs to meet part of their own loss out of their own pockets.'

[39] Whereby a finding of contributory negligence no longer acts as a complete defence to the plaintiff's claim: see n. 26 above. It is easy to see why, when the common law rule as to the effect of contributory negligence applied, the doctrine of imputed contributory negligence was considered by many to be somewhat offensive.

[40] Atiyah (n. 37 above), 410.

and principle support Rogers C.J.'s alternative finding that management's actions could be imputed to the company. These findings assume real importance when related to his Honour's later finding that the plaintiff's non-executive directors had not been negligent. Although the chief executive/chairman *was* held negligent, his negligence was less extensive than that of those members of senior management who were responsible for controlling the FX operation. If it had been found that only the negligence of the chief executive/chairman, and not also that of the other relevant members of senior management, was to be treated as contributory negligence of the company, the apportionment of blame to the company *vis-à-vis* the auditors would have been less.[41]

2.3.3. AVAILABILITY OF CONTRIBUTORY NEGLIGENCE AS A DEFENCE FOR AUDITORS

The issue of whether *as a matter of principle* an auditor ought to be able to utilize a defence of contributory negligence against a corporate client plaintiff is one of the most important aspects of the *AWA* case. It is a very important issue *per se*, but it assumed added significance in *AWA* due to Rogers C.J.'s findings on the matters discussed in Subsections 2.3.1 and 2.3.2 above.

There appears not to be any English authority on the matter,[42] but Rogers C.J. noted that: 'There is a respectable body of authority [in Australia and the US] for the proposition that, whether the action be laid in contract or in tort, a defence of contributory negligence against a company, based on the allegedly negligent conduct of a servant or director, is not available to an auditor whose duty it is to check the conduct of such persons.'[43]

The earliest relevant Australian case is *Pacific Acceptance Corporation Ltd.* v. *Forsyth*.[44] The defendant auditors seem to have conceded that a defence of contributory negligence was not available where the client company's action was one in contract. The auditors sought relief from liability pursuant to Section 365 of the Companies Act 1961 (NSW)—the equivalent of the UK Companies Act 1985, Section 727.[45] Before opining that,'in reality', the auditors' reliance upon Section 365 'was an attempt to raise contributory negligence whilst conceding that it was not open', Moffitt J. stated:

I do not find merit in a submission which in effect is that, although the auditors were

---

[41] The judgment under discussion did not deal with the question of apportionment. On the apportionment issue see (1993) 9 ACSR 383.

[42] See, however, *De Meza and Stuart* v. *Apple, Van Straten, Shena and Stone* [1974] 1 Lloyd's Rep. 508, where Brabin J. held the plaintiff firm of solicitors contributorily negligent, where the solicitors had sued a firm of auditors (on appeal, Roskill L.J. expressly declined to comment on Brabin J.'s finding on contributory negligence: [1975] Lloyd's Rep. 498, 509).

[43] At 842.

[44] (1970) 92 WN (NSW) 29.

[45] See discussion under Subsection 2.4, below.

negligent, they should be excused because the directors also were negligent. To excuse an auditor because the directors or management were also at fault, and in particular to excuse him when he failed to perform his duty with independence and to check on management and the board, would be to apply s. 365 to negate a fundamental reason for the appointment of the auditor. If there is a complaint that other officers of the company also failed in their duty and contributed thereby to the loss, then the proper course is to take such action, if any, as in the circumstances is open to the auditor for contribution from the officers at fault so that the company's loss can be shared between those proved at fault after precise allegations and proper investigation, rather than being cut down or excused to the detriment of the company because others as well as the auditor were at fault.[46]

In *Simonius Vischer & Co.* v. *Holt & Thompson*,[47] where the defendant auditors *did* argue contributory negligence, Moffitt P. in the NSW Court of Appeal said, obiter:

Where the action for professional negligence is against an auditor, it is difficult to see how a finding of contributory negligence, according to usual concepts, could be made. If, as where the audit is of a public company, the audit contract or the undertaking of an audit is found to impose a duty to be exercised so as to safeguard the interests of shareholders, it is difficult to see how the conduct of any servant or director could constitute the relevant negligence, so as to defeat the claim against the auditor, whose duty is to check the conduct of such persons and, where appropriate, report it to the shareholders.[48]

The reasoning of Moffitt P. in *Simonius Vischer* has been applied in subsequent Australian cases.[49]

The question whether a defence of contributory negligence against a corporate client is available to auditors has arisen in many US cases.[50] Essentially, there are two lines of US authority: the *Craig* v. *Anyon*[51] line, where a defence of contributory negligence has been allowed; and the *National Surety Corporation* v. *Lybrand*[52] line, where such a defence has normally not been allowed. Both *Craig* v. *Anyon* and *National Surety* are decisions of the Appellate Division of the New York Supreme Court.

---

[46] At 124–5.
[47] [1979] 2 NSWLR 322.
[48] At 329–30.
[49] *WA Chip & Pulp Co. Pty. Ltd.* v. *Arthur Young & Co.* (1987) 12 ACLR 25, 43–4 (Pidgeon J.), [1989] WAR 100, 104 (WA Full Court: Burt C.J., who dissented on other grounds; the majority did not need to discuss this point); *Walker* v. *Hungerfords* (1987) 44 SASR 532, 553 (Bollen J.), (1988) 49 SASR 93, 96 (SA Full Court: King C.J., with whom Jacobs & Millhouse JJ. concurred).
[50] See: Note, 'The Legal Responsibility of Public Accountants', 35 *Yale LJ* 76 (1925); C. S. Hawkins, 'Professional Negligence Liability of Public Accountants' 12 *Vanderbilt Law Review* 797 (1959), 809–11; E. R. Dinallo, 'The Peculiar Treatment of Contributory Negligence in Accountants' Liability Cases' 65 *New York University Law Review* 329 (1990); T. M. Dodd, 'Accounting Malpractice and Contributory Negligence: Justifying Disparate Treatment Based Upon the Auditor's Unique Role' 80 *Georgetown Law Journal* 909 (1992).
[51] 208 NYS 259 (1925); affirmed without reasons: 152 NE 431 (1926).
[52] 9 NYS 2d 554 (1939).

Although the above discussion suggests that the cases are inconsistent, the court in the latter case did not find *Craig* v. *Anyon* to be wrongly decided. Rather, *Craig* v. *Anyon* was distinguished. It is the ground of distinction elucidated in *National Surety* that has come to be widely accepted as the law in US jurisdictions: 'Negligence of the employer is a defence only when it has contributed to the accountant's failure to perform his contract and to report the truth.'[53] The *National Surety* approach, therefore, involves a general denial of the defence. The defence can be pleaded successfully only in exceptional circumstances. However, Moffitt P. in *Simonius Vischer*, and the other Australian courts adopting Moffitt P.'s approach, did not acknowledge that the defence would be available in the exceptional circumstances set out in *National Surety*, and it is contended that the defence should be denied even in such circumstances.[54] To explain this contention, it is necessary (*a*) to extract the rationale of the court in *National Surety* for holding that in the usual case an auditor may not rely upon a defence of contributory negligence against a corporate client, and (*b*) to contrast this with the reasoning of Moffitt P. in *Simonius Vischer*.

The rationale of the court in *National Surety* is found in the statement that '[a]ccountants . . . are commonly employed for the very purpose of detecting defalcations which the employer's negligence has made possible'.[55] However, it is the contention of this chapter that this is not the fundamental justification for denying auditors the defence of contributory negligence. *The* policy argument for denying the defence to auditors is presented—concisely—in the judgment of Moffitt P. in *Simonius Vischer*, and is explained in greater detail in the next paragraph. It is not argued that the rationale of *National Surety*, and like reasoning such as '[t]he widespread availability of such a defence would devalue the auditor's responsibilities and duties',[56] are not valid points. That these would be weighty arguments in favour of a restriction on the availability of the defence, were the defence otherwise available, is accepted. The point sought to be made is that these arguments tell only half the story. They fail to identify the importance in this matter of the relationship between the auditors and the collective body of shareholders.

The House of Lords has recently, and emphatically, held that the principal underlying purpose of the appointment and work of auditors is to provide the collective body of shareholders with information upon which to make an informed appraisal of the stewardship of the company's directors

---

[53] At 563. This reasoning is not to be found on the face of the judgment in *Craig* v. *Anyon*. None the less, as noted by Dodd (n. 50 above), 926, '[d]uring the last half century, a majority of [US] courts addressing this issue have followed the holding of *National Surety*'.

[54] The one exceptional area where the defence may sometimes be pleaded successfully is where the plaintiff is a small closely-held company. See discussion below, in the final two paragraphs of this subsection.

[55] At 563.

[56] Marshall and Beltrami (n. 25 above), 421.

and management.[57] The vital distinction to be drawn when considering the availability to auditors of the defence of contributory negligence—and which was not drawn either by Rogers C.J. in *AWA* or by the American courts in the cases discussed—is between the different manifestations of 'the company'. First, there is the board of directors or, as in *AWA*, the senior management whose negligent acts and omissions are attributed to the company (the acts and omissions upon which the auditors seek to rely as evidencing contributory negligence). Secondly, there is the collective body of shareholders primarily for whose benefit, according to *Caparo*, the auditors have carried out their duties. Allowing auditors to claim contributory negligence in respect of the negligence of directors or management would serve to decrease or even possibly wipe out the award payable to 'the company' in respect of the auditors' negligence. The 'losers' in the scenario would be the shareholders, 'the residual claimants on the firm's income stream'.[58] But is this not an unsustainable result given that the principal purpose of the audit is to help to enable the shareholders collectively to make an informed appraisal of the stewardship of the directors and management?

Returning briefly to *National Surety*, if the New York Supreme Court's rationale—that part of the auditors' job is detection of defalcations made possible by directors' negligence—*were* the fundamental justification for denying the defence, one can easily see how the defence could be granted exceptionally where 'an intervening circumstance ... such as the employer's own misconduct ... prevent[ed] the [auditor] from properly performing its duties'.[59] That is, by failing to recognize *explicitly* the

---

[57] *Caparo Industries plc* v. *Dickman* [1990] 2 AC 605, 626 *per* Lord Bridge, 630–1 *per* Lord Oliver, 661–2 *per* Lord Jauncey. Many would argue that the auditor's role is wider. See e.g. R. Baxt, 'The Liability of Auditors—The Pendulum Swings Back' (1990) 8 *Company and Securities Law Journal* 249; C. Humphrey, S. Turley, and P. Moizer, *The Audit Expectations Gap in the UK* (Research Board, Institute of Chartered Accountants in England and Wales, Sept. 1992); Auditing Practices Board, *The Future Development of Auditing* (London, Nov. 1992); cf. Committee on the Financial Aspects of Corporate Governance, *Report* (London, 1 Dec. 1992), app. 6.

[58] Terminology from D. R. Fischel, 'The Corporate Governance Movement' 35 *Vanderbilt Law Review* 1,259, 1,262 (1982). The discussion in the text should not be construed as resting the denial of the defence *solely* upon the fact that it is the shareholders rather than the directors who 'lose' if auditors are allowed to claim contributory negligence. This alone is not the basis for denying the defence. That it cannot be is demonstrated by considering the simple case of a negligent act of a company's board which harms a third party. The company could not argue as a defence that, although it was the company in the form of the board that harmed the plaintiff, the plaintiff should not obtain relief because it would be the company in the form of the collective body of shareholders, rather than the board, that would suffer if the plaintiff were to be awarded damages. The policy reason for denying the defence rests upon the following: (i) as affirmed in *Caparo*, the principal purpose of the audit is to assist the general meeting in assessing the board's stewardship; *and* (ii) allowing the defence would be detrimental to the general body of shareholders.

[59] *Holland* v. *Arthur Andersen & Co.* 469 NE 2d 419, 427 (1984). If the company's negligent conduct *has* so hindered the auditors, the court may take this into account in determining whether or not the auditors were negligent. As Marshall and Beltrami (n. 25 above) at 423, point

importance in this matter of the relationship between the auditors and the collective body of shareholders, such an exceptional allowing of the defence seems acceptable. However, once the reasoning of their Lordships in *Caparo* is taken into account, and applied to the contributory-negligence problem, it becomes clear that the defence should be no more available in the '*National Surety* exceptional circumstances' than anywhere else.

The approach supported in this subsection necessarily is at odds with that of some other commentators. It has been argued that 'the contributory negligence defence should be as available to accountants as it is to other professionals'.[60] Adoption of the reasoning in this subsection of necessity involves refutation of this argument. The case of auditors can be contrasted to those of, for example, a solicitor sued in negligence by a client and a doctor sued by a patient. In the latter cases, the client/patient guilty of contributory negligence is the same person (*a*) for whose benefit the solicitor/doctor was acting, and (*b*) who suffered loss or injury as a result of the solicitor's/ doctor's negligence. In the case of auditors, however, the company management guilty of negligent conduct is distinct from the party (the collective body of shareholders), (*a*) primarily for whose benefit the auditors were acting, and (*b*) that suffered loss as a result of the auditors' negligence.[61]

As mentioned, Rogers C.J. upheld the auditors' defence of contributory negligence on the facts. His Honour found that the negligence of AWA's senior management was contributory negligence of AWA on the bases: (i) that instances of management's negligence which, 'while leading to the same loss as did the auditors' negligence, were not matters for the auditors at all',[62] could be considered contributory negligence; or, alternatively (ii) that on the *National Surety* test, many of management's acts and omissions hindered the auditors and contributed to their failure to perform properly their contract. His Honour placed weight on the following:

[T]he primary complaints of the plaintiff are failure on the part of the auditors to report on the insufficiency and inappropriateness of the plaintiff's internal controls. Now that was not the principal purpose of the audit. It was something that the auditors discovered, in the course of preparing to do their audit, and which . . . they should have drawn to the attention of the plaintiff's board.[63]

out: 'Although the duty of the auditor remains the same, the activities of the company have a direct effect on the performance of that duty.' The authors say (ibid.) of the New Zealand case of *Nelson Guarantee Corporation Ltd.* v. *Hodgson* [1958] NZLR 609: 'In view of the maladministration of the company, although the auditors delivered what might *in other circumstances have been a negligent report*, they were found not to have breached the standard of the reasonably competent and cautious auditor' [emphasis added].

[60] Dinallo (n. 50 above), 331; later, Dinallo criticizes the 'peculiar treatment of auditors', believing that this may be due to 'a belief that the accounting profession is somehow unique' (at 351–2). See too Marshall and Beltrami (n. 25 above), 422: 'there is nothing out of the ordinary or unusual about the situation of auditors such that the normal principles of contributory negligence do not apply.'

[61] See also Dodd (n. 50 above), 930–3.

[62] At 854.   [63] At 846.

The complaint is not that the auditors have failed to detect some error or misstatement in the accounts. Rather, the failure is to report on matters crucial, but ancillary, to the audit, namely, the state of internal controls and records and books.[64]

It is submitted that neither of Rogers C.J.'s grounds described in (i) and (ii), above, is supportable. Each is overridden by the policy argument for denying the defence. Further, the fact that the auditors' negligence related to matters ancillary to the audit does not alter the position. Although ancillary to the audit, the relevant matters were of such a nature that it was part of the auditors' duty of care to report upon them. They failed to do so, and were found negligent. Here, the policy argument for denying the defence of contributory negligence to auditors *vis-à-vis* corporate client plaintiffs applies none the less.

However, in situations such as in *AWA*, it is open to the auditors to issue a third-party notice[65] against any negligent company officer(s) seeking contribution in respect of the officer's breach of duty of care and skill owed to the company. In theory at least, this option allows the auditors to overcome the unsatisfactory aspects of the rule of joint and several liability. Any company officers liable in respect of the same damage as that caused by the auditors' negligence could be served with a third-party notice, and ordered to pay contribution to the auditors. Importantly, in contrast to the scenario which would ensue if it were possible to plead successfully a defence of contributory negligence, the third-party procedure (in theory at least) mitigates the effects of the rule of joint and several liability *without* causing detriment to the general body of shareholders. The policy argument for denying to auditors the defence of contributory negligence does not, therefore, apply in the case of such third-party proceedings. In practice, though, the option of bringing third party proceedings may prove to be of little assistance to the auditors, as the officers may have insufficiently deep pockets to meet any contribution ordered recoverable from them. Unfortunately for auditors, the courts should not redress this inequity by allowing claims of contributory negligence against client companies because, given the primary purpose of auditors' appointment and functions, as a matter of policy it would be indefensible to do so.

There seems, however, to be room for an exception in the case of companies where there is no shareholder body distinct from the negligent and/or wrongdoing directors. In small quasi-partnerships, as opposed to companies with a distinct shareholder body, the purpose of the audit is much less the assisting of an informed appraisal by shareholders of the stewardship of the directors.[66] In a Canadian case, *H. E. Kane Agencies Ltd.*

---

[64] At 849.

[65] See Rules of the Supreme Court 1965, Ord. 16, and Civil Liability (Contribution) Act 1978, s. 1(1). It was this course that the defendant auditors ultimately took against AWA's chairman/chief executive (see n. 78 below).

[66] This is evidenced by the fact that certain small companies in Australia can choose not to appoint an auditor: Corporations Law, s. 326; cf. the position in the UK, where this is not

v. *Coopers & Lybrand*,[67] the defendant auditors pleaded successfully a defence of contributory negligence where the plaintiff company was a closely held family company, and appears to have had no shareholders other than those involved in management. Hoyt J. referred to Moffitt J.'s comments in *Pacific Acceptance* and *Simonius Vischer*, and continued:

While these remarks may be appropriate in situations involving public companies or in the case of third party actions such as investors or purchasers who rely on these [auditors'] statements I think that contributory negligence is appropriate in circumstances like this . . . Although the business was incorporated it was run almost exclusively by Harold Kane who acted as president, general manager and bookkeeper. At that time his son Charles Kane had full responsibility, apart from accounting functions, for the travel agency.[68]

The exceptional recognition of a defence of contributory negligence, where a closely held company has sued its auditors for breach of duty of care, probably is best construed as analogous to the court piercing the corporate veil. In cases such as *Kane*, where the directors who acted negligently are also the only shareholders in the company, there would appear to be no policy grounds for an unqualified denial to auditors of the defence of contributory negligence. In appropriate circumstances the defence should be granted. Appropriate circumstances would seem to be those covered by the *National Surety* test: where the company's negligence has contributed to the auditors' failure to perform its contract.

2.4. RELIEF FROM LIABILITY

The auditors sought relief under Section 1,318 of the Australian Corporations Law from their liability for breach of contract. Section 1,318 is the equivalent of the UK Companies Act 1985, Section 727. Rogers C.J. rejected the plaintiff's contention that the section is available only in claims for breach of tortious, statutory, or fiduciary obligations and not available in an action for damages for breach of contract. His Honour then held that if he

---

possible except for dormant companies: Companies Act 1985, s. 250 (but see EEC Council Directive 78/660, art. 51(2); Department of Trade and Industry, *Consultative Document: Accounting and Audit Requirements of Small Firms* (London, 1985); 'Audit Law Remit May be Reduced', *Financial Times*, 23 Nov. 1992, p. 8, where it was reported that the UK government is considering dropping the audit requirement at least for companies with turnover below the VAT registration threshold).

[67] (1983) 44 NBR 2d 374.

[68] At 391. Marshall and Beltrami (n. 25 above), 424–5, interpret the distinction drawn in *Kane* as follows: 'where the company is a small, closely held company [t]he company's system of control is often dependent on the close involvement of the directors, who are better acquainted with the employees and officers. If there is fraud by an employee of the company, a director may be more likely to have his suspicions aroused than would his counterpart in a large, anonymous, public company.' With respect, it is submitted that Hoyt J. based the distinction between the small company at hand and public companies upon the fact that in *Kane* there was no separate shareholder body (or indeed 'investors or purchasers') primarily for whose benefit—had there been such a body—the auditors' work would have been performed.

was 'wrong . . . as to the availability of a defence of contributory negligence . . . the same facts . . . would enliven the operation of' Section 1318.[69] Although it may well be that '[t]he section is appropriate to operate as a provision for the proper allocation of fault',[70] it is submitted that the reasoning expounded in the previous subsection applies equally to deny auditors the use of this provision in claims brought against them by a client company. Moffitt J. expressed this view in *Pacific Acceptance*.[71]

2.5. AUDITORS' CLAIMS AGAINST AWA'S NON-EXECUTIVE DIRECTORS AND CHAIRMAN/CHIEF EXECUTIVE

The auditors filed 'cross-claims' against the plaintiff's former non-executive directors and chief executive/chairman, seeking contribution. This is equivalent procedurally to the issuing of third-party notices pursuant to Order 16 of the Rules of the Supreme Court 1965.

In this area, two preliminary issues confronted Rogers C.J. which, given a statutory amendment in 1978, would not arise in the UK. For this reason, these matters receive only brief treatment. First, the NSW statute governing contribution is, in relevant respects, identical to the provisions in the Law Reform (Married Women and Tortfeasors) Act 1935. Section 6(1)(c) of the UK Act, and Section 5(1)(c) of the NSW Act,[72] refer to damage suffered 'as a result of a tort' and to 'tortfeasor[s]'. It was argued for the directors that a claim for contribution cannot be made under the Act by a defendant who has been sued in contract. Finding that the auditors had a concurrent liability in contract and tort, Rogers C.J. followed a short line of Australian authority which has adopted Glanville Williams' view[73] that a defendant sued in contract, but concurrently liable in contract and tort, is a 'tortfeasor' within the meaning of the Act.[74] As a matter of policy this is defensible; however, it is less clear that the legislature intended the Act to be utilized in this way.[75]

---

[69] At 856.

[70] Ibid.

[71] See the passage quoted in the text accompanying n. 46, above. Rogers C.J. recognized the conflict with the approach of Moffitt J. (ibid.).

[72] The Law Reform (Miscellaneous Provisions) Act 1946 (NSW).

[73] G. L. Williams, *Joint Torts and Contributory Negligence* (London, 1951), 129.

[74] At 856–8.

[75] The common-law rule was that contribution was disallowed unless the defendant and the person from whom contribution was sought were liable to a 'common demand': *Merryweather* v. *Nixan* (1799) 8 TR 186; *Weld-Blundell* v. *Stephens* [1920] AC 956, 976 *per* Lord Dunedin. The Law Revision Committee, whose report led to the 1935 UK provision, recommended the overturning of the common-law rule in respect of tort: *Third Interim Report* (Cmd. 4637 (1934)), para. 7. The Committee suggested that consideration be given later to extending the reform to other areas of the law. In 1977 the Law Commission recommended changes that are reflected in the 1978 Act (see text): *Law of Contract, Report on Contribution* (Law Com. No. 79 (HMSO, London, 1977)). The Commission's recommendations were based on the belief that contribution was not possible under the 1935 Act unless the relevant wrongdoers were liable in tort (paras. 7, 33, 58, 81(a), (d), (f)). Further, the NSW Law Reform Committee is currently considering legislative change for the stated reason that, under s. 5(1)(c) of the NSW Act, no

In any event, the 1935 UK Act now applies only where the relevant damage occurred before 1 January 1979. The Civil Liability (Contribution) Act 1978,[76] Section 1(1), which applies to claims arising on or after 1 January 1979, puts the matter beyond doubt: 'any person liable in respect of any damage suffered by another person may recover contribution from any other person liable in respect of the same damage (whether jointly with him or otherwise).'

Secondly, the non-executive directors argued that no claim for contribution could be made against them as, even if they had breached their duty of care and skill, they were not 'tortfeasors' under Section 5(1)(c) of the NSW Act. The directors' main argument was that the duty of care and skill is imposed by equity rather than common law, and that a director cannot be sued for liquidated damages at common law in an action for negligence. Not surprisingly, Rogers C.J. found that the weight of judicial and academic opinion favours the view that the duty of care and skill is a common-law duty.[77] This interesting point simply would not arise in the UK because Section 1(1) of the 1978 Act amply covers breach of any of the duties imposed on directors.

Rogers C.J. found that the non-executive directors had *not*, but that the chief executive/chairman *had*, been negligent.[78] His Honour noted the general proposition of *Re City Equitable Fire Insurance Co. Ltd.*[79] that a director need not exhibit, in the performance of his or her duties, a greater degree of skill than may reasonably be expected from a person of his or her knowledge and experience. His Honour also noted that what constitutes the proper performance of the duties of a director of a particular company traditionally has been considered to be dependent upon: (i) the actual knowledge and experience of the director; (ii) the nature and extent of the company's business; and (iii) the distribution of responsibilities in the company in question.[80]

'right of contribution is available where the liability of one or both of the wrongdoers arises other than in tort': *Annual Report* (Sydney, 1991), para. 4.20.

[76] An Act which applies only in England, Wales, and Northern Ireland. The legislation applying in Scotland is the Law Reform (Miscellaneous Provisions) (Scotland) Act 1940.

[77] And there would appear to be little doubt that a director *can* be sued for liquidated damages at common law in an action for negligence: see e.g. *Dorchester Finance Co. Ltd.* v. *Stebbing* [1989] BCLC 498; L. S. Sealy, 'The Director as Trustee' [1967] *CLJ* 83, 102, n. 6.

[78] Initially, his Honour proposed to take the chief executive's negligence into account as part of the contributory negligence of AWA. However, in later proceedings (reported at (1993) 9 ASCR 383) Rogers C.J. accepted that the defendant auditors had a right of *election* as to whether (1) to have the chief executive's negligence treated as part of the contributory negligence of AWA, or (2) to instead claim contribution from the chief executive in respect of his share of the responsibility for the plaintiff's loss. The auditors elected option (2). His Honour apportioned responsibility as: defendant auditors: 80 per cent; plaintiff: 20 per cent (this being the contributory negligence of AWA's senior management). The chief executive was ordered to pay, as contribution to the auditors, an amount of 10 per cent of the 80 per cent of AWA's loss for which the auditors were liable.

[79] [1925] Ch. 407, 428.

[80] At 864. See *Re City Equitable*, ibid., at 426.

Speaking of non-executive directors, his Honour said that 'there is no objective standard of the reasonably competent company director to which they may aspire. The very diversity of companies and the variety of business endeavours do not allow of a uniform standard.'[81] As far as the common-law duty of care and skill is concerned, these comments apply equally to executive directors: there is no uniform standard. Under the traditional view of the common-law duty of skill and care, the standard of skill required of *both* executive and non-executive directors (*a*) depends on the nature of the company and the distribution of responsibilities within it, and (*b*) is 'partly objective (the standard of the reasonable man) and partly subjective (the reasonable man is deemed to have the knowledge and experience of the particular individual)'.[82] However, his Honour recognized that, in the case of an executive director, the contract of service will either expressly or impliedly require the director to 'exercise the care and skill to be expected of a person in that position'.[83] Thus, in contrast to the traditional position under the common-law duty of care and skill, contractual principles require an executive director to exercise the skill and care of a reasonable executive director in the circumstances of the company in question. Under the contractual duty, whilst the nature of the company's business and the distribution of responsibilities between the directors and other officers still will be relevant considerations, the actual knowledge and experience of the executive director in question would appear to be irrelevant. However, Rogers C.J. noted counsel's submission that 'no claim was made against [H], based on his office as chief executive, for any breach of contract'.[84] Thus, the chief executive's conduct was examined—and found to have been deficient—under the common-law standard of skill and care.

Rogers C.J. adopted the two other well-known propositions of *Re City Equitable*:[85] (i) a director is not bound to give continuous attention to the affairs of the company; the duties are of an intermittent nature to be performed at periodic board meetings and at meetings of any committee of the board upon which the director happens to be placed (applying to non-executives only); (ii) a director is justified in trusting some other official to perform honestly all duties that, having regard to the exigencies of business, the intelligent devolution of labour and the articles of association, may properly be left to such an official.[86] As a result of these principles, especially (i), it is commonly said that directors are much more likely to breach their duty as a result of positive action as opposed to a failure to act.[87] Certainly,

---

[81] At 867.
[82] L. C. B. Gower, *Principles of Modern Company Law* (5th edn., London, 1992), 587.
[83] At 867, confirming the textbook writers' view that *Lister* v. *Romford Ice and Cold Storage Co. Ltd.* [1957] AC 555 entails an objective duty of care for executive directors.
[84] At 769.
[85] n. 79 above.
[86] See also *Dovey* v. *Cory* [1901] AC 477.
[87] See e.g. Gower (n. 82 above), 587.

most old cases bear this out.[88] But in terms of a legal foundation, where would this leave those who have lately propounded a formal monitoring role for non-executives?[89] Failure to monitor is a failure to act; on the old authorities, failure to act is unlikely to constitute a breach of duty. In *AWA*, the case against the non-executive directors was essentially that they had been negligent as a result of failure to fulfil a supervisory role.

The remainder of this subsection is structured as follows. There is an outline of the findings made by Rogers C.J. in relation to (i) the non-executives, and (ii) the chief executive/chairman. Then there is discussion of recent developments (including statements of Rogers C.J. in *AWA*) indicating that it is no longer the case that part-time directors can escape liability in negligence simply by not acting.

The non-executive directors: Rogers C.J. found that the non-executives had a general, undetailed knowledge of FX matters.[90] The board had laid down certain basic principles ('extremely scanty policy guidelines')[91] in regard to FX, *but* had *properly* left it in the hands of senior management to implement the principles and supervise the FX operations.[92] As alarmingly high monthly profit figures for FX operations were reported, the board expressed grave concerns to both the senior management and the auditors. It was found that senior management and the auditors had failed to relay to the board serious problems about which they were aware, and had even

---

[88] See e.g. *Re Cardiff Savings Bank (Marquis of Bute's* case) [1892] 2 Ch. 100, 109 *per* Stirling J.; cf. *Charitable Corporation* v. *Sutton* (1742) 2 Atk. 400; *Re Denham & Co.* (1883) 25 Ch.D. 752. The director in *Re Denham* who had not attended a board meeting or taken part in the company's affairs for four years was held not liable in negligence for losses suffered by the company as a result of other directors' fraud. Most commentators interpret the decision as supporting the view that failure to act does not amount to breach of the duty of skill and care. However, Chitty J. held that the director had been 'guilty of considerable negligence in the discharge of the duties of his office' (at 766). The director was held *not liable* because Chitty J. found that, given his lack of accounting knowledge and business acumen, even if he had made an enquiry when he should have, it would not have uncovered the fraud (at 768). Properly construed, therefore, the case is one where the director was found to be in breach of his duty of diligence but, because of his lack of accounting skill, there was no causative link between his lack of diligence and the company's loss. It is an illustration of the interrelationship between the concepts of 'diligence' or 'care' on the one hand, and 'skill' on the other. The subjective component of the duty of skill operated so as to render not liable the director who had failed to exercise the required degree of diligence or care. If the director in *Re Denham* had possessed accounting knowledge, presumably it would have been found that an enquiry made at the appropriate time would have uncovered the fraud (and that something would have been done to rectify the situation). In this circumstance, there would have existed the causative link between the director's lack of diligence and the company's loss, and it is submitted that the director would have been found liable.

[89] See e.g. Committee on the Financial Aspects of Corporate Governance, *Report* (London, 1 Dec. 1992), paras. 4.4–4.6, Code of Best Practice, para. 1.1; Institutional Shareholders' Committee, *The Role and Duties of Directors—A Statement of Best Practice* (London, 1991), 3; J. Charkham, 'Corporate Governance and the Market for Control of Companies', *Bank of England Panel Paper No. 25* (London, 1989), 12–13.

[90] At 773.

[91] At 833.

[92] At 774, 874.

positively reassured the board in circumstances where to do so was grossly misleading.[93] His Honour made the important legal finding that the directors were *entitled* to rely upon the reassurances given to them by senior management and the auditors, and the important factual finding that the directors actually *did* so rely.[94] There was 'no evidence to suggest that the non-executive directors ever became aware, or should have become aware, of the deficiencies in internal controls and books of account', or that their policy guide-lines were not being followed.[95] The non-executives were found not to have breached their duties of care and skill.

The chief executive/chairman: H, the chief executive, was found to have been negligent in (a) failing, in the face of dire warning signs, to make enquiries of senior management which might have led to a better insight into K's activities; and (b) failing to inform the non-executive directors of important information and warnings received from the auditors,[96] a bank with which K dealt, and the company's external corporate advisors. Neither H nor the non-executive directors took action to investigate deeply into the FX operation, but only H was found negligent. But there were important differences between H and the non-executive directors. First, H did virtually nothing after having been informed that there were problems with FX. The non-executives did nothing apart from expressing concerns to and asking questions of management and the auditors. In circumstances where it was reasonable for them to do so, they relied upon reassurances from senior management, H, and the auditors that there were no problems with the FX operation. The evidence showed that the non-executives, unlike H, never became aware, nor should have become aware, of the problems with the FX operation.

Secondly, the nature of H's position as chief executive required that he should have taken greater steps to investigate the FX operation. The totality of apparently inexplicable profit figures, warnings from a bank with which K dealt and from AWA's external corporate advisors, and the information from the auditors on 13 March, 'called for much more action from [H] than merely implementation of the auditors' suggestions. [H] was the chief executive, not the auditors. It was for [H] to decide on the appropriate action.'[97] Rogers C.J. found that H had 'accepted explanations and information from [AWA's general manager] and other members of senior management without attempting at any point to review the various matters for concern in the context of their cumulative effect'.[98] In one instance H's delegation to and reliance upon a senior executive was found to have been 'so

---

[93] See n. 15 above.
[94] At 772, 774, 775, 874.
[95] At 774, 874.
[96] See discussion under Subsection 2.1 above.
[97] At 875.
[98] Ibid.

extreme as to amount to neglect'.[99] The combination of factors referred to earlier required H, as the chief executive, to make more specific enquiries and to decide on the appropriate action.

Rogers C.J. initially proposed to take the negligence of H into account as part of the contributory negligence of AWA. However, in later proceedings, Rogers C.J. accepted that the defendant auditors had a right of election as to whether (1) to have H's negligence treated a part of the contributory negligence of AWA, or (2) to instead claim contribution from H in respect of his share of the responsibility for AWA's loss. The auditors elected the latter option.

Developments in the requirements of diligence and skill: Although the non-executives in *AWA* were found not to have been negligent, it is clear from Rogers C.J.'s judgment that the directors would not, as they might seventy or eighty years ago, have escaped liability if they had simply not attended meetings or not acted. Professor Gower's prediction[100] was proven correct when Rogers C.J. stated: 'it is of the essence of the responsibilities of directors that they take reasonable steps to place themselves in a position to guide and monitor the management of the company . . . A director is obliged to obtain at least a general understanding of the business of the company . . .'.[101] The non-executives in *AWA* were not negligent, because they had properly left the implementation of certain matters to senior management, they had made diligent enquiries and expressed their grave concerns at relevant times, and they were entitled to rely upon the (ultimately defective and misleading) replies from management and the auditors. Rogers C.J. interpreted the directors' duty of diligence as requiring them to take some steps to monitor management's handling of the FX operation, particularly when put on alert by the extraordinary profit figures. Had the directors not pursued the FX matters in the way that they did, a finding of negligence would likely have resulted.

So, the nineteenth-century decisions on the diligence required of directors are unlikely to be given any significant weight by Australian courts.[102] The following comments of Rogers C.J. indicate strongly the reasons why this should be so:

---

[99] At 877.

[100] '[I]t may be that today the courts would require a degree of diligence somewhat greater than that suggested in the old decisions. Certainly, today most public companies expect all their directors to do some homework to familiarise themselves with the company's operations . . .': (n. 82 above), 587–8.

[101] At 864. The first sentence is an adaptation of a proposition of Tadgell J. in *Commonwealth Bank of Australia* v. *Friedrich* (1991) 5 ACSR 115, 184. See also *Re Australasian Venezolana Pty. Ltd.* (1962) 4 FLR 60, 66.

[102] In the Australian context consideration must also be given to s. 232(4) of the Corporations Law: 'In the exercise of his or her powers and the discharge of his or her duties, an officer of a corporation must exercise the degree of care and diligence that a reasonable person in a like position in a corporation would exercise in the corporation's circumstances' (which applies in addition to, not in derogation of, the common-law duty: s. 232(11)).

Of necessity, as the complexities of commercial life have intensified the community has come to expect more than formerly from directors whose task is to govern the affairs of companies to which large sums of money are committed by way of equity capital or loan. The affairs of a company with a large annual turnover, large stake in assets and liabilities, the use of very substantial resources and hundreds, if not thousands of employees *demands an appreciable degree of diligent application* by its directors if they are to attempt to do their duty.[103]

The indications are that the old authorities will, similarly, be afforded little weight by courts in the UK. This view is based primarily upon the compelling fact that the level of diligence required—or not required—by the old cases is discordant with modern commercial practice and shareholder expectations. Additional support for the view exists in the approach adopted by Foster J. in a relatively recent decision on the duty of care and skill, and in the legislature's enactment of a wrongful trading provision.

In *Dorchester Finance Co. Ltd.* v. *Stebbing*,[104] two non-executive directors of a money-lending company, at which there would appear never to have been board meetings, had signed blank cheques which facilitated the making of inadequately secured loans by the company. The single executive director of the company who had organized the loans, which proved irrecoverable, was clearly liable, but the non-executives argued that they were entitled to rely upon the company's auditors. Foster J. stated:

For a chartered accountant and an experienced accountant to put forward the proposition that a non-executive director has no duties to perform I find quite alarming. It would be an argument which, if put forward by a director with no accounting experience, would involve total disregard of many sections of the Companies Act 1948 . . . The signing of blank cheques by [the non-executives] was in my judgment negligent, as it allowed [the executive director] to do as he pleased. Apart from that they not only failed to exhibit the necessary skill and care in the performance of their duties as directors, but also failed to perform any duty at all as directors of [the company].[105]

It is manifest that Foster J. postulated a reasonable degree of diligence on the part of directors, whether with or without accounting knowledge.

Section 214 of the Insolvency Act 1986, known as the wrongful trading provision, empowers the court, on the application of a liquidator, to declare that a director is liable to contribute to the company's assets.[106] The liquidator may apply where the company is in insolvent liquidation, and where at some time before the commencement of the winding up the director knew or ought to have concluded that there was no reasonable prospect that the company would avoid going into insolvent liquidation (s.

---

[103] At 865 (Emphasis added).
[104] [1989] BCLC 498 (decided in 1977).
[105] Ibid., at 505.
[106] See generally: D. D. Prentice, 'Creditor's Interests and Director's Duties' (1990) 10 *OJLS* 265; F. Oditah, 'Wrongful Trading' [1990] *LMCLQ* 205.

214(2)). Subsection 3 provides a defence where the court is satisfied that the director took every step with a view to minimizing the potential loss to the company's creditors that he ought to have taken. For present purposes, the crucial provision is Subsection 4, which provides that for the purposes of Subsections 2 and 3:

the facts which a director of a company ought to know or ascertain, the conclusions which he ought to reach and the steps which he ought to take are those which would be known or ascertained, or reached or taken, by a reasonably diligent person having both—

(a) the general knowledge, skill and experience that may reasonably be expected of a person carrying out the same functions as are carried out by that director in relation to the company, and

(b) the general knowledge, skill and experience that that director has.

Important also is Subsection 5, which provides that the reference in Subsection 4 to the functions carried out in relation to a company by a director of the company includes any functions which he does not carry out but which have been entrusted to him.

Section 214(4) contains criteria relating to both the concepts of 'diligence' and 'skill'. The standard of diligence contained in the subsection is an objective standard: the court must determine what a director exercising reasonable diligence would have known, ascertained, concluded, and done.[107] On the other hand, clauses (a) and (b) provide objective and subjective standards, respectively, in relation to skill (and knowledge and experience). In *Re Produce Marketing Consortium Ltd. (No. 2)*,[108] Knox J. made it clear that clause (a) provides a minimum standard of knowledge, skill, and experience. Thus, clause (b) can operate only so as to *increase* the standard.[109] The standards of skill and diligence under Section 214(4) can be contrasted with those under the common-law duty of care and skill, as traditionally stated. The standard of skill set out in *Re City Equitable* embodies no minimum standard, and the old authorities suggest that there is no requirement of a reasonable level of diligence.

The relevance of Section 214 in the present context may be unapparent. As the provision applies only where a company has gone into insolvent liquidation, on the surface it is of relevance only to the position of directors *vis-à-vis* creditors and not to directors *vis-à-vis* shareholders or the company as a going concern. However, there are two reasons, the second more important than the first, why Section 214 (especially subsection 4) *is* of importance to the present discussion. First, the provision[110] probably has a

---

[107] Coupled with ss. 5, this ensures that a director cannot simply by doing nothing escape the reach of the provision.

[108] [1989] BCLC 520, 550.

[109] See Prentice (n. 106 above), p. 269 n. 30.

[110] Together with other provisions such as those in the Company Directors Disqualification Act 1986.

'positive' deterrent effect upon the directors of solvent companies: 'the fact that the possible personal liability is so extensive and insolvent liquidation always a possibility (however remote) should ensure some raising of standards'.[111] Secondly, the adoption by the legislature of objective criteria may serve as a guide to the courts in their construction of the common-law duty of care and skill.[112] It is submitted that the next fully argued case in the UK on the common law duty will see the adoption of objective criteria at least in relation to the requirement of diligence, and possibly in relation to the standard of skill.[113] There has already been a dictum supporting this view. In *Norman* v. *Theodore Goddard*,[114] after deciding not to call for argument on the point, Hoffmann J. said he was 'willing to assume' that the requirements of the common-law duty of care and skill are 'accurately stated in s 214(4) of the Insolvency Act 1986'.[115] His Lordship decided the case on the basis that the director was entitled to rely upon the representations of the solicitor who, in effect, defrauded the company.

Two points need to be made about the last submission. The inability of a shareholder to bring a derivative action in respect of a simple breach of the duty of care and skill[116] has in the past presented a procedural obstacle to the development of the duty. The absence of a case[117] reflecting contemporary expectations as to the diligence of directors is explicable largely on this ground. Unfortunately, the same obstacle probably will continue to hinder development of the duty. *Theodore Goddard*, like *AWA*, involved third-party proceedings against the director.

The second matter concerns the fact that Section 214(4) contains an objectively measured minimum standard of skill. There can be little argument with the contention that an objectively assessed requirement of *diligence* is appropriate not only for Section 214 but also for the common-law duty of care and skill.[118] However, arguably it is defensible to have differing standards of *skill* for (i) directors of companies near to or in insolvency, and (ii) directors of solvent companies. Without accepting this view, grounds in

[111] J. H. Farrar, N. E. Furey, and B. M. Hannigan, *Farrar's Company Law* (3rd edn., London, 1991), 399; see also Gower (n. 82 above), 589.

[112] The same argument applies in relation to the Australian 'insolvent trading' provision: Corporations Law, s. 592; see S. Sievers, 'Directors' Duty of Care, Skill and Diligence—Further Developments' (1992) 10 *Company and Securities Law Journal* 337; L.D. Griggs, 'Inactive Directors—Under Attack' (1992) 11 *U Tas. LR* 75, 88-9.

[113] See A. L. Mackenzie, 'A Company Director's Obligations of Care and Skill' [1982] *JBL* 460, 464: standards developed up to 1925 are no longer appropriate.

[114] [1991] BCLC 1028. See also *Department of Health and Social Security v. Evans* [1984] BCLC 125.

[115] Ibid. at 1030.

[116] *Pavlides v. Jensen* [1956] Ch. 565—as opposed to negligence from which the defendant directors benefit: *Daniels v. Daniels* [1978] 1 Ch. 406.

[117] Apart from *Dorchester Finance* (n. 104 above).

[118] As Rogers C.J. said, 'it is of the essence of the responsibilities of directors that they take *reasonable steps* to place themselves in a position to guide and monitor the management of the company' (at 864, emphasis added).

support would seem to include: (a) that the perverse incentives (for directors and shareholders) existing, as a result of the effects of limited liability, where a company becomes insolvent[119] justify a higher standard in this situation; (b) in the case of a solvent company, that the shareholders elected the board and have the power to remove the directors.[120] When considering whether there ought to be an objectively measured standard of skill under the common-law duty, it of course also needs to be borne in mind that non-executives are commonly elected because of their specialist knowledge. A geologist or a medical scientist may provide valuable input to the board of a suitable public company, but may have extremely limited accounting and financial knowledge. On the other hand, it is reasonable, as Rogers C.J. pointed out, to expect that directors should 'obtain at least a general understanding of the business of the company'.[121] Also, Hoffmann J. in *Theodore Goddard* was prepared to accept that the common-law duty now embraces an objective standard of skill.

On balance it is contended that a minimum level of skill *should* be required by the courts. The director's actual knowledge, skill, and experience should be of relevance only where these attributes would serve to add to an objectively determined standard. Although the suggested minimum standard is said to be formulated objectively, it would not necessarily be uniform as between different companies or even as between different directors in the same company. This is because the minimum objective standard should be set having regard to (i) the nature of the company, (ii) the distribution of responsibilities between the directors and other officers, and (iii) the knowledge, skill, and experience that the court would reasonably expect of a director 'carrying out the same functions as [the defendant] director' in the company concerned. To use the terminology of Hirst J. in *DHSS* v. *Evans*, the court should 'determine the issue by reference to a reasonable director placed in the position of the director in question'.[122] The actual knowledge and experience of the particular director should, if appropriate, be applied so as to bolster this objective standard.[123] However, the director's personal

---

[119] See Prentice (n. 106 above).

[120] Companies Act 1985, s. 303; *Overend Gurney & Co. v. Gurney* (1869) LR 4 Ch. App. 701, 720; cf. Farrar (n. 111 above), 396: 'This argument ignores the extent to which the board has become a self-perpetuating body through the directors' control of the proxy machinery and the passive role adopted by the average shareholder'; L. S. Sealy, 'Directors' "Wider" Responsibilities—Problems Conceptual, Practical and Procedural' (1987) 13 *Mon. ULR* 164, 173.

[121] At 864.

[122] n. 114 above, at 136—a case concerning the Social Security Act 1975, s. 152(4) (a provision that was repealed by the Insolvency Act 1985, s. 216). See also Mackenzie (n. 113 above), 470: 'the careful formulation of a number of different objective standards, the application of each depending on the particular role the director is occupying in the company'; V. Finch, 'Company Directors: Who Cares About Skill and Care?' (1992) 55 *MLR* 179, 203: 'a director [should] exhibit the skill and care reasonably to be expected of a person who has undertaken their kind of role in their kind of company.'

[123] Cf. Finch, ibid., at 203–4.

attributes should not be allowed to lower the minimum objectively determined standard.[124]

It will be apparent that on this suggested approach the court is required to consider the concept of a 'reasonable director'. Trebilcock was somewhat troubled by this, explaining that it is 'an extraordinarily nebulous concept'.[125] However, in the context of a claim against three directors in respect of the non-payment by their company of national insurance contributions, Hirst J. has recently interpreted and applied a provision of the Social Security Act 1975 which in effect required consideration of 'a reasonable director placed in the position of the director in question'.[126] His Lordship was comfortable with the concept of a 'reasonable director', given that it was to be applied having regard to the nature of the company in question and the nature of the defendant director's position and responsibilities. Coupled with the approach of Hoffmann J. in *Theodore Goddard*, this suggests that the courts would find it within their competence to apply the objective test recommended for the duty of care and skill.

The suggested future approach to the common-law duty of care and skill, illustrated using the case of a non-executive director in a public company, is therefore as follows. Assume that over a period of twelve months an executive officer defrauds his company. The fraud is later uncovered and a differently constituted board sues, amongst others, one of the former non-executive directors (for breach of duty of care and skill). In scenario 1, the court finds that during the twelve-month period the non-executive director failed to take reasonable steps (whether by not acting at all or by doing too little) to monitor the company's executive management. Here, (a) the director will be found to have failed to display the requisite degree of diligence. That alone will not render the director liable. However, if the court also finds, on the assumption that the director possessed *both* a reasonable level of knowledge, skill, and experience[127] *and* her actual knowledge and experience, that the director would have uncovered the problem *if* reasonable monitoring steps had been taken (and if the court finds that the uncovering of the problem would have led to an appropriate solution to the problem), (b) the director will be liable to the company in negligence.[128] In scenario 2, the court finds that during the twelve-month

---

[124] 'The director in question cannot . . . pray in aid his own lack of ability or his own inferiority of intellect, still less his lack of interest in the management of the company': *DHSS* v. *Evans* (n. 114 above), 136.

[125] M. J. Trebilcock, 'The Liability of Company Directors for Negligence' (1969) 32 *MLR* 499, 511.

[126] *DHSS* v. *Evans* (n. 114 above). That provision has now been repealed (see n. 122 above).

[127] The 'reasonable' level of knowledge, skill, and experience being the level of those attributes which the court decides would have been possessed by a 'reasonable director' placed squarely in the shoes of the defendant director (but ignoring her actual knowledge and experience): see n. 122 above, and accompanying text.

[128] Cf. discussion in n. 88 above. Professor Gower's submission (n. 82 above, at 587) that it

period the non-executive director took all reasonable steps to monitor the company's executive management. The director has therefore met the standard of diligence required. However, she still may be liable in negligence if in carrying out her duties she did not meet the required standard of skill. That is, she will be liable if the court finds that, had she possessed a reasonable level of knowledge, skill, and experience,[129] her diligent activities would have uncovered the problem (and if the court finds that the uncovering of the problem would have led to an appropriate solution to the problem).

Linking this analysis to *AWA*, and to the discussion under Subsection 2.3.3 above, Rogers C.J. would have said that the negligence of a non-executive director could be relied upon by the auditors as contributory negligence of the company. This view is rejected for the reasons set out under Subsection 2.3.3. However, it is accepted that the negligence of a non-executive director, as a concurrent cause of the company's loss, could be the subject of third-party proceedings (seeking contribution) brought by the auditors.

3. Other Aspects Concerning Corporate Governance

Some of Rogers C.J.'s general comments in the area of corporate governance are discussed in Subsections 3.1–3.5 below. There are other aspects of the case which although not discussed by Rogers C.J., might be of interest to those engaged in the corporate governance debate in the UK. Three of these are addressed in Subsections 3.6–3.8.

3.1. COMBINATION OF ROLES OF CHAIRMAN AND CHIEF EXECUTIVE

A recent survey of UK listed companies found that about one-quarter of companies combined the roles of chairman and chief executive,[130] despite concern as to the accompanying conflicts of interest.[131] Rogers C.J. noted that H, the plaintiff's chief executive/chairman, 'uneasily straddled' the most senior management position with the senior board position.[132] H 'was not only the channel of communication between the board and management but also between management and the board'.[133] There was the potential, which unfortunately was realized in this case, for problems and information that ought to have come from management to the board not to get there.

---

would be 'next to impossible' to prove a causative link between failure to act and the company's loss is, with respect, too pessimistic.

[129] See n. 127 above.
[130] 'Boards' Linguistic Silence Speaks Volumes', *Financial Times*, 9 July 1992, p. 10.
[131] See e.g. Institutional Shareholders' Committee (n. 89 above), 2.
[132] At 865.
[133] At 867–8.

This gives further support to the Cadbury Committee's belief that the roles ought to be separate, given 'the importance and particular nature of the chairman's role'.[134]

3.2. OUTMODED COMPANIES LEGISLATION

Rogers C.J. noted that '[c]ompanies legislation has not sought to determine the proper division of functions between the board and management'.[135] It is true that, as the corporate governance debate has progressed, so has the relevant English (and Australian) companies legislation stood still. The standard Table A 'management article'[136] provides for the business of the company to be 'managed' by the directors. But, with the non-executive board members joining their executive colleagues for full-board meetings perhaps only once a month or even once a quarter, it is clear that the board of directors, as an organ, does not manage the day-to-day affairs of the average large public company. This task is the domain of executive management, which usually is composed both of executive directors and of executive officers who are not also members of the board.[137] However, the boards of a small minority of large public companies consist entirely of executive directors. In such cases it is possible to say of the board that, even if *as an organ* it does not manage the company's business, it is at least entirely *composed of* those who (usually with other executives below board level) manage the company.

3.3. SCOPE FOR MEANINGFUL MONITORING BY NON-EXECUTIVES

Importantly, Rogers C.J. commented *generally* upon the monitoring role of non-executives in large public companies. After earlier asking, rhetorically: 'What knowledge of the affairs of an international conglomerate like IBM or General Motors can a non-executive director be required or expected to have?'[138] his Honour reached the conclusion that 'the opportunity for non-executive directors [in large public companies] to exercise meaningful control over management is as slight as the ability of ministers to control a vast bureaucracy'.[139]

---

[134] Committee on the Financial Aspects of Corporate Governance (hereafter 'Cadbury Committee'), *Report* (London, 1 Dec. 1992), para. 4.9.

[135] At 865.

[136] The Companies (Table A–F) Regulations 1985, S. I. 1985/805, art. 70.

[137] Rogers C.J. stated, at 866: 'The board of a large public corporation cannot manage the corporation's day to day business. That function must by business necessity be left to the corporation's executives.' Of course, the articles of association usually permit the directors to delegate some or all of their powers (see e.g. Table A, art. 72), and the law permits directors to rely upon others: *Dovey* v. *Corey* [1901] AC 477; cf. *Re Leeds Banking Co.* (*Howard's* case) (1866) LR 1 Ch. App. 561.

[138] At 865.

[139] At 878. See also at 832–3.

However, at least one judge takes a more optimistic and demanding view, than did Rogers C.J., of the scope for monitoring by non-executives. Extrajudicially, Chancellor William Allen of the Delaware Court of Chancery has recently set out a relatively rigorous standard of monitoring for American 'outside' directors.[140]

3.4. ROTATION OF AUDIT PARTNERS

The defendant firm in *AWA* had been auditors to the plaintiff company for many years. D, the partner in charge of audits of AWA's accounts during the two audits in question, had been the audit partner for AWA's accounts for some twelve or thirteen years.[141] Rogers C.J. noted that D and the plaintiff's general manager and internal auditor were friends of long standing.[142] His Honour continued that if D had reported to the board the absence of internal controls and records, and more significantly the failure of senior management to rectify the deficiencies after having been notified of the problems by the auditors, it would likely 'have reflected badly on [D's] two friends'.[143] His Honour concluded: 'The difficulties which may arise from too close a relationship between auditor and management have been recognised in recent proposals to require a change of auditor at least every 7 years.'[144]

In the UK the balance of opinion is against any compulsory rotation of audit *firms*. However, it now seems probable that a requirement for rotation of audit *partners* (at least every seven years) will be introduced by way of amendment to *The Guide to Professional Ethics* of the institutes of chartered accountants of England and Wales, Scotland, and Ireland.[145] Whether or not the relationship between AWA's general manager, internal auditor, and auditor actually contributed to the auditors' negligent performance during 1986/7,[146] the situation seems to reinforce the view that rotation of audit partners is appropriate *at least* on the ground that, 'in the public interest, independence must always be seen to be achieved rather than just claimed as a result of professional training, attitudes and in-house procedures'.[147]

---

[140] See Martin Lipton, Ch. 8 above, p. 115. See also *Francis v United Jersey Bank* 432 A 2d 814, 822 (1981); The American Law Institute, *Principles of Corporate Governance: Analysis and Recommendations* (Proposed Final Draft, 31 Mar. 1992), Parts III and IIIA.

[141] See at 775.

[142] At 766.

[143] At 766–7.

[144] At 767.

[145] See Chartered Accountants Joint Ethics Committee, *Rotation of Audit Partners—A Consultation Paper* (Milton Keynes, 19 Oct. 1992), para. 12. The large institutional shareholder body, the National Association of Pension Funds Ltd., suggested in Sept. 1991 that rotation of audit partners be made compulsory: 'Institutions Want Fuller Financial Information', *Financial Times*, 2 Sept. 1991, p. 14. The main impetus for change came, however, from the Cadbury Committee: *Draft Report* (London, 27 May 1992), para. 5.12.

[146] No finding was made on this point.

[147] *Rotation of Audit Partners—A Consultation Paper* (n. 145 above) para. 1.

3.5. SOLIDARY LIABILITY

'Solidary liability' refers to what is essentially the 'several' aspect of joint and several liability under the common law. The effect of the rule is a particular concern of auditors.[148] Rogers C.J. expressed the concern as follows:

[A] well insured defendant, who may perhaps be responsible for only a minor fault, in comparison with the fault of other persons, may nonetheless be made liable, at least in the first instance, for the entirety of the damage suffered by the plaintiff. The defendant may indeed seek contribution from other persons responsible for the major damage. Why should the whole of the burden of possibly insolvent wrongdoers fall entirely on a well insured, or deep pocket, defendant?[149]

This is not an appropriate forum for detailed discussion of the matter. However, even assuming for the sake of argument that the present law is unsatisfactory and in need of reform,[150] in cases such as *AWA* where auditors are sued by their client company it is inappropriate for the courts, and it would be inappropriate for the legislature, to attempt to 'ease the burden' on auditors by allowing a defence of contributory negligence against the company. Sound policy supports this view.[151]

3.6. AUDIT COMMITTEE

Although not mentioned in the judgment, it seems that the plaintiff company's board did not have an 'audit committee'. Of course, proposals have been forwarded in both the UK and Australia that listed companies be required to establish audit committees.[152] Although this is necessarily speculation, it is considered likely that the relevant information would have come to the board's attention sooner had an audit committee of non-executive directors been in operation. The discipline of meeting with a committee of non-executive directors *specifically* for the purpose of

---

[148] See Department of Trade and Industry, *Report of the Study Teams, Professional Liability* (HMSO, London, 1989)—Report of the Steering Group, paras. 4.7–4.8; Report of the Auditors Study Team, paras. 3.23–3.30, 9.4–9.5.

[149] At 877.

[150] The writer does not support such a view, and neither did the NSW Law Reform Commission in a paper referred to by Rogers C.J. (at 877). In its *Interim Report on Solidary Liability* (LRC 65 (Sydney, 1990)), the Commission states, at para. 45: 'In the Commission's opinion, consideration of arguments concerning fairness as between the plaintiff and tortfeasors weigh in favour of retention of solidary liability and against a system of proportionate liability. It is the Commission's opinion that the existing system of solidary liability coupled with rights of contribution between tortfeasors best reflects the substantive rights and responsibilities of a plaintiff on the one hand and of tortfeasors on the other.'

[151] See discussion under Subsection 2.3.3, above.

[152] See e.g. Cadbury Committee, *Report* (1 Dec. 1992), para. 4.35; the Institute of Chartered Accountants in England and Wales, *Report of the Study Group on the Changing Role of the Non-Executive Director* (London, 1991), para. 4.10; Australian Senate Standing Committee on Legal and Constitutional Affairs, *Report on the Social and Fiduciary Duties and Obligations of Company Directors* (Canberra, 1989), paras. 8.15–8.16.

discussing matters relating to the auditors' work would, it is submitted, probably have led to an earlier disclosure by the auditors to the board (via the audit committee) of the company's internal control and reporting problems.

If UK best practice is any guide, there is some firm support for this belief. Guidebooks of two of the leading accounting firms set out model questions for audit-committee members to put to executive management, the internal auditors, and the external auditors. Amongst those directed to the external auditors, Arthur Andersen suggests: 'Has the audit identified any areas of serious concern relative to the overall control environment?'[153] Similarly, Ernst & Young suggest: 'What were the most significant internal control weaknesses uncovered by the internal and external auditors during the period?' 'Have the internal and external auditors' comments on internal controls been addressed?' 'What are the auditors' opinions on the internal control system, on the quality of the accounting records, and on the timeliness, completeness and accuracy of reports to management?'[154]

3.7. SHORT-TERMISM

It may be that *AWA* provides an illustration of short-termism, an issue which has been widely debated in the UK.[155] It will be recalled from the discussion under Section 2.1 that the defendants' second audit of AWA was not a statutory audit, but an investigating accountant's report in anticipation of a hostile takeover bid. The relevant events in *AWA* occurred during the height of a takeover boom in Australia. Interestingly, the potential takeover bidder feared by AWA's senior management was one of the Australian entrepreneurial companies which became insolvent when the economy went into recession.

A recurring point throughout the judgment is that the senior management of AWA were very careful to treat K with 'kid gloves'.[156] Rogers C.J. found: '[K] was regarded as essential to the continued profit-making performance of AWA. That in turn was essential to repel apprehended predators such as

[153] Arthur Andersen & Co., *Audit Committees for the 1990s* (1992), 29.

[154] Ernst & Young, *New Directions for Audit Committees* (1992), 47–8. See also Cadbury Committee, *Report* (1 Dec. 1992), para. 5.26. Of course, it can be argued that the non-executive directors of AWA *did* ask pertinent questions, both of executive management and of the external auditors, and that the deficiencies in internal controls and reporting nevertheless were not brought to light. The point made in the text is that the problems in AWA may well have been divulged by the external auditors had there been in existence an audit committee, precisely because of the institutionalization of the non-executive review mechanism.

[155] See e.g. Confederation of British Industry, *Investing for Britain's Future: Report of the CBI City/Industry Task Force* (London, 1987); P. Marsh, *Short-Termism on Trial* (Institutional Fund Managers' Association, London, 1990); A. Cosh, A. Hughes, *et al.*, 'Takeovers and Short-Termism in the UK', *Institute for Public Policy Research Industrial Policy Paper No. 3* (London, 1990); The National Association of Pension Funds Ltd., *Creative Tension?* (London, 1990).

[156] See at 772, 825, 830, 876.

Skase.'[157] One might perhaps conclude that the distraction of a possible hostile bid caused AWA's senior management to adopt an excessively short-term approach in the FX area. The point is not so much that the impending bid may have caused management to concentrate their energies in areas other than FX. Rather, the bid threat might well have caused management consciously to adopt a lenient policy on the controls to be applied to the (apparently very profitable) FX operation. The 'kid gloves' approach seems to have been employed largely because of the need to maintain short-term profits in the face of a possible hostile bid.

3.8. FOREIGN-EXCHANGE MANAGEMENT AND INSTITUTIONAL INVESTORS IN THE UK

Following the loss by Allied-Lyons plc of £150 million on foreign-exchange dealings in early 1991, corporate treasury policy has become a prominent issue with British institutional investors. First, discussions between the Association of Corporate Treasurers (ACT), the National Association of Pension Funds Ltd. (NAPF), and the Association of British Insurers (ABI) resulted in the ACT organizing a study of important issues for institutional shareholders. The resultant document,[158] published in August 1992, sets out some basic information about foreign-exchange management, together with questions appropriate for investors to put to management.

More recently, Mr Hugh Jenkins, the chief executive of Prudential Portfolio Managers Ltd., the largest shareholder in many UK listed companies, called for greater disclosure of corporate treasury policies in companies' accounts.[159] It has been reported that, as a consequence of Mr Jenkins's motion, the ACT is setting up a working party (involving the NAPF, the ABI, and the Accounting Standards Board) to develop guidelines on the appropriate levels of disclosure of corporate treasury management activities.[160] Of further interest, in the light of the discussion under Section 3.6, above, is that Mr Jenkins also suggested that companies' audit committees should monitor systems of risk control and ensure that internal control systems are adequate.[161]

---

[157] At 772.
[158] J. Grout and D. Ross, *Foreign Exchange Management in Non-Financial Corporations: A Checklist of Major Issues for Institutional Investors* (Association of Corporate Treasurers, London, 1992).
[159] 'Pru Chief Issues Plea for Greater Treasury Detail', *Financial Times*, 16 Oct. 1992, p. 31.
[160] Ibid. See also 'Survey: Corporate Treasury Management', *Financial Times*, 11 Nov. 1992, s. III, p. I.
[161] Ibid.

INDEX